CHRISTMAS COOKING
150 recipes for the festive season

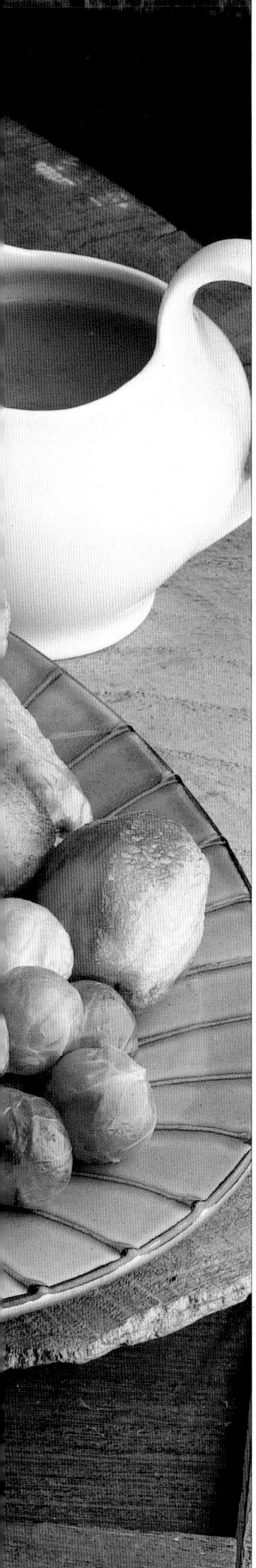

CHRISTMAS COOKING
150 recipes for the festive season

MAKE CHRISTMAS SPECIAL WITH THIS TRADITIONAL
COLLECTION OF CLASSIC RECIPES, SHOWN IN
180 INSPIRATIONAL PHOTOGRAPHS

Editor: Emma Holley

southwater

This edition is published by Southwater,
an imprint of Anness Publishing Ltd, Blaby Road, Wigston,
Leicestershire LE18 4SE; info@anness.com

Web: www.southwaterbooks.com; www.annesspublishing.com

If you like the images in this book and would like to investigate
using them for publishing, promotions or advertising, please visit
our website www.practicalpictures.com for more information.

Publisher: Joanna Lorenz
Editor: Anne Hildyard
Jacket Design: Jonathan Davison
Production Controller: Mai-Ling Collyer

© Anness Publishing Ltd 2012

NOTES
Bracketed terms are intended for American readers.

For all recipes, quantities are given in both metric and imperial
measures and, where appropriate, in standard cups and spoons.
Follow one set of measures, but not a mixture, because they are
not interchangeable.

Standard spoon and cup measures are level. 1 tsp = 5ml, 1 tbsp =
15ml, 1 cup = 250ml/8fl oz. Australian standard tablespoons are
20ml. Australian readers should use 3 tsp in place of 1 tbsp for
measuring small quantities.

American pints are 16fl oz/2 cups. American readers should use
20fl oz/2.5 cups in place of 1 pint when measuring liquids.
Electric oven temperatures in this book are for conventional ovens.
When using a fan oven, the temperature will probably need to be
reduced by about 10–20°C/20–40°F. Since ovens vary, you should
check with your manufacturer's instruction book for guidance.
The nutritional analysis given for each recipe is calculated per
portion (i.e. serving or item), unless otherwise stated. If the recipe
gives a range, such as Serves 4–6, then the nutritional analysis will
be for the smaller portion size, i.e. 6 servings.
The analysis does not include optional ingredients, such as
salt added to taste.
Medium (US large) eggs are used unless otherwise stated.

Main front cover image shows Christmas Star Cakes – for recipe,
see page 74

Previously published as part of a larger volume,
500 Christmas Recipes

Contents

Introduction

Christmas is a time of celebration, of getting together with friends and family for social gatherings and parties. Food plays an important part in the festive season, and traditionally indulgent meals can be thoroughly enjoyed in the knowledge that it is just once a year. This lovely collection of inspirational recipes will help you plan all your meals over the holiday period, whether for family meals or for entertaining. All courses are covered: included are soups,

appetizers and starters, dips and party nibbles, pâtés, terrines and mousses, fish and shellfish, poultry and game, meat dishes, vegetarian main courses, side dishes, hot and cold desserts, cakes, cookies and edible gifts and sauces, stuffings, preserves and drinks.

For the big day, why not serve up a classic Christmas dinner of Chestnut and Whitebean Soup, Gravlax with Mustard and Dill Sauce, Roast Turkey with a stuffing of fruit, sausagemeat, mushroom or herby liver – served with all the trimmings: Hasselback Potatoes, Roast Parsnips with Honey and Mustard and Festive Brussels Sprouts, followed by Christmas Pudding with Brandy Butter. Or, spice up your Christmas meals with a few festive recipes with a twist – try Scallops with Black Bean Sauce, Cardamom Chicken Mousselines, Salmon with Cucumber Sauce and a sumptuous Chocolate Amaretto Marquise for dessert. Vegetarians will love Filo Vegetable Pie or Festive Lentil and Nut Roast. There are also lots of treats to make to give away as gifts, such as Chocolate Citrus Candies, Truffle Christmas Puddings and Orange, Mint and Coffee Meringues, and children will love the Gingerbread Family.

Since most home cooks may have to cater for quite a few people throughout the holiday time, planning ahead is important, so that when the day comes, the cook can enjoy the festivities knowing that everything in the kitchen is under control. There are recipes to take you through the whole holiday period: simply look up the recipes you need, whether you want a light lunch, brunch, supper for entertaining or some quick ideas for dips, nibbles or party treats to serve unexpected guests.

If you have a lot of guests to entertain, a party buffet can be a good option. Try serving a selection of dips and party nibbles: Grilled Chicken Balls on Skewers with Yakitori Sauce, Smoked Salmon with Warm Potato Cakes, Fragrant Spiced Lamb on Poppadums and Russian Pancakes with Mixed Topping should be very well received by your guests. For an impressive seafood dish, try Hake au Poivre with Pepper Relish, or what could be more luxurious for a festive occasion than

Lobster Noodles – or a tasty Game Terrine. If you want to ring the changes as well as make life easier for yourself, serve Coq au Vin, a delicious dish that can be made ahead and reheated later. To ensure that your Christmas catering goes smoothly, the 180 tempting festive recipes in this

collection are organized so that you can quickly find the recipes you want; they are clearly explained in step-by-step instructions and illustrated with inspiring photographs so that you can see what you are aiming to create. Packed full of great recipes, ideas, tips, and with nutritional information for every dish to help you plan your menus, this book is an invaluable resource for all your Christmas meals.

Cream of Pea and Spinach Soup

Although best made with peas, spinach and mint picked fresh from the garden, these are out of season at Christmas time. Frozen peas are a perfectly good substitute for fresh, and the soup will not suffer as a result.

Serves 6

25g/1oz/2 tbsp butter
1 onion, finely chopped
675g/1½lb frozen peas
1.5ml/¼ tsp sugar
1.2 litres/2 pints/5 cups chicken
   or vegetable stock
handful of fresh mint leaves
450g/1lb young spinach leaves
150ml/¼ pint/⅔ cup double
   (heavy) cream
salt and ground black pepper
15ml/1 tbsp chopped fresh
   chives, to garnish

1 Melt the butter in a large pan and add the onion. Cook over low heat for about 8–10 minutes, stirring occasionally, until they are soft and just turning brown.

2 Add the peas, sugar, stock and half the mint. Cover the pan and simmer gently for 10 minutes, until the peas are almost tender.

3 Stir the spinach into the peas and simmer gently for a further 5 minutes, until the spinach leaves have just wilted.

4 Leave to cool slightly. Add the remaining mint and process or blend until smooth. Return the soup to the rinsed-out pan and season to taste with salt and pepper.

5 Stir in the cream and reheat gently without boiling. Serve immediately, garnished with chopped chives.

> **Variation**
> Tender broccoli is also delicious with peas and spinach in this soup, if it is in season. Add the chopped stems for about 10 minutes and the tops of the chopped florets for 5 minutes when adding the spinach.

Chestnut and White Bean Soup

This substantial soup is a great dish to make at Christmas, when chestnuts are plentiful and at their best. Chestnuts have a long history of cultivation in Europe, and were eaten long before potatoes. You can freeze chestnuts if you buy too many – so long as you remember to peel them first.

Serves 4

100g/3¾oz/½ cup dried white
   beans, soaked overnight in cold
   water and drained
90g/3½oz peeled chestnuts,
   thawed if frozen
1 bay leaf
50ml/2fl oz/¼ cup olive oil
1 onion, chopped
salt

1 Put the beans, chestnuts and bay leaf in a large pan. Pour in 1 litre/3¾ pints/4 cups water and bring to the boil. Lower the heat, cover the pan with a lid and simmer the beans for about 1½ hours, until they are tender.

2 Heat the oil in a frying pan. Add the onion and cook over low heat, stirring occasionally, for 5 minutes, until softened. Do not allow the oil to overheat.

3 Add the onion and its cooking oil to the soup. Stir well, seasoning to taste with salt. Remove and discard the bay leaf. Mash the beans and chestnuts with a fork or vegetable masher, so they are crushed into the soup but not smooth.

4 Ladle the soup into four warmed soup bowls and serve immediately, while it is piping hot and freshly laced with the olive oil and chopped onion.

> **Cook's Tip**
> If using fresh chestnuts, do not store them for more than a week. The easiest way to shell them and remove their inner skins is to make a small cut in each one and par-boil or roast in the oven at 180°C/350°F/Gas 4 for about 5 minutes. Remove the shells and rub off the skins with a dish towel. Peeled frozen chestnuts are a simpler option.

Cream of Pea Soup Energy 121kcal/506kJ; Protein 6.1g; Carbohydrate 9.2g, of which sugars 5.2g; Fat 7g, of which saturates 4.2g; Cholesterol 18mg; Calcium 113mg; Fibre 3g; Sodium 123mg.
Chestnut and Bean Soup Energy 184kcal/773kJ; Protein 6.2g; Carbohydrate 20.5g, of which sugars 3.1g; Fat 9.2g, of which saturates 1.4g; Cholesterol 0mg; Calcium 39mg; Fibre 5.1g; Sodium 8mg.

Creamy Mushroom Soup with Savoury Croûtes

This classic soup will brighten up a festive meal, especially with the addition of delicious cheese and mushroom croûtes.

Serves 6
1 onion, chopped
1 garlic clove, chopped
25g/1oz/2 tbsp butter
450g/1lb/6 cups chestnut or brown cap (cremini) mushrooms, roughly chopped
15ml/1 tbsp plain (all-purpose) flour
45ml/3 tbsp dry sherry
900ml/1½ pints/3¾ cups vegetable stock
150ml/¼ pint/⅔ cup double (heavy) cream
salt and ground black pepper
sprigs of fresh chervil, to garnish

For the croûtes
15ml/1 tbsp olive oil, plus extra for brushing
1 shallot, chopped
115g/4oz/1½ cups button (white) mushrooms, finely chopped
15ml/1 tbsp chopped fresh parsley
6 brown cap (cremini) mushrooms
6 slices baguette
1 small garlic clove
115g/4oz/1 cup soft goat's cheese

1 Cook the onion and garlic in the butter for 5 minutes. Add the mushrooms, cover and cook for 10 minutes, stirring often. Stir in the flour and cook for 1 minute. Stir in the sherry and stock and bring to the boil, then simmer for 15 minutes. Cool slightly, then purée it in a food processor or blender.

2 For the croûtes, heat the oil in a small pan. Add the shallot and button mushrooms, and cook for 8–10 minutes, until softened. Drain well and transfer to a food processor. Add the parsley and process until finely chopped.

3 Preheat the grill (broiler). Brush the mushrooms with oil and grill (broil) for 5–6 minutes. Toast the baguette, rub with the garlic and top with goat's cheese. Add the grilled mushrooms and fill these with the chopped mushroom mixture.

4 Return the soup to the pan and stir in the cream. Season, then reheat gently. Ladle the soup into six bowls. Float a croûte in the centre of each and garnish with chervil.

Cauliflower Soup with Broccoli

Creamy cauliflower soup is a classic winter dish and is given real bite by adding chunky cauliflower and broccoli florets. Crusty bread piled high with bacon and melting Cheddar cheese transforms this dish into a real festive treat.

Serves 4
1 onion, chopped
1 garlic clove, chopped
50g/2oz/¼ cup butter
2 cauliflowers, broken into florets
1 large potato, cut into chunks
900ml/1½ pints/3¾ cups chicken stock
225g/8oz broccoli, broken into florets
150ml/¼ pint/⅔ cup single (light) cream
6 rindless streaky (fatty) bacon rashers (strips)
1 small baguette, cut in 4 pieces
225g/8oz/2 cups medium-mature (sharp) Cheddar cheese, grated
salt and ground black pepper
roughly chopped fresh parsley, to garnish

1 Cook the onion and garlic in the butter for 4–5 minutes. Add half the cauliflower, all the potato and the stock. Bring to the boil, reduce the heat and simmer for 20 minutes.

2 Boil the remaining cauliflower for about 6 minutes, or until just tender. Use a draining spoon to remove the florets and refresh under cold running water, then drain well. Cook the broccoli in the water for 3–4 minutes, until just tender. Drain, refresh under cold water, then drain. Add to the cauliflower.

3 Cool the soup slightly, then purée it until smooth and return it to the rinsed pan. Add the cream and seasoning, then heat gently. Add the cauliflower and broccoli and heat through.

4 Preheat the grill (broiler) to high. Grill (broil) the bacon until crisp, then cool slightly. Ladle the soup into flameproof bowls.

5 Place a piece of baguette in each bowl. Sprinkle grated cheese over the top and grill for 2–3 minutes, until the cheese is melted and bubbling. Take care when serving the hot bowls.

6 Crumble the bacon and sprinkle it over the melted cheese, then sprinkle the parsley over the top and serve immediately.

Creamy Mushroom Soup Energy 368kcal/1533kJ; Protein 10.3g; Carbohydrate 25.1g, of which sugars 3.1g; Fat 25g, of which saturates 14.5g; Cholesterol 61mg; Calcium 99mg; Fibre 2.4g; Sodium 399mg.
Cauliflower Soup Energy 737kcal/3071kJ; Protein 34.8g; Carbohydrate 45.5g, of which sugars 9.2g; Fat 46.2g, of which saturates 26.4g; Cholesterol 121mg; Calcium 589mg; Fibre 6.6g; Sodium 1206mg.

Lobster Bisque

Bisque is a luxurious, velvety soup, which can be made with any crustaceans. A lobster version, laced with brandy, will go down a treat at a Christmas dinner party.

Serves 6
500g/1¼lb cooked lobster
75g/3oz/6 tbsp butter
1 onion, chopped
1 carrot, diced
1 celery stick, diced

45ml/3 tbsp brandy, plus extra for
    serving (optional)
250ml/8fl oz/1 cup dry white wine
1 litre/1¾ pints/4 cups fish stock
15ml/1 tbsp tomato purée (paste)
75g/3oz/scant ½ cup long
    grain rice
1 fresh bouquet garni
150ml/¼ pint/⅔ cup double
    (heavy) cream, plus extra
    to garnish
salt, ground white pepper and
    cayenne pepper

1 Cut the lobster into pieces. Melt half the butter in a large pan, add the vegetables and cook over low heat until soft. Add the lobster and stir for 30–60 seconds.

2 Pour over the brandy and set it alight. When the flames die down, add the wine and boil until reduced by half. Pour in the fish stock and simmer for 2–3 minutes. Remove the lobster.

3 Stir in the tomato purée and rice, add the bouquet garni and cook until the rice is tender. Meanwhile, remove the lobster meat from the shell and return the shells to the pan. Dice the lobster meat and set it aside.

4 When the rice is cooked, discard all the larger pieces of lobster shell. Transfer the mixture into a blender or food processor and process to a purée.

5 Press the purée through a sieve (strainer) placed over a clean pan. Stir, then heat until almost boiling. Season with salt, pepper and cayenne, then lower the heat and stir in the cream.

6 Dice the remaining butter and whisk it into the bisque. Add the diced lobster meat and serve immediately. If you like, pour a small spoonful of brandy into each soup bowl and swirl in a little extra double cream to garnish.

Spicy Pumpkin and Prawn Soup

The natural sweetness of the pumpkin is balanced by chillies, shrimp paste and dried shrimp in this colourful soup. The cooked shellfish adds further colour and a decent amount of bite, making this dish a real delight to the senses. This tasty warming soup would be ideal for serving as part of a festive feast.

Serves 4–6
2 garlic cloves, crushed
4 shallots, finely chopped
2.5ml/½ tsp shrimp paste
1 lemon grass stalk, chopped
2 fresh green chillies, seeded
    and chopped

15ml/1 tbsp dried shrimp, soaked
    for 10 minutes in warm water
600ml/1 pint/2½ cups
    chicken stock
450g/1lb pumpkin, peeled,
    seeded and cut into
    2cm/¾in chunks
600ml/1 pint/2½ cups
    coconut cream
30ml/2 tbsp fish sauce
5ml/1 tsp sugar
115g/4oz peeled cooked
    prawns (shrimp)
salt and ground black pepper

To garnish
2 fresh red chillies, seeded and
    thinly sliced
10–12 fresh basil leaves

1 Put the garlic, shallots, shrimp paste, lemon grass, green chillies and salt to taste in a mortar. Drain the dried shrimp, discarding the soaking liquid, and add them to the mortar, then use a pestle to grind the mixture into a paste. Alternatively, place all the ingredients in a food processor or blender and process until you have a paste.

2 Bring the chicken stock to the boil in a large pan. Add the ground paste and stir well to dissolve. Add the pumpkin chunks and simmer for 10–15 minutes, or until tender.

3 Stir in the coconut cream, then bring the soup back to simmering point. Do not let it boil. Add the fish sauce, sugar and ground black pepper to taste.

4 Add the prawns and cook for a further 2–3 minutes, until they are heated through. Serve in warm soup bowls, garnished with chillies and basil leaves.

Lobster Bisque Energy 406kcal/1684kJ; Protein 20.3g; Carbohydrate 13.7g, of which sugars 3.1g; Fat 25.2g, of which saturates 15g; Cholesterol 153mg; Calcium 84mg; Fibre 0.7g; Sodium 365mg.
Spicy Prawn Soup: Energy 73kcal/310kJ; Protein 6.5g; Carbohydrate 10.4g, of which sugars 9.8g; Fat 0.9g, of which saturates 0.4g; Cholesterol 56mg; Calcium 102mg; Fibre 1.3g; Sodium 399mg.

Salmon Soup with Salsa and Rouille

This elegant seafood soup is perfect for serving at a Christmas gathering.

Serves 4

90ml/6 tbsp olive oil
1 onion, chopped
1 leek, chopped
1 celery stick, chopped
1 fennel bulb, roughly chopped
1 red (bell) pepper, seeded and sliced
3 garlic cloves, chopped
grated rind and juice of 2 oranges
1 bay leaf
400g/14oz can chopped tomatoes
1.2 litres/2 pints/5 cups fish stock
pinch of cayenne pepper

800g/1¾lb salmon fillet, skinned
300ml/½ pint/1¼ cups double (heavy) cream
salt and ground black pepper
4 thin slices baguette, to serve

For the ruby salsa

2 tomatoes, peeled, seeded and diced
½ small red onion, very finely chopped
15ml/1 tbsp cod's roe
15ml/1 tbsp chopped fresh sorrel

For the rouille

120ml/4fl oz/½ cup mayonnaise
1 garlic clove, crushed
5ml/1 tsp sun-dried tomato paste

1 Heat the oil in a large pan. Add the onion, leek, celery, fennel, pepper and garlic. Cover and cook gently for 20 minutes.

2 Add the orange rind and juice, bay leaf and tomatoes to the pan. Cover with a lid and cook for 4–5 minutes, stirring occasionally. Add the stock and cayenne, cover the pan again and simmer gently for about 30 minutes.

3 Add the salmon and poach it for 8–10 minutes, until just cooked. Lift out the fish and flake it coarsely, discarding bones.

4 Mix all the salsa ingredients and set aside. For the rouille, mix the mayonnaise with the garlic and the sun-dried tomato paste. Toast the baguette slices on both sides and set aside.

5 Purée the soup and strain it back into the rinsed pan. Stir in the cream, seasoning and salmon. Heat gently but do not boil.

6 To serve, ladle the soup into bowls. Top the baguette slices with rouille, float on the soup and spoon over the salsa.

Seafood Chowder

Like most chowders, this is a substantial slow-cooker dish, and could be served with crusty bread for a tasty lunch or supper.

Serves 4

25g/1oz/2 tbsp butter
1 small leek, sliced
1 small garlic clove, crushed
1 celery stalk, chopped
2 smoked streaky (fatty) bacon rashers (strips), finely chopped
200g/7oz/generous 1 cup drained, canned corn kernels

450ml/¾ pint/scant 2 cups milk
5ml/1 tsp plain (all-purpose) flour
450ml/¾ pint/scant 2 cups hot chicken or vegetable stock
115g/4oz/generous ½ cup easy-cook (converted) rice
4 large scallops, with corals
115g/4oz white fish fillet, such as monkfish
15ml/1 tbsp chopped fresh parsley, plus extra to garnish
pinch of cayenne pepper
45ml/3 tbsp single (light) cream (optional)
salt and ground black pepper

1 Melt the butter in a frying pan, add the leek, garlic, celery and bacon and cook, stirring frequently, for 10 minutes, until soft but not browned. Transfer the mixture to the ceramic cooking pot and switch the slow cooker on to high.

2 Place half the corn kernels in a food processor or blender. Add about 75ml/2½fl oz/⅓ cup of the milk and process until the mixture is well blended and fairly thick and creamy.

3 Sprinkle the flour over the leek mixture and stir in. Gradually add the remaining milk, stirring after each addition. Stir in the stock, followed by the corn mixture. Cover the slow cooker with the lid and cook for 2 hours.

4 Add the rice to the pot and cook for 30 minutes. Meanwhile, pull the corals away from the scallops and slice the white flesh into 5mm/¼in slices. Cut the fish into bitesize chunks. Add the scallops and fish to the chowder and gently stir to combine. Cover and cook for 15 minutes.

5 Add the corals, parsley and cayenne pepper and cook for 5–10 minutes, or until the vegetables, rice and fish are tender. Add the cream, if using. Serve hot, garnished with fresh parsley.

Salmon Soup Energy 1153kcal/4772kJ; Protein 44.9g; Carbohydrate 13.7g, of which sugars 12.5g; Fat 102.5g, of which saturates 34.9g; Cholesterol 225mg; Calcium 127mg; Fibre 4.7g; Sodium 268mg.
Seafood Chowder Energy 355Kcal/1497kJ; Protein 18.5g; Carbohydrate 45.9g, of which sugars 10.8g; Fat 12.1g, of which saturates 5.8g; Cholesterol 49mg; Calcium 179mg; Fibre 1.5g; Sodium 655mg.

Chicken, Leek and Celery Soup

This makes a substantial main course soup with fresh crusty bread.

Serves 4–6
1.3kg/3lb chicken
1 small head of celery, trimmed
1 onion, coarsely chopped
1 bouquet garni
3 large leeks
65g/2½oz/5 tbsp butter
2 potatoes, cut into chunks
150ml/¼ pint/⅔ cup dry
   white wine
30–45ml/2–3 tbsp single (light)
   cream (optional)
salt and ground black pepper
90g/3½oz pancetta, grilled until
   crisp, to garnish

1 Cut the breasts from the chicken and set aside. Chop the rest of the chicken carcass into eight to ten pieces and place in a pan. Chop four or five of the celery sticks and add them to the pan with the onion and bouquet garni. Pour in 2.4 litres/ 4 pints/10 cups water to cover the ingredients and bring to the boil. Reduce the heat, cover the pan, then simmer for 1½ hours.

2 Remove the chicken and cut off and reserve the meat. Strain the stock, then return it to the pan and boil rapidly until it has reduced to about 1.5 litres/2½ pints/6¼ cups.

3 Set about 150g/5oz leeks aside. Slice the remaining leeks and the remaining celery, reserving any celery leaves. Melt half the butter in a pan. Add the sliced leeks and celery, cover and cook over low heat for 10 minutes, until soft but not brown. Add the potatoes, wine and 1.2 litres/2 pints/5 cups of the stock. Season, bring to the boil and reduce the heat. Part-cover and simmer for 15–20 minutes, or until the potatoes are cooked.

4 Dice the reserved uncooked chicken. Melt the remaining butter in a pan and fry the chicken for 5–7 minutes, until cooked. Slice the remaining leeks, add to the chicken and fry, stirring occasionally, for a further 3–4 minutes, until just cooked.

5 Purée the soup and diced chicken from the stock. Season and add more stock if the soup is thick. Stir in the cream and chicken and leek mixture. Reheat gently and serve, topped with pancetta and the chopped reserved celery leaves.

Celeriac and Bacon Soup

Versatile, yet often overlooked, celeriac is a winter vegetable that makes excellent soup.

Serves 4
50g/2oz/¼ cup butter
2 onions, chopped
675g/1½lb celeriac, roughly diced
450g/1lb potatoes, roughly diced
1.2 litres/2 pints/5 cups
   vegetable stock
150ml/¼ pint/⅔ cup single
   (light) cream
salt and ground black pepper
sprigs of fresh thyme,
   to garnish

For the topping
1 small Savoy cabbage
50g/2oz/¼ cup butter
175g/6oz rindless streaky (fatty)
   bacon, roughly chopped
15ml/1 tbsp roughly chopped
   fresh thyme
15ml/1 tbsp roughly chopped
   fresh rosemary

1 Melt the butter in a pan. Add the onions and cook for 4–5 minutes, until softened. Add the celeriac. Put a lid on sthe pan and cook gently for 10 minutes.

2 Stir in the potatoes and stock. Bring to the boil, reduce the heat and simmer for 20 minutes or until the vegetables are very tender. Leave to cool slightly. Using a slotted spoon, remove about half the celeriac and potatoes from the soup and set them aside.

3 Purée the soup in a food processor or blender. Return it to the rinsed-out pan with the reserved celeriac and potatoes.

4 Prepare the topping. Discard the tough outer leaves from the cabbage. Roughly tear the remaining leaves, discarding any hard stalks, and blanch them in boiling salted water for 2–3 minutes. Refresh under cold running water and drain.

5 Melt the butter in a large frying pan and cook the bacon for 3–4 minutes. Add the cabbage, thyme and rosemary, and stir-fry for 5–6 minutes, until tender. Season well.

6 Add the cream to the soup and season it well, then reheat gently. Ladle the soup into bowls and pile the cabbage mixture in the middle. Garnish with sprigs of fresh thyme.

Chicken Soup Energy 294kcal/1246kJ; Protein 40.5g; Carbohydrate 22.1g, of which sugars 5.9g; Fat 2.8g, of which saturates 0.7g; Cholesterol 105mg; Calcium 69mg; Fibre 4.8g; Sodium 124mg.
Celeriac Soup Energy 462kcal/1919kJ; Protein 12.3g; Carbohydrate 24.3g, of which sugars 7.3g; Fat 35.8g, of which saturates 20.4g; Cholesterol 97mg; Calcium 144mg; Fibre 4.3g; Sodium 954mg.

Cream of Duck Soup

This rich soup is ideal to begin a festive meal.

Serves 4
2 duck breast fillets
4 rindless streaky (fatty) bacon
   rashers (strips), chopped
1 onion, chopped
1 garlic clove, chopped
2 carrots, diced
2 celery sticks, chopped
4 large mushrooms, chopped
15ml/1 tbsp tomato purée (paste)
2 duck legs, chopped into pieces
15ml/1 tbsp plain
   (all-purpose) flour
45ml/3 tbsp brandy
150ml/¼ pint/⅔ cup port

300ml/½ pint/1¼ cups red wine
900ml/1½ pints/3¾ cups
   chicken stock
1 bay leaf
2 sprigs fresh thyme
15ml/1 tbsp redcurrant jelly
150ml/¼ pint/⅔ cup double
   (heavy) cream
salt and ground black pepper

For the blueberry relish
150g/5oz/1¼ cups blueberries
15ml/1 tbsp caster
   (superfine) sugar
grated rind and juice of 2 limes
15ml/1 tbsp chopped
   fresh parsley
15ml/1 tbsp balsamic vinegar

1 Score the skin and fat on the duck breast fillets. Brown in a hot heavy pan, skin down, for 8–10 minutes. Turn and cook for 5–6 minutes, until tender. Remove the duck. Drain off some of the duck fat, leaving about 45ml/3 tbsp in the pan.

2 Add the bacon, onion, garlic, carrots, celery and mushrooms and cook for 10 minutes, stirring. Stir in the tomato purée and cook for 2 minutes. Remove the skin and bones from the duck legs and chop the flesh. Add to the pan and cook for 5 minutes.

3 Stir in the flour, then the brandy, port, wine and stock. Boil, stirring. Stir in the bay, thyme and jelly. Reduce the heat and simmer for 1 hour. Strain the soup and simmer for 10 minutes.

4 Mix all the ingredients for the blueberry relish in a mixing bowl, crushing some berries as you mix.

5 Discard the skin and fat from the duck breast fillets. Cut the meat into strips and add to the soup with the cream. Season and reheat, then ladle into bowls and serve, topped with relish.

Duck Broth with Spiced Dumplings

Handle the dumplings gently for a light texture to match their delicious flavour.

Serves 4
1 duckling, about 1.8kg/4lb,
   with liver
1 large onion, halved
2 carrots, thickly sliced
½ garlic bulb
1 bouquet garni
3 cloves
bunch of chives, in short lengths

For the spiced dumplings
2 thick slices white bread
60ml/4 tbsp milk
2 rashers (strips) rindless streaky
   (fatty) bacon
1 shallot, finely chopped
1 garlic clove, crushed
1 egg yolk, beaten
grated rind of 1 orange
2.5ml/½ tsp paprika
50g/2oz/½ cup plain
   (all-purpose) flour
salt and ground black pepper

1 Set the duck liver aside. Cut off the breasts and set them aside. Put the carcass into a pan and pour in enough water to cover. Bring to the boil and skim the scum off the surface.

2 Add the onion, carrots, garlic, bouquet garni and cloves to the pan. Reduce the heat, cover, then simmer for 2 hours, skimming off any scum occasionally.

3 Lift the carcass from the broth. Remove all meat from the carcass and shred it finely, then set it aside. Strain the broth and skim off any fat. Return the broth to the pan and then simmer, uncovered, until reduced to 1.2 litres/2 pints/5 cups.

4 For the dumplings, soak the bread in the milk for 5 minutes. Remove the skin and fat from the duck breasts. Mince (grind) the meat with the duck liver and bacon. Squeeze the milk from the bread, then mix the bread into the meat with the shallot, garlic, egg yolk, orange rind, paprika, flour and seasoning.

5 Shape the mixture into balls, a little smaller than walnuts to make 20 small dumplings. Bring a pan of lightly salted water to the boil. Poach the dumplings for 4–5 minutes, until just tender.

6 Boil the broth. Add the dumplings. Divide the shredded duck among bowls and ladle in the broth. Sprinkle with chives.

Cream of Duck Soup Energy 642kcal/2673kJ; Protein 39.2g; Carbohydrate 14.2g, of which sugars 13.6g; Fat 35g, of which saturates 17.2g; Cholesterol 252mg; Calcium 83mg; Fibre 2.8g; Sodium 384mg.
Duck Broth Energy 289kcal/1214kJ; Protein 29.9g; Carbohydrate 19g, of which sugars 2.8g; Fat 13g, of which saturates 3.1g; Cholesterol 196mg; Calcium 63mg; Fibre 1.3g; Sodium 373mg.

Crab Salad with Coriander

Crab is delicious when it is simply dressed and served in a mixed salad, as with this festive treat. The crab's richness is blended with cream, which contrasts with the apples and spring onions.

Serves 6
1 romaine lettuce
2 eating apples

juice of 1 lemon
1 bunch spring onions
  (scallions), chopped
150ml/¼ pint/⅔ cup
  whipping cream
135ml/4½fl oz crème fraîche
30ml/2 tbsp chopped fresh
  coriander (cilantro), plus
  extra to garnish
brown and white meat of 2 crabs
salt

1 Shred the lettuce and arrange in a shallow serving bowl, reserving four bowl-shaped leaves. Peel, quarter and core the apples, then cut into small dice. Put in a bowl, add the lemon juice and toss together. Add the spring onions and mix together.

2 Whisk the cream in a large bowl until it stands in soft peaks, then fold in the crème fraîche. Add the apple mixture and chopped coriander to the bowl and mix in.

3 Mix together the brown and white crab meat and season with salt to taste. Fold the meat into the cream mixture. Check the seasoning and place in the centre of the reserved lettuce leaves. Serve garnished with chopped coriander.

Cook's Tip
This dish makes a great appetizer before a Christmas meal as it can be prepared a few hours ahead. Let the salad come to room temperature before serving.

Variation
For a more substantial dish, which can be served as a light lunch or supper, simply accompany the crab salad with chopped hard-boiled eggs.

Hot Crab Soufflés

These delicious little soufflés must be served as soon as they are ready, so ensure your Christmas guests are at the table before taking the soufflés out of the oven.

Serves 6
50g/2oz/¼ cup butter
45ml/3 tbsp fine wholemeal
  (whole-wheat) breadcrumbs
4 spring onions (scallions),
  finely chopped

15ml/1 tbsp Malayan or mild
  Madras curry powder
25g/1oz/¼ cup plain
  (all-purpose) flour
105ml/7 tbsp coconut milk
  or milk
150ml/¼ pint/⅔ cup
  whipping cream
4 egg yolks
225g/8oz white crab meat
mild green Tabasco sauce
6 egg whites
salt and ground black pepper

1 Use some of the butter to grease six ramekin dishes or a 1.75 litre/3 pint/7½ cup soufflé dish.

2 Sprinkle the fine wholemeal breadcrumbs into the ramekins or soufflé dish. Roll the dishes or dish around to coat the base and sides completely, then tip out the excess breadcrumbs. Preheat the oven to 200°C/400°F/Gas 6.

3 Melt the remaining butter in a pan, add the spring onions and Malayan or mild Madras curry powder and cook over low heat for about 1 minute, until softened. Stir in the flour and cook for a further 1 minute.

4 Gradually add the coconut milk or milk and the cream, stirring constantly. Cook until smooth and thick. Off the heat, stir in the egg yolks, then the crab. Season with salt, ground black pepper and Tabasco sauce.

5 In a grease-free bowl, beat the egg whites stiffly with a pinch of salt. With a metal spoon stir one-third into the crab mixture then fold in the rest. Spoon into the dishes or dish.

6 Bake until well risen, golden brown and just firm to the touch. Individual soufflés will take 8 minutes; a large soufflé will take 15–20 minutes. Serve immediately.

Hot Crab Soufflés Energy 270kcal/1122kJ; Protein 14g; Carbohydrate 11.6g, of which sugars 2.2g; Fat 18.9g, of which saturates 12.1g; Cholesterol 181mg; Calcium 123mg; Fibre 1g; Sodium 426mg.
Crab Salad Energy 382kcal/1585kJ; Protein 20.6g; Carbohydrate 6.4g, of which sugars 6.2g; Fat 30.6g, of which saturates 19.3g; Cholesterol 151mg; Calcium 188mg; Fibre 1.4g; Sodium 571mg.

Scallops with Black Bean Sauce

When scallops are fresh, they taste exquisite when simply steamed in their shells. Here they are served with a little flavoursome sauce made from Chinese wine, black bean sauce and fresh ginger, which perfectly complements the sweet, tender flesh of the scallops.

Serves 4
8 scallops, preferably in the shell
30ml/2 tbsp Chinese wine
15ml/1 tbsp fermented
 black beans
15ml/1 tbsp chopped fresh
 root ginger
2.5ml/½ tsp sugar
15ml/1 tbsp sliced spring onions
 (scallions), to garnish

1 Preheat the oven to 160°C/325°F/Gas 3. Spread the scallop shells in a single layer on a baking sheet. Heat them for a few moments until they gape, then remove them from the oven.

2 Hold a scallop in a clean dish towel, flat side up. Using a long, flexible knife, run the blade along the inner surface of the flat shell to cut through the muscle that holds the shells together. Ease the shells apart completely.

3 Lift off the top shell. Pull out and discard the black intestinal sac and the yellowish frilly membrane. Cut the white scallop and orange coral from the bottom shell and rinse briefly under cold water. Remove and discard the white ligament attached to the scallop flesh.

4 Mix the wine, black beans, ginger and sugar in a shallow dish. Add the scallops and marinate for 30 minutes.

5 Return the scallops and marinade to the half shells and place them in a steamer. If you have bought shelled scallops, divide them – and the marinade – among four ramekins. Steam for 10 minutes. Serve immediately, garnished with spring onions.

Cook's Tip
Scallops are at their best in the autumn and early winter so are ideal for serving over the festive season.

Toast Skagen

This luxurious dish makes an ideal opener to a festive dinner party. It is quick and easy to prepare so you can spend more time with your guests.

Serves 6–8
1kg/2¼lb shell-on cooked
 prawns (shrimp)
250ml/8fl oz/1 cup sour cream
250ml/8fl oz/1 cup thick
 mayonnaise
30ml/2 tbsp chopped fresh dill,
 plus fronds to garnish
30ml/2 tbsp chopped fresh chives
a squeeze of lemon juice
25–50g/1–2oz/2–4 tbsp butter
8 slices bread, halved
salt and ground black pepper
5ml/1 tsp red lumpfish roe,
 to garnish

1 Carefully remove the shells from the prawns, keeping them intact. Put the sour cream, mayonnaise, chopped dill, chives and lemon juice in a large bowl.

2 Season the mixture with salt and ground black pepper to taste, then stir in the prawns.

3 Melt the butter in a large frying pan, add the bread slices and fry until golden brown on both sides.

4 Serve the prawn mixture piled on top of the fried bread slices and garnish each serving with a small amount of the lumpfish roe and a frond of fresh dill.

Cook's Tip
You can use peeled prawns (shrimp) for this dish, but those with their shell on taste and look better.

Variation
If you can't find lumpfish roe then salmon roe is ideal as a substitute to use as a garnish, as its beautiful orange colour and large eggs make the dish look rather special and festive. Grated horseradish is another good accompaniment.

Scallops Energy 75kcal/319kJ; Protein 12.3g; Carbohydrate 3.9g, of which sugars 0.9g; Fat 0.8g, of which saturates 0.2g; Cholesterol 24mg; Calcium 19mg; Fibre 0.3g; Sodium 91mg.
Toast Skagen Energy 415kcal/1726kJ; Protein 14.5g; Carbohydrate 15.2g, of which sugars 2.5g; Fat 33.4g, of which saturates 9.2g; Cholesterol 180mg; Calcium 128mg; Fibre 0.7g; Sodium 1065mg.

Prawn Salad with Spicy Marinade

This warm salad is a real treat on a cold wintry day. Serve with garlic and herb bread for a more substantial meal for your festive guests.

Serves 8
225g/8oz large, cooked, shelled
   prawns (shrimp)
225g/8oz smoked streaky (fatty)
   bacon rashers (strips), chopped
mixed lettuce leaves

30ml/2 tbsp chopped fresh
   chives, to garnish

For the spicy marinade
1 garlic clove, crushed
finely grated rind of 1 lemon
15ml/1 tbsp lemon juice
60ml/4 tbsp olive oil
1.5ml/¼ tsp chilli paste, or a
   large pinch dried ground chilli
15ml/1 tbsp light soy sauce
salt and ground black pepper

1 In a glass bowl, mix the prawns with the garlic, lemon rind and juice, 45ml/3 tbsp of oil, the chilli paste and soy sauce. Season with salt and black pepper. Cover the bowl with a piece of clear film (plastic wrap) and leave to marinate in a cool place for at least one hour.

2 Gently cook the bacon in the remaining oil in the pan until crisp. Drain well on kitchen paper and set aside.

3 Wash and dry the lettuce, tear the leaves into bitesize pieces and arrange them in individual bowls or on plates.

4 Just before serving, put the prawns with their marinade into a large frying pan. Bring the mixture to the boil.

5 Add the bacon to the pan with the prawns and cook for one minute. Spoon the prawns and bacon over the salad and sprinkle with chives. Serve immediately.

> **Cook's Tip**
> This dish is handy to make over the festive season as the ingredients can be prepared in advance. If you do this, cook the marinated prawns (shrimp) and bacon just before serving, spoon them over the salad and serve immediately.

Seafood Salad

This crustacean salad is delicious served with a glass of cold beer when enjoying a festive drink with friends.

Serves 6–8
200g/7oz fresh asparagus spears
1kg/2¼lb shell-on cooked
   prawns (shrimp)
200g/7oz can mussels in brine
100g/3½oz can crab meat in
   brine or the meat from 2 large
   cooked crabs
200g/7oz small mushrooms, sliced
1 cos or romaine lettuce

For the dressing
105ml/7 tbsp mayonnaise
5ml/1 tsp tomato purée (paste)
pinch of salt
1 garlic clove, crushed
15ml/1 tbsp chopped fresh dill

For the garnish
1 potato
vegetable oil, for deep-frying
4 baby tomatoes or cherry
   tomatoes, quartered
2 lemons, cut into wedges
1 bunch fresh dill

1 Stand the asparagus spears upright in a deep pan, pour in enough boiling water to come three-quarters of the way up the stalks and simmer for about 10 minutes until tender. Drain and, when cool enough to handle, cut into 5cm/2in lengths.

2 Remove the shells from the prawns, keeping them intact. If using canned mussels and crab, drain the brine. Mix the prawns with the mussels, crab, asparagus and mushrooms.

3 To make the potato garnish, finely grate the potato and rinse under cold running water. Pat dry the potato on a dish towel. Heat the oil in a deep-fryer or pan to 180–190°C/350–375°F or until a cube of bread browns in 30 seconds. Add the potato and fry until golden brown, then remove with a slotted spoon. Drain on kitchen paper and leave to cool.

4 For the dressing, mix together the mayonnaise, tomato purée, salt, garlic and dill. Add the dressing to the fish mixture and mix carefully, keeping the prawns and mussels whole.

5 To serve, chop the lettuce finely and place on individual plates. Place the salad on the lettuce and garnish with the fried potato, tomatoes, lemon wedges and dill.

Prawn Salad Energy 298kcal/1240kJ; Protein 18.8g; Carbohydrate 28.1g, of which sugars 1.6g; Fat 12.1g, of which saturates 2g; Cholesterol 146mg; Calcium 102mg; Fibre 1.4g; Sodium 586mg.
Seafood Salad Energy 594kcal/2531kJ; Protein 113.3g; Carbohydrate 2.8g, of which sugars 1.2g; Fat 14.6g, of which saturates 2.9g; Cholesterol 1337mg; Calcium 565mg; Fibre 0.9g; Sodium 7723mg.

Gravlax with Mustard and Dill Sauce

Gravlax may be widely available commercially but, for a festive treat, the home-made version really has no comparison. The key to making successful gravlax is in the mustard and dill sauce with which the fish is served.

Serves 6–8
1kg/2¼lb fresh salmon, filleted
   and boned, with skin on
50g/2oz/½ cup sea salt
50g/2oz/½ cup caster
   (superfine) sugar

10ml/2 tsp crushed
   white peppercorns
200g/7oz/2 cups chopped fresh
   dill with stalks
fresh dill fronds, to garnish

For the mustard and dill sauce
115g/4oz Dijon mustard
115g/4oz/generous ½ cup sugar
15ml/1 tbsp vinegar
5ml/1 tsp salt
ground black pepper
300ml/½ pint/1¼ cups
   vegetable oil
115g/4oz/2 cups chopped fresh
   dill fronds

1 Using tweezers, remove any pinbones from the salmon. Then mix the salt and sugar together. Sprinkle a little on to the centre of a sheet of foil and place half the salmon fillet, skin side down, on top. Sprinkle the salmon with a little more salt mixture.

2 Sprinkle the white pepper on the flesh side of both salmon fillets and then add the chopped dill to both fillets. Place the second salmon fillet, skin side up, on top of the first fillet and finally sprinkle over the remaining salt mixture.

3 Wrap the foil around the salmon fillets and leave in the refrigerator for 48 hours, turning the salmon every 12 hours.

4 To make the sauce, put the mustard, sugar, vinegar and salt and pepper into a bowl and mix them all together. Then very slowly drizzle the oil into the mixture, whisking it all the time until you end up with a thick, shiny sauce. Finally add the chopped fresh dill to the mixture.

5 When the salmon has marinated slice it thinly, from one end, at an angle of 45 degrees. Serve on individual serving plates or on one large dish with the sauce. Garnish with dill fronds.

Salmon and Scallop Brochettes

With their delicate colours, really superb flavour and attractive lemon grass skewers, these brochettes make the perfect opener for a sophisticated dinner party at Christmas time.

Serves 4
8 lemon grass stalks
225g/8oz salmon fillet, skinned
8 shucked queen scallops, with
   their corals if possible

8 baby (pearl) onions, peeled
   and blanched
½ yellow (bell) pepper, cut into
   8 squares
25g/1oz/2 tbsp butter
juice of ½ lemon
salt, ground white pepper
   and paprika

For the sauce
30ml/2 tbsp dry vermouth
50g/2oz/¼ cup butter
5ml/1 tsp chopped fresh tarragon

1 Preheat the grill (broiler) to medium-high. Cut off the top 7.5–10cm/3–4in of each lemon grass stalk. Reserve the bulb ends to use in another dish.

2 Cut the salmon fillet into twelve 2cm/¾in cubes. Thread the salmon, scallops, corals if available, onions and pepper squares on to the lemon grass and arrange the brochettes in a grill pan.

3 Melt the butter in a small pan, add the lemon juice and a pinch of paprika and stir well to combine. Brush the mixture all over the brochettes.

4 Grill (broil) the skewers for about 2–3 minutes on each side, turning and basting the brochettes every minute, until the fish and scallops are just cooked through, but are still very juicy and succulent. Transfer to a platter and keep hot while you make the tarragon butter sauce.

5 Pour the dry vermouth and the leftover cooking juices from the brochettes into a small pan. Bring to the boil and continue to boil fiercely to reduce the liquid by half.

6 Add the butter and melt, then stir in the chopped fresh tarragon and salt and ground white pepper to taste. Pour the butter sauce over the brochettes and serve.

Gravlax Energy 543kcal/2258kJ; Protein 26.4g; Carbohydrate 21g, of which sugars 20.7g; Fat 39.8g, of which saturates 5.4g; Cholesterol 63mg; Calcium 58mg; Fibre 0.3g; Sodium 428mg.
Salmon Brochettes Energy 321kcal/1336kJ; Protein 23.5g; Carbohydrate 4.8g, of which sugars 2.7g; Fat 22.4g, of which saturates 11.1g; Cholesterol 92mg; Calcium 36mg; Fibre 0.6g; Sodium 231mg.

Melon and Prosciutto Salad

Cool fragrant melon wrapped with air-dried ham makes a delicious appetizer. If making this dish outside the festive period, when strawberries are in season, serve with a fruity salsa.

Serves 4
1 large cantaloupe, Charentais or Galia melon
175g/6oz prosciutto or Serrano ham, thinly sliced

For the salsa
225g/8oz/2 cups strawberries
5ml/1 tsp caster (superfine) sugar
30ml/2 tbsp groundnut (peanut) or sunflower oil
15ml/1 tbsp orange juice
2.5ml/½ tsp finely grated orange rind
2.5ml/½ tsp finely grated fresh root ginger
salt and ground black pepper

1 Halve the melon and scoop the seeds out with a spoon. Cut the rind away with a paring knife, then slice the melon thickly. Chill until ready to serve.

2 To make the salsa, hull the strawberries and cut them into large dice. Place in a small mixing bowl with the sugar and crush lightly to release the juices.

3 Add the oil, orange juice, rind and ginger and mix until all the ingredients are combined. Season to taste with salt and pepper.

4 Arrange the sliced melon on a serving plate, lay the ham over the top and serve with a bowl of salsa, handed round separately for diners to help themselves.

Cook's Tip
Prosciutto means 'ham' in Italian, and is a term generally used to describe seasoned, salt-cured and air-dried hams. Parma ham is the most famed prosciutto. Italian prosciuttos are designated prosciutto cotto, or cooked, and prosciutto crudo, or raw – although edible due to curing. They are labelled according to the place of origin, such as prosciutto di Parma and prosciutto di San Daniele. Buy it in supermarkets and Italian delicatessens.

Figs with Prosciutto and Roquefort

In this easy, stylish dish, figs and honey balance the richness of the ham and cheese. Serve with warm bread for a simple light appetizer before any rich festive meal.

Serves 4
8 fresh figs
75g/3oz prosciutto
45ml/3 tbsp clear honey
75g/3oz Roquefort cheese
ground black pepper

1 Preheat the grill (broiler). Quarter the figs and place on a foil-lined grill rack. Tear each slice of prosciutto into two or three pieces. Crumple the pieces of prosciutto and place them on the foil beside the figs. Brush the figs all over with about 15ml/1 tbsp of the clear honey and cook under the grill until lightly browned all over.

2 Crumble the Roquefort cheese and divide among four plates, setting it to one side. Add the honey-grilled figs and ham and pour over any cooking juices caught on the foil. Drizzle the remaining honey over the figs, ham and cheese, and serve seasoned with plenty of ground black pepper.

Cook's Tip
Fresh figs are a delicious treat, whether you choose dark purple, yellowy green or green-skinned varieties. When they are ripe, you can split them open with your fingers to reveal the soft, sweet flesh full of edible seeds.

Variations
• *Any thinly sliced cured ham can be used instead of prosciutto: Westphalian, Bayonne, Culatello or Serrano.*
• *The figs could be replaced with fresh pears. Slice two ripe but firm dessert pears in quarters and remove the cores. Toss in olive oil and cook on a hot ridged grill or griddle pan for 2 minutes on each side. Drizzle balsamic vinegar over and cook for 1 minute more until nicely coloured.*

Carpaccio with Rocket

Invented in Venice, carpaccio is named in honour of the Renaissance painter. In this sophisticated Italian dish, raw beef is lightly dressed with lemon juice and olive oil, and it is traditionally served with shavings of Parmesan cheese. Use very fresh meat of the best quality and ask the butcher to slice it very thinly.

Serves 4

1 garlic clove, peeled and
  cut in half
1 1/2 lemons
50ml/2fl oz/1/4 cup extra virgin
  olive oil
2 bunches rocket (arugula)
4 very thin slices of beef fillet
115g/4oz Parmesan
  cheese, shaved
salt and ground black pepper

1 Rub the cut side of the garlic over the inside of a bowl. Squeeze the lemons into the bowl, then whisk in the olive oil. Season with salt and ground black pepper, then leave to stand for at least 15 minutes.

2 Carefully wash the bunches of rocket and tear off any thick stalks. Spin dry or pat dry with kitchen paper. Arrange the rocket around the edge of a large serving platter or divide it among four individual plates.

3 Place the sliced beef in the centre of the platter and pour the dressing over, ensuring that the meat gets an even covering.

4 Arrange the Parmesan shavings on top of the meat slices and serve immediately.

Variation

You can also serve meaty fish, such as tuna, in the same way if you have festive guests who eat fish but not meat. Place a fresh tuna steak between sheets of clear film (plastic wrap) and pound with a rolling pin to flatten. Roll it up tightly and wrap in clear film. Place in the freezer for 4 hours until firm. Unwrap the fish and cut the fish crossways into slices as thin as possible. Serve in the same way as the beef carpaccio.

Steak Tartare on Toast

Steak tartare is delicious used to top toast or spread on a baguette for a festive appetizer. The key to a successful and, above all, safe steak tartare is to use only ultra-fresh beef of superior quality, and to chop it only at the very last minute.

Serves 4

2 fresh egg yolks
15ml/1 tbsp Dijon mustard
15ml/1 tbsp tomato ketchup
10ml/2 tsp Worcestershire sauce
Tabasco sauce, to taste
75ml/5 tbsp vegetable oil
2 shallots, finely chopped

30ml/2 tbsp capers, rinsed
6 cornichons (small pickled
  gherkins), finely chopped
30ml/2 tbsp finely chopped parsley
500g/1 1/4lb fresh sirloin steak,
  finely minced (ground) or
  finely chopped
4 slices good quality white bread,
  toasted, crusts removed
15g/1/2oz/1 tbsp
  unsalted butter
salt and ground black pepper

For the garnish
4 lettuce leaves
16 tomato slices
4 cornichons
4 fresh parsley sprigs

1 Place the egg yolks in a large stainless steel bowl. Add the mustard. With a wire whisk, mix in the ketchup, Worcestershire sauce and Tabasco, with a little salt and pepper. Slowly whisk in the oil until the mixture is smooth. Fold in the shallots, capers, cornichons and the chopped parsley.

2 Add the chopped or minced (ground) raw meat to the bowl and mix well, using a spoon or clean hands. Shape into four patties by hand or use a small round mould.

3 Spread the toasted bread with the butter. Place a patty of the steak tartare on each slice of toast and press it down to cover the surface of the toast evenly.

4 Using a paring knife, score diamond shapes into the meat. Garnish four plates with lettuce leaves and top with the toast. Place four tomato slices alongside. Slice each cornichon lengthways, keeping one end intact, then fan the slices out. Place one fan on each slice of toast and garnish with a fresh parsley sprig. Serve immediately.

Carpaccio Energy 244kcal/1013kJ; Protein 17.3g; Carbohydrate 0.1g, of which sugars 0.1g; Fat 19.4g, of which saturates 7.9g; Cholesterol 44mg; Calcium 384mg; Fibre 0.4g; Sodium 336mg.
Steak Tartare Energy 538kcal/2237kJ; Protein 29.7g; Carbohydrate 20.4g, of which sugars 5.5g; Fat 38.3g, of which saturates 12.7g; Cholesterol 184mg; Calcium 84mg; Fibre 1.5g; Sodium 318mg.

Guacamole

Serve this classic Mexican dip at a festive party. Nachos or tortilla chips are the perfect accompaniment.

Serves 4

2 ripe avocados
2 fresh red chillies, seeded
1 garlic clove
1 shallot
30ml/2 tbsp olive oil, plus
   extra to serve
juice of 1 lemon
salt
5ml/1 tsp flat leaf parsley leaves,
   to garnish

1 Halve the avocados, remove their stones (pits) and, using a spoon, scoop out their flesh into a bowl.

2 Mash the flesh well with a potato masher or a large fork until it is slightly coarse.

3 Finely chop the fresh red chillies, garlic and shallot, then stir into the mashed avocado. Drizzle in the olive oil and lemon juice and mix well. Add salt to taste.

4 Spoon the mixture into a small serving bowl. Drizzle over a little olive oil and sprinkle with a few flat leaf parsley leaves. Serve immediately with tortilla chips for dipping.

Cook's Tip
• Avocado flesh will discolour quickly when exposed to the air. If preparing this in advance for a Christmas party, ensure that it is tightly covered with clear film (plastic wrap).
• Ripe avocados will yield slightly when squeezed on the ends. To speed up the ripening process, place avocados in a paper bag and set them aside at room temperature.

Variation
Make a completely smooth guacamole by whizzing the ingredients in a blender or food processor. For a chunkier version, add a diced tomato or red (bell) pepper.

Tsatziki

Cool, creamy and refreshing, tzatziki is wonderfully easy to make and even easier to eat. Serve this classic Greek dip with slices of toasted pitta bread as part of a festive buffet spread, as a healthy appetizer or with a selection of chargrilled vegetables.

Serves 4

1 mini cucumber
4 spring onions (scallions)
1 garlic clove
200ml/7fl oz/scant 1 cup Greek
   (US strained plain) yogurt
45ml/3 tbsp chopped fresh mint
fresh mint sprig, to garnish
   (optional)
salt and ground black pepper

1 Trim the ends from the mini cucumber, then cut the flesh into dice about 5mm/¼in in size.

2 Cut the ends from the spring onions, keeping plenty of the green parts, and the garlic, then chop both very finely.

3 Beat the yogurt until smooth, if necessary, then gently stir in the cucumber, onions, garlic and mint.

4 Transfer the mixture to a serving bowl and add salt and plenty of ground black pepper to taste. Chill until ready to serve and then garnish with a small mint sprig, if you like.

Cook's Tip
Choose Greek (US strained plain) yogurt for this dip – it has a higher fat content than most yogurts, which gives the tsatziki a deliciously rich, creamy texture.

Variation
A similar, but smoother, dip can be made in the food processor. Peel one mini cucumber and process with two garlic cloves and 75g/3oz/3 cups mixed fresh herbs to a purée. Stir the purée into 200ml/7fl oz/scant 1 cup sour cream, and season to taste with salt and ground black pepper.

Guacamole Energy 156kcal/645kJ; Protein 2.1g; Carbohydrate 3.7g, of which sugars 2.5g; Fat 14.7g, of which saturates 3.1g; Cholesterol 0mg; Calcium 26mg; Fibre 3.5g; Sodium 11mg.
Tsatziki Energy 67kcal/279kJ; Protein 4g; Carbohydrate 2.3g, of which sugars 1.6g; Fat 5.3g, of which saturates 2.6g; Cholesterol 0mg; Calcium 107mg; Fibre 0.3g; Sodium 39mg.

Hummus

This nutritious dip is great served as a dip with crudités at a festive party or spread over hot toast.

Serves 4
400g/14oz can chickpeas, drained
2 garlic cloves
30ml/2 tbsp tahini or smooth peanut butter
60ml/4 tbsp olive oil
juice of 1 lemon
2.5ml/½ tsp cayenne pepper
15ml/1 tbsp sesame seeds
sea salt

1 Rinse the chickpeas well and place in a food processor or blender with the garlic and a good pinch of sea salt. Process until very finely chopped.

2 Add the tahini or smooth peanut butter and process until fairly smooth. With the motor still running, slowly pour in the olive oil and the lemon juice.

3 Stir in the cayenne pepper and add more salt, to taste, if necessary. If the mixture is too thick, stir in a little cold water. Transfer the purée to a serving bowl.

4 Heat a small non-stick pan and add the sesame seeds. Cook for 2–3 minutes, shaking the pan, until the seeds are golden. Allow to cool, then sprinkle over the purée. Serve immediately on toasted bread or with crudités.

Cook's Tip
Tahini is a classic ingredient in this Middle Eastern dip. It is a thick, smooth and oily paste, which is made from sesame seeds. It is usually available from health food stores and large supermarkets, in light and dark varieties.

Variation
The peanut butter would not be used in a traditional recipe but it is a useful substitute if tahini is not available.

Saucy Tomato Dip

This versatile dip is delicious and can be made up to a day in advance, so is ideal for serving at a Christmas drinks party.

Serves 4
1 shallot
2 garlic cloves
handful of fresh basil leaves, plus extra to garnish
500g/1¼lb ripe tomatoes
30ml/2 tbsp olive oil
2 fresh green chillies, halved and seeds removed
salt and ground black pepper

1 Peel and halve the shallot and garlic cloves. Place in a blender or food processor with the basil leaves, then process the ingredients until they are very finely chopped.

2 Halve the tomatoes and add to the shallot mixture. Pulse the power until the mixture is well blended and all the tomatoes are finely chopped.

3 With the motor still running, slowly pour in the olive oil. Add salt and black pepper to taste.

4 Finely slice the fresh green chillies into tiny strips and stir them into the tomato mixture. Serve at room temperature. Garnish with a few torn basil leaves.

Cook's Tip
You may need to wear a pair of kitchen gloves while preparing chillies or cut them up with a knife and fork if you find that they irritate your skin. Wash your hands in warm, soapy water after preparing the chillies.

Variation
This dip is best made with full-flavoured, sun-ripened tomatoes. Over the festive period, when tomatoes are out of season, you can use a drained 400g/14oz can of plum tomatoes instead.

Hummus Energy 210kcal/880kJ; Protein 10.3g; Carbohydrate 16.9g; of which sugars 0.6g; Fat 11.8g; of which saturates 1.6g; Cholesterol 0mg; Calcium 146mg; Fibre 5.5g; Sodium 223mg.
Saucy Tomato Dip Energy 81kcal/336kJ; Protein 2.3g; Carbohydrate 4.2g, of which sugars 4.2g; Fat 6.2g, of which saturates 0.9g; Cholesterol 0mg; Calcium 24mg; Fibre 1.3g; Sodium 15mg.

Smoked Salmon with Warm Potato Cakes

Although the ingredients are timeless, this combination makes an excellent modern dish, which is deservedly popular as an appetizer or as a substantial canapé to serve with festive drinks. It also makes a perfect brunch dish to serve on Christmas Day, accompanied by lightly scrambled eggs and freshly squeezed orange juice. Choose wild fish if possible.

Serves 6

450g/1lb potatoes, cooked
  and mashed
75g/3oz/²⁄₃ cup plain
  (all-purpose) flour
2 eggs, beaten
2 spring onions
  (scallions), chopped
a little freshly grated nutmeg
50g/2oz/¹⁄₄ cup butter, melted
150ml/¹⁄₄ pint/²⁄₃ cup sour cream
12 slices of smoked salmon
salt and ground black pepper
chopped fresh chives, to garnish

1 Put the potatoes, flour, eggs and spring onions into a large mixing bowl. Season with salt, ground black pepper and a little nutmeg, and add half the butter.

2 Mix thoroughly until the mixture is well combined and shape into 12 small potato cakes.

3 Heat the remaining butter in a non-stick frying pan and cook the potato cakes until browned on both sides.

4 To serve, mix the sour cream with some salt and pepper. Fold a piece of smoked salmon and place on top of each potato cake. Top the salmon with the cream and then the chives and serve immediately.

> **Cook's Tip**
> If it is more convenient, you can make the potato cakes in advance and keep them overnight in the refrigerator. When required, warm them through in a hot oven about 15 minutes before assembling and serving.

Russian Pancakes with Mixed Toppings

These mini pancakes make delicious festive canapés. They can be made with caviar or smoked salmon, or with crème fraîche, soused herring and onion.

Makes 20

25g/1oz fresh yeast
5ml/1 tsp caster (superfine) sugar
50ml/2fl oz/¹⁄₄ cup warm water
2 egg yolks
250ml/8fl oz/1 cup warm milk
2.5ml/¹⁄₂ tsp salt

175g/6oz/1¹⁄₂ cups plain white
  (all-purpose) flour
3 egg whites
150ml/¹⁄₄ pint/²⁄₃ cup rapeseed
  (canola) oil

For the toppings
slices of smoked salmon
pickled herring, chopped
chopped onion
crème fraîche
caviar
lemon wedges and dill, to garnish

1 Put the yeast, sugar and warm water in a bowl and blend until smooth. Leave in a warm place for 20 minutes until frothy.

2 Mix the egg yolks, 200ml/6fl oz/³⁄₄ cup of the warm milk and the salt in a bowl. Stir in the yeast mixture and the flour, a little at a time, to form a smooth batter. Leave to rise in a warm place for 4–5 hours, stirring three or four times.

3 Stir the remaining 50ml/2fl oz/¹⁄₄ cup of the milk into the batter. Whisk the egg whites in a dry bowl until they form soft peaks. Fold into the batter and set aside for 30 minutes.

4 Heat the oil in a frying pan and add 25–30ml/1¹⁄₂–2 tbsp of batter for each pancake. Fry over medium heat until set and risen, then cook the other side. Cook the remaining batter to make 20 pancakes. Let your guests choose their own toppings.

> **Cook's Tip**
> Start the batter a minimum of 3 hours before frying for the yeast to rise fully. Stir the batter 3–4 times while rising.

Salmon with Potato Cakes Energy 326kcal/1365kJ; Protein 21.9g; Carbohydrate 22.9g, of which sugars 2.3g; Fat 17g, of which saturates 8.6g; Cholesterol 119mg; Calcium 70mg; Fibre 1.2g; Sodium 1315mg.
Russian Pancakes Energy 89kcal/372kJ; Protein 2g; Carbohydrate 7.6g, of which sugars 0.7g; Fat 5.9g, of which saturates 0.9g; Cholesterol 21mg; Calcium 30mg; Fibre 0.3g; Sodium 16mg.

Butterfly Prawn Skewers with Chilli and Raspberry Dip

The success of this dish depends upon the quality of the prawns, so it is worthwhile getting really good ones, which have a fine flavour and firm texture.

Serves 4–6
*30 raw king prawns
  (jumbo shrimp), peeled*

*15ml/1 tbsp sunflower oil
sea salt*

*For the chilli
and raspberry dip*
30ml/2 tbsp raspberry vinegar
15ml/1 tbsp sugar
115g/4oz/²⁄₃ cup raspberries
*1 large fresh red chilli, seeded
  and finely chopped*

1 If using wooden skewers, soak 30 of them in cold water for 30 minutes so that they don't burn during cooking.

2 Make the dip by mixing the vinegar and sugar in a small pan. Heat gently until the sugar has dissolved, stirring constantly, then add the raspberries.

3 When the raspberry juices start to flow, transfer the mixture into a sieve (strainer) set over a bowl. Push the raspberries through the sieve using the back of a ladle or wooden spoon. Discard the seeds left in the sieve.

4 Stir the chilli into the purée and leave to cool. When the dip is cold, cover and place in a cool place until it is needed.

5 Preheat the grill (broiler). Remove the dark spinal vein from the prawns using a small, sharp knife. Make an incision down the curved back and butterfly each prawn.

6 Mix the sunflower oil with a little sea salt in a bowl. Add the prawns and toss to coat them completely. Thread the prawns on to the drained skewers, spearing them head first.

7 Grill (broil) the prawns for about 5 minutes, depending on their size, turning them over once. Serve immediately while hot, with the chilli and raspberry dip.

Breaded Tiger Prawn Skewers with Parsley

Fresh parsley and lemon are all that is required to create a lovely tiger prawn dish. They are quick and easy to make so will be ideal for a festive buffet.

Serves 4
*900g/2lb raw tiger prawns (jumbo
  shrimp), peeled*

60ml/4 tbsp olive oil
45ml/3 tbsp vegetable oil
*75g/3oz/1¼ cups very fine
  dry breadcrumbs*
1 garlic clove, crushed
*15ml/1 tbsp chopped
  fresh parsley*
salt and ground black pepper
lemon wedges, to serve

1 Slit the tiger prawns down their backs and, using the point of a sharp knife, remove the dark vein. Rinse the prawns under cold running water and dry them thoroughly between sheets of kitchen paper.

2 Put the olive and vegetable oils in a large bowl and add the prawns. Stir to ensure the oils are well combined and the prawns are evenly coated.

3 Add the fine breadcrumbs, crushed garlic and chopped parsley to the bowl of prawns. Season with salt and plenty of ground black pepper. Using your hands, or a wooden spoon, toss the prawns thoroughly to give them an even coating of the breadcrumb mixture.

4 Cover the bowl with clear film (plastic wrap) and leave to marinate for 1 hour in a cool place.

5 Carefully thread the breaded tiger prawns on to four metal or wooden skewers, curling them up as you work, so that the tails of the prawns are skewered neatly in the middle.

6 Preheat the grill (broiler) to a moderate heat. Place the prawn skewers in the grill pan and cook for about 2–3 minutes on each side until they are golden and cooked through. Serve immediately with the lemon wedges.

Prawns Skewers Energy 156kcal/635kJ; Protein 12.5g; Carbohydrate 7.3g, of which sugars 0.5g; Fat 8g, of which saturates 1.3g; Cholesterol 157mg; Calcium 64mg; Fibre 0.3g; Sodium 316mg.
Tiger Prawn Skewers Energy 415kcal/1734kJ; Protein 42.2g; Carbohydrate 14.9g, of which sugars 0.8g; Fat 21.1g, of which saturates 2.8g; Cholesterol 439mg; Calcium 227mg; Fibre 1.1g; Sodium 574mg.

Grilled Chicken Balls on Skewers with Yakitori Sauce

These tasty morsels make a great low-fat appetizer or snack to serve at a Christmas drinks party.

Serves 4
300g/11oz skinless chicken, minced (ground)
2 eggs
2.5ml/½ tsp salt
10ml/2 tsp plain (all-purpose) flour
10ml/2 tsp cornflour (cornstarch)
90ml/6 tbsp dried breadcrumbs
2.5cm/1in piece fresh root ginger, grated

For the yakitori sauce
60ml/4 tbsp sake
75ml/5 tbsp Japanese soy sauce
15ml/1 tbsp mirin (rice wine)
15ml/1 tbsp sugar
2.5ml/½ tsp cornflour (cornstarch) blended with 5ml/1 tsp water

1 Soak eight bamboo skewers for about 30 minutes in water. Put all the ingredients for the chicken balls, except the ginger, in a food processor and process to blend well.

2 Shape the mixture into a small ball about half the size of a golf ball. Make a further 30–32 balls in the same way.

3 Squeeze the juice from the grated ginger into a small mixing bowl. Discard the pulp. Preheat the grill (broiler).

4 Add the ginger juice to a small pan of boiling water. Add the chicken balls, and boil for about 7 minutes, or until the colour of the meat changes and the balls float to the surface. Scoop the balls out using a slotted spoon and drain on kitchen paper.

5 In a small pan, mix all the ingredients for the yakitori sauce, except the cornflour liquid. Bring to the boil, then simmer until the sauce has reduced slightly. Add the cornflour liquid and stir until thickened. Transfer to a small bowl.

6 Drain the skewers and thread three to four balls on each. Grill (broil) for a few minutes, turning frequently until they brown. Brush with sauce and return to the heat. Repeat twice, then serve immediately.

Fragrant Spiced Lamb on Mini Poppadums

Crisp, melt-in-the-mouth mini poppadums make a great base for these divine little bites. Top them with a drizzle of yogurt and a spoonful of mango chutney, then serve immediately. To make an equally tasty variation, you can use chicken or pork in place of the lamb.

Makes 25
30ml/2 tbsp sunflower oil
4 shallots, finely chopped
30ml/2 tbsp medium curry paste
300g/11oz minced (ground) lamb
90ml/6 tbsp tomato purée (paste)
5ml/1 tsp caster (superfine) sugar
200ml/7fl oz/scant 1 cup coconut cream
juice of 1 lime
60ml/4 tbsp chopped fresh mint leaves
25 mini poppadums
vegetable oil, for frying
salt and ground black pepper
natural (plain) yogurt and mango chutney, to drizzle
red chilli slivers and mint leaves, to garnish

1 Heat the oil in a wok over medium heat and add the shallots. Stir fry for 4–5 minutes, until softened, then add the curry paste. Stir-fry for 1–2 minutes.

2 Add the lamb and stir-fry over high heat for 4–5 minutes, then stir in the tomato purée, sugar and coconut cream.

3 Cook the lamb over a gentle heat for 25–30 minutes, or until the meat is tender and all the liquid has been absorbed. Season with salt and pepper and stir in the lime juice and mint leaves. Remove from the heat and keep warm.

4 Fill a separate wok one-third full of oil and deep-fry the mini poppadums for about 30–40 seconds, or until puffed up and crisp. Drain on kitchen paper.

5 Place the poppadums on a large serving platter. Put a spoonful of spiced lamb on each one, then top with a little yogurt and mango chutney. Serve immediately, garnished with slivers of red chilli and mint leaves.

Grilled Chicken Balls Energy 332kcal/1398kJ; Protein 30.4g; Carbohydrate 29g, of which sugars 7.4g; Fat 9.7g, of which saturates 2.6g; Cholesterol 339mg; Calcium 84mg; Fibre 0.6g; Sodium 325mg.
Fragrant Spiced Lamb Energy 63kcal/260kJ; Protein 2.7g; Carbohydrate 2.7g, of which sugars 1.3g; Fat 4.7g, of which saturates 1.4g; Cholesterol 9mg; Calcium 7mg; Fibre 0.3g; Sodium 45mg.

Skewered Lamb with Onion Salsa

This tasty appetizer is ideal for festive entertaining. The refreshing salsa is quick and easy to make and is the ideal accompaniment to the lamb. They are also great cooked on a barbecue, if making them in summer.

Serves 4
225g/8oz lean lamb, cubed
2.5ml/½ tsp ground cumin
5ml/1 tsp paprika
15ml/1 tbsp olive oil
salt and ground black pepper

For the salsa
1 red onion, very thinly sliced
1 large tomato, seeded
　and chopped
15ml/1 tbsp red wine vinegar
3–4 fresh basil or mint leaves,
　coarsely torn
small fresh mint leaves,
　to garnish

1 Place the lamb in a bowl with the cumin, paprika, oil and seasoning. Toss well until the lamb is coated with spices.

2 Cover the bowl with clear film (plastic wrap). Set aside in a cool place for a few hours, or in the refrigerator overnight, so that the lamb absorbs the flavours.

3 Spear the marinated lamb cubes on to four small skewers. Ensure that the cubes are not to tightly packed together.

4 To make the salsa, put the sliced onion, tomato, red wine vinegar and basil or mint leaves in a small bowl and stir together until thoroughly blended. Season to taste with salt, garnish with mint, then set aside while you cook the lamb.

5 Cook the skewers under a preheated grill (broiler) for 5–10 minutes, turning frequently, until the lamb is well browned. Serve while hot, with the salsa.

Cook's Tip
If using wooden or bamboo skewers, soak them first in cold water for at least 30 minutes to prevent them from burning under the grill (broiler) during cooking.

Bacon-wrapped Beef on Skewers

These tasty little skewers are packed with Asian flavours thanks to the tangy marinade. Serve as part of a festive buffet spread or as nibbles for Christmas guests.

Serves 4
225g/8oz beef fillet (tenderloin)
　or rump (round) steak, cut
　across the grain into 12 strips
12 thin rashers (strips) of streaky
　(fatty) bacon
ground black pepper
chilli sambal, for dipping

For the marinade
15ml/1 tbsp groundnut
　(peanut) oil
30ml/2 tbsp fish sauce
30ml/2 tbsp soy sauce
4–6 garlic cloves, crushed
10ml/2 tsp sugar

1 To make the marinade, mix all the ingredients in a large bowl until the sugar dissolves. Season generously with black pepper.

2 Add the beef strips to the marinade, stir to coat them thoroughly, and set aside for about an hour.

3 Preheat a griddle pan over high heat until very hot. Remove the beef strips from the marinade and roll up each strip, then wrap it in a slice of bacon. Thread the rolls on to the skewers, so that you have three rolls on each one.

4 Cook the bacon-wrapped rolls on the hot griddle for about 4–5 minutes, turning once during the cooking process, until the bacon is golden and crispy. Serve immediately, with a bowl of chilli sambal on the side for dipping.

Cook's Tip
These tasty skewers can also be cooked under a preheated grill (broiler), or over hot coals on the barbecue. Simply cook for 6–8 minutes, turning every couple of minutes so that the bacon is browned but not burned. Serve them as an appetizer ahead of the main course – they will whet the appetite without being too filling.

Skewered Lamb Energy 135kcal/563kJ; Protein 11.4g; Carbohydrate 2g, of which sugars 1.6g; Fat 9.2g, of which saturates 3.4g; Cholesterol 43mg; Calcium 10mg; Fibre 0.5g; Sodium 51mg.
Bacon-wrapped Beef Energy 282kcal/1172kJ; Protein 21.7g; Carbohydrate 1.1g, of which sugars 1.1g; Fat 21.3g, of which saturates 7.1g; Cholesterol 69mg; Calcium 7mg; Fibre 0g; Sodium 745mg.

Grilled Vegetable Terrine

A colourful, layered terrine, this appetizer uses a variety of Mediterranean vegetables.

Serves 6
2 large red (bell) peppers, quartered, cored, seeded
2 large yellow (bell) peppers, quartered, cored, seeded
1 large aubergine (eggplant), sliced lengthways
2 courgettes (zucchini), sliced lengthways
90ml/6 tbsp olive oil
1 large red onion, thinly sliced
75g/3oz/½ cup raisins
15ml/1 tbsp tomato purée (paste)
15ml/1 tbsp red wine vinegar
400ml/14fl oz/1⅔ cups tomato juice
15g/½oz/2 tbsp powdered gelatine
fresh basil leaves, to garnish

For the dressing
90ml/6 tbsp extra virgin olive oil
30ml/2 tbsp red wine vinegar
salt and ground black pepper

1 Place the peppers skin side up under a hot grill (broiler) and cook until the skins are blackened. Transfer to a bowl and cover. Leave to cool. Arrange the aubergine and courgette slices on separate baking sheets. Brush them with oil and cook under the grill, turning occasionally, until they are tender and golden.

2 Heat the remaining olive oil in a frying pan, and add the onion, raisins, tomato purée and red wine vinegar. Cook gently until the mixture is syrupy. Set aside and leave to cool.

3 Lightly oil a 1.75 litre/3 pint/7½ cup terrine, then line it with clear film (plastic wrap), leaving a little hanging over the sides. Pour half the tomato juice into a pan, and sprinkle with the gelatine. Dissolve over low heat, stirring frequently.

4 Place a layer of red peppers in the base of the terrine, and pour in enough tomato juice with gelatine to cover. Continue layering the vegetables, pouring tomato juice over each layer. Finish with a layer of red peppers. Pour the remaining tomato juice into the terrine. Cover and chill until set.

5 To make the dressing, whisk together the oil and vinegar, and season. Turn out the terrine and remove the clear film. Serve in slices, drizzled with dressing and garnished with basil leaves.

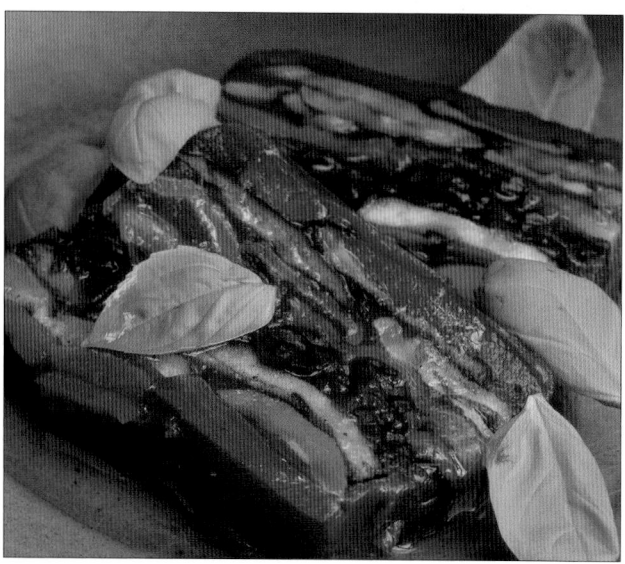

Asparagus and Egg Terrine

For festive entertaining, this terrine is a delicious choice.

Serves 8
150ml/¼ pint/⅔ cup milk
150ml/¼ pint/⅔ cup double (heavy) cream
40g/1½oz/3 tbsp butter
40g/1½oz/3 tbsp plain (all-purpose) flour
75g/3oz herbed or garlic cream cheese
675g/1½lb asparagus, cooked
vegetable oil, for brushing
2 eggs, separated
15ml/1 tbsp chopped fresh chives
30ml/2 tbsp chopped fresh dill
salt and ground black pepper
fresh dill sprigs, to garnish

For the hollandaise sauce
15ml/1 tbsp white wine vinegar
15ml/1 tbsp fresh orange juice
4 black peppercorns
1 bay leaf
2 egg yolks
115g/4oz/½ cup butter, melted and cooled slightly

1 Heat the milk and cream in a small pan to just below boiling point. Melt the butter in a medium pan, stir in the flour and cook over low heat, stirring constantly, to a thick paste. Gradually stir in the milk, whisking as it thickens. Stir in the cream cheese, season to taste and leave to cool slightly.

2 Trim the asparagus to fit the width of a 1.2 litre/2 pint/5 cup loaf tin (pan) or terrine. Lightly oil the tin and then base line with baking parchment. Preheat the oven to 180°C/350°F/Gas 4.

3 Beat the egg yolks into the sauce. Whisk the whites until stiff. Fold in with the chives, dill and seasoning. Layer the asparagus and egg mixture in the tin, starting and finishing with the asparagus. Cover with foil, place in a roasting pan and half fill with hot water. Cook for 45–55 minutes, until firm. Cool, then chill.

4 To make the sauce, put the vinegar, orange juice, peppercorns and bay leaf in a pan and heat gently until reduced by half. Cool the sauce slightly, then whisk in the egg yolks, then the butter, over a very gentle heat. Season to taste and continue whisking until thick. Keep the sauce warm over a pan of hot water.

5 Invert the terrine on to a serving dish, remove the paper and garnish with the dill. Serve in slices with the warmed sauce.

Vegetable Terrine Energy 296kcal/1229kJ; Protein 3.5g; Carbohydrate 20.2g, of which sugars 19.7g; Fat 22.9g, of which saturates 3.4g; Cholesterol 0mg; Calcium 42mg; Fibre 3.8g; Sodium 169mg.
Asparagus Terrine Energy 359kcal/1483kJ; Protein 6.6g; Carbohydrate 7.1g, of which sugars 3.2g; Fat 34.1g, of which saturates 20.2g; Cholesterol 175mg; Calcium 87mg; Fibre 1.6g; Sodium 179mg.

Shrimp, Egg and Avocado Mousses

A light creamy mousse, with lots of texture and a great mix of flavours, will go down a treat at Christmas time.

Serves 6
a little olive oil
20ml/4 tsp powdered gelatine
juice and rind of 1 lemon
60ml/4 tbsp mayonnaise
60ml/4 tbsp chopped fresh dill
5ml/1 tsp anchovy essence (paste)
5ml/1 tsp Worcestershire sauce
1 large avocado, ripe but just firm

4 hard-boiled eggs, peeled
   and chopped
175g/6oz/1 cup cooked peeled
   prawns (shrimp), coarsely
   chopped if large
250ml/8fl oz/1 cup double
   (heavy) or whipping cream,
   lightly whipped
2 egg whites, whisked
salt and ground black pepper
fresh dill or parsley sprigs,
   to garnish
warmed multigrain bread or toast,
   to serve

1 Prepare six small ramekins. Lightly grease the dishes with olive oil, then wrap a baking parchment collar around the top of each and secure with tape. This makes sure that you can fill the dishes as high as you like and that the extra mixture will be supported while it is setting. The mousses will, therefore, look really dramatic when you remove the paper. Alternatively, prepare just one small soufflé dish.

2 Dissolve the gelatine in the lemon juice with 15ml/1 tbsp hot water in a small bowl set over hot water, until clear, stirring occasionally. Allow to cool slightly, then blend in the lemon rind, mayonnaise, dill, anchovy essence and Worcestershire sauce.

3 In a medium bowl, mash the avocado flesh. Add the eggs and prawns. Stir in the gelatine mixture and then fold in the cream, egg whites and seasoning to taste. When evenly blended, spoon into the ramekins or soufflé dish and chill for 3–4 hours. Garnish with the herbs and serve with bread.

> **Cook's Tip**
> *Other seafood can be a good alternative to prawns (shrimp).*
> *Use the same quantity of smoked trout, or cooked crab meat.*

Smoked Salmon Pâté

This pâté is in individual ramekins lined with smoked salmon so that it looks really special. It is the ideal appetizer for an elaborate dinner party or special feast over the festive season. Taste as you are making it; add more lemon juice and seasoning if necessary.

Serves 4
350g/12oz thinly sliced smoked
   salmon (wild if possible)
150ml/¼ pint/⅔ cup double
   (heavy) cream
finely grated rind and juice of
   1 lemon
salt and ground black pepper
Melba toast, to serve

1 Line four small ramekin dishes with clear film (plastic wrap), then line the dishes with 115g/4oz of the smoked salmon cut into strips long enough to flop over the edges.

2 In a food processor fitted with a metal blade, process the rest of the salmon with the double cream, lemon rind and juice, salt and plenty of ground black pepper.

3 Pack the lined ramekins with the smoked salmon pâté, pressing it down gently. Wrap the loose strips of smoked salmon over the top of the pâté.

4 Cover the ramekins with clear film and chill for at least 30 minutes in the refrigerator.

5 To serve the pâtés, invert the ramekins on to plates. Serve, accompanied by slices of Melba toast.

> **Cook's Tip**
> *Melba toast was created by the celebrated chef Auguste Escoffier for opera singer Dame Nellie Melba. It is sold packaged in most supermarkets but is easy to make at home. Simply toast a slice of bread under a grill (broiler), cut off the crusts and then carefully cut it in half to make two slices of half the thickness. Return the halved slices of bread to the grill to brown the untoasted sides.*

Shrimp Mousses Energy 384kcal/1589kJ; Protein 12g; Carbohydrate 2.1g, of which sugars 1.7g; Fat 38.9g, of which saturates 15.7g; Cholesterol 245mg; Calcium 88mg; Fibre 1.3g; Sodium 230mg.
Smoked Salmon Pâté Energy 311kcal/1293kJ; Protein 22.9g; Carbohydrate 0.8g, of which sugars 0.8g; Fat 24.1g, of which saturates 13.2g; Cholesterol 82mg; Calcium 36mg; Fibre 0g; Sodium 1654mg.

Cardamom Chicken Mousselines

These mousselines are made in the slow cooker and make an elegant appetizer. They should be served warm, not hot, so when they are cooked, turn off the slow cooker and leave to cool for half an hour before eating.

Serves 6

350g/12oz skinless chicken
  breast fillets
1 shallot, finely chopped

115g/4oz/1 cup full-fat soft white
  (farmer's) cheese
1 egg, lightly beaten
2 egg whites
crushed seeds of 2 cardamom pods
60ml/4 tbsp white wine
150ml/¼ pint/⅔ cup double
  (heavy) cream
oregano sprigs, to serve

For the tomato vinaigrette

350g/12oz ripe tomatoes
10ml/2 tsp balsamic vinegar
30ml/2 tbsp olive oil

1 Chop the chicken and put in a food processor with the shallot. Process until fairly smooth. Add the cheese, beaten egg, egg whites, cardamom seeds and wine and season with salt and pepper. Process again until the ingredients are blended.

2 Gradually add the cream, using the pulsing action, until the mixture has a smooth and creamy texture. Transfer to a bowl, cover with clear film (plastic wrap) and chill for 30 minutes.

3 Meanwhile, prepare six 150ml/¼ pint/⅔ cup ramekins or dariole moulds that will all fit in the slow cooker. Lightly grease the base of each one, then line. Pour about 2cm/¾ in hot water into the ceramic cooking pot and switch the cooker to high.

4 Divide the mixture among the dishes. Cover with foil and put in the ceramic cooking pot. Add more hot water to come halfway up the dishes. Cover and cook for 2½–3 hours until firm.

5 Meanwhile, peel, quarter, seed and dice the tomatoes. Place in a bowl and sprinkle with the vinegar and salt. Stir well.

6 To serve, unmould the mousselines on to warmed plates. Place tomato vinaigrette around each, then drizzle over a little olive oil and add black pepper. Garnish with sprigs of oregano.

Chicken and Pistachio Pâté

This simplified pâté can be made using either chicken pieces or left-over turkey meat. Serve it as part of a festive buffet accompanied by a herb mayonnaise.

Serves 10–12

900g/2lb boneless chicken meat
1 skinless chicken breast fillet
  (about 175g/6oz)
25g/1oz/⅔ cup fresh
  white breadcrumbs
120ml/4fl oz/½ cup
  whipping cream

1 egg white
4 spring onions (scallions),
  finely chopped
1 garlic clove, finely chopped
75g/3oz cooked ham, cut into
  1cm/½in cubes
50g/2oz/⅓ cup shelled
  pistachio nuts
45ml/3 tbsp chopped
  fresh tarragon
pinch of grated nutmeg
5ml/1 tsp salt
7.5ml/1½ tsp pepper
green salad, to serve

1 Trim all the fat, tendons and connective tissue from the 900g/2lb chicken meat and cut into 5cm/2in cubes. Put in a food processor fitted with the metal blade and pulse to chop the meat to a smooth purée, in two or three batches if necessary.

2 Preheat the oven to 180°C/350°F/Gas 4. Cut the chicken breast fillet into 1cm/⅜in cubes.

3 In a large mixing bowl, soak the breadcrumbs in the cream. Add the puréed chicken, egg white, spring onions, garlic, ham, pistachio nuts, tarragon, nutmeg and salt and pepper. Using a wooden spoon or your fingers, mix until very well combined.

4 Lay out a piece of extra-wide strong foil about 45cm/18in long on a work surface and lightly brush oil on a 30cm/12in square in the centre. Spoon the chicken mixture on to the foil to form a log shape about 30cm/12in long and about 9cm/3½in thick across the width of the foil. Bring together the long sides and fold over to enclose. Twist the ends and tie with string.

5 Transfer to a baking dish and bake for 1½ hours. Leave to cool in the dish and chill until cold, preferably overnight. Serve the pâté sliced, with a green salad.

Cardamon Mousselines Energy 191kcal/795kJ; Protein 18.1g; Carbohydrate 2g, of which sugars 2g; Fat 11.6g, of which saturates 5g; Cholesterol 96mg; Calcium 30mg; Fibre 0.7g; Sodium 130mg.
Chicken Pâté Energy 189kcal/790kJ; Protein 22.5g; Carbohydrate 2.8g, of which sugars 0.8g; Fat 9.8g, of which saturates 3.9g; Cholesterol 54mg; Calcium 26mg; Fibre 0.4g; Sodium 203mg.

Chicken and Pork Terrine

Serve this delicate pâté with warm, crusty bread as an elegant appetizer before the main Christmas Day meal.

Serves 6–8

225g/8oz rindless, streaky
   (fatty) bacon rashers (strips)
375g/13oz chicken breast
   fillet, skinned
15ml/1 tbsp lemon juice

225g/8oz lean minced
   (ground) pork
½ small onion, finely chopped
2 eggs, beaten
30ml/2 tbsp chopped
   fresh parsley
5ml/1 tsp salt
5ml/1 tsp green peppercorns,
   lightly crushed
fresh green salad, radishes and
   lemon wedges, to serve

1 Preheat the oven to 160°C/325°F/Gas 3. Put the bacon rashers on a board and stretch them using the back of a knife so that they can be arranged in over-lapping slices over the base and sides of a 900g/2lb loaf tin (pan).

2 Cut 115g/4oz of the chicken into strips about 10cm/4in long. Sprinkle with lemon juice and set aside.

3 Place the rest of the chicken in a food processor or blender with the minced pork and the chopped onion. Process briefly until the mixture is fairly smooth.

4 Add the eggs, parsley, salt and peppercorns to the meat mixture and process again briefly. Spoon half the mixture into the loaf tin and then level the surface.

5 Arrange the chicken strips on top, then spoon in the remaining meat mixture and smooth the top. Give the tin a couple of sharp taps to knock out any pockets of air.

6 Cover with a piece of oiled foil and put in a roasting pan. Pour in enough hot water to come halfway up the sides of the loaf tin. Bake for about 45–50 minutes, until firm.

7 Allow the terrine to cool in the tin before turning out and chilling. Serve sliced, with a fresh green salad, radishes and wedges of lemon to squeeze over.

Duck Liver Pâté and Redcurrant Sauce

This tasty pâté is easy to prepare and will keep for about a week in the refrigerator if the butter seal is not broken.

Serves 4–6

1 onion, finely chopped
1 large garlic clove, crushed
115g/4oz/½ cup butter
225g/8oz duck livers
10–15ml/2–3 tsp chopped fresh
   mixed herbs, such as parsley,
   thyme or rosemary
15–30ml/1–2 tbsp brandy

50–115g/2–4oz/¼ –½ cup
   clarified butter, or melted
   unsalted butter
salt and ground black pepper
a sprig of flat leaf parsley,
   to garnish

For the redcurrant sauce
30ml/2 tbsp redcurrant jelly
15–30ml/1–2 tbsp port
30ml/2 tbsp redcurrants

For the Melba toast
8 slices white bread,
   crusts removed

1 Cook the onion and garlic in 25g/1oz/2 tbsp of the butter in a pan over gentle heat, until just turning colour.

2 Add the duck livers to the pan with the herbs and cook together for about 3 minutes, or until the livers have browned on the outside but are still pink in the centre. Allow to cool.

3 Dice the remaining butter, then process the liver mixture in a food processor, gradually working in the cubes of butter by dropping them down the chute, to make a smooth purée.

4 Add the brandy, then check the seasoning and transfer to a 450–600ml/¾–1 pint dish. Seal the pâté with clarified or unsalted butter. Cool, and then chill until required.

5 For the sauce, put the jelly, port and redcurrants into a pan. Bring to the boil, then simmer to reduce a little. Leave to cool.

6 To make the Melba toast, toast the bread on both sides, then slice vertically to make 16 very thin slices. Place the untoasted side face up on a grill (broiler) rack and grill (broil) until browned. Serve the chilled pâté garnished with parsley and accompanied by Melba toast and the redcurrant sauce.

Chicken Terrine Energy 191kcal/798kJ; Protein 22g; Carbohydrate 0.6g, of which sugars 0.4g; Fat 11.3g, of which saturates 3.8g; Cholesterol 115mg; Calcium 15mg; Fibre 0.1g; Sodium 417mg.
Duck Liver Pâté Energy 794kcal/3312kJ; Protein 101.3g; Carbohydrate 11.3g, of which sugars 9.9g; Fat 36.8g, of which saturates 19g; Cholesterol 2213mg; Calcium 73mg; Fibre 1.3g; Sodium 608mg.

Chicken Liver and Brandy Pâté

This rich pâté is quick and easy to make and tastes so much better than anything you can buy in the supermarkets. Serve as an appetizer with Melba toast or crackers.

Serves 4

350g/12oz chicken livers
50g/2oz/¼ cup butter
30ml/2 tbsp brandy
30ml/2 tbsp double
    (heavy) cream
salt and ground black pepper

1 Trim any fat from the chicken livers and discard. Chop the livers roughly. Heat the butter in a large frying pan.

2 Add the chicken livers to the pan and cook over medium heat for 3–4 minutes, stirring occasionally, until evenly browned all over and cooked through.

3 Pour the brandy into the pan with the chicken livers and allow to bubble for a few minutes. Remove the pan from the heat and set aside to cool slightly.

4 Place the livers and brandy in a food processor or blender. Pour in the double cream and season with salt and plenty of ground black pepper.

5 Process the mixture until smooth and then spoon it into ramekin dishes. Level the surface of each dish and chill overnight in the refrigerator to set. Serve garnished with sprigs of fresh parsley to add a little colour.

Cook's Tips
• If you can't find any fresh chicken livers, look out for them in the freezer section of large supermarkets. Ensure that they are fully defrosted before using.
• This is a useful dish for serving on Christmas Day as it can be made a few days in advance, which helps to take some of the strain off the busy festive period. If you are making the pâté more than 1 day ahead, seal the surface of each portion in the ramekin dish with a layer of melted butter.

Game Terrine

Any game can be used to make this country terrine – hare, rabbit, pheasant or pigeon – so choose the best meat your butcher has to offer.

Serves 8

225g/8oz rindless, unsmoked
    streaky (fatty) bacon
    rashers (strips)
225g/8oz lamb's or pig's liver,
    minced (ground)

450g/1lb minced (ground) pork
1 small onion, finely chopped
2 garlic cloves, crushed
10ml/2 tsp mixed dried herbs
225g/8oz game of your choice
60ml/4 tbsp port or sherry
1 bay leaf
50g/2oz/½ cup plain
    (all-purpose) flour
300ml/½ pint/1¼ cups aspic jelly,
    made up as packet instructions
salt and ground black pepper

1 Stretch each rasher with the back of a knife, then use to line a 1 litre/1¾ pint/4 cup terrine. The terrine must have a lid to help seal in the flavours during cooking.

2 Mix the minced meats with the onion, garlic and mixed dried herbs. Season well with plenty of salt and ground black pepper.

3 Cut the game into thin strips, and place in a large mixing bowl with the port or sherry. Season with salt and pepper.

4 Put one-third of the minced mixture into the terrine. Press the mixture well into the corners. Cover with half the strips of the game and repeat these layers, ending with a minced layer. Level the surface and lay the bay leaf on top.

5 Preheat the oven to 160°C/325°F/Gas 3. Put the flour into a small bowl and mix it to a firm dough with 30–45ml/2–3 tbsp cold water. Cover the terrine with a lid and seal it with the flour paste. Place the terrine in a roasting pan and pour in hot water to come halfway up the sides of the tin. Bake for 2 hours.

6 Remove the lid and weigh the terrine down with a 2kg/4½lb weight. Leave to cool. Remove any fat from the surface and cover with warmed aspic jelly. Leave overnight before turning out on to a serving plate. Serve in thin slices with a mixed salad.

Chicken Liver Pâté Energy 227kcal/942kJ; Protein 15.7g; Carbohydrate 0.2g, of which sugars 0.2g; Fat 16.3g, of which saturates 9.6g; Cholesterol 369mg; Calcium 13mg; Fibre 0g; Sodium 144mg.
Game Terrine Energy 266kcal/1112kJ; Protein 27.1g; Carbohydrate 6.4g, of which sugars 1.4g; Fat 14g, of which saturates 5g; Cholesterol 182mg; Calcium 25mg; Fibre 0.3g; Sodium 432mg.

Spiced Pork Pâté

This pâté has an Asian twist: it is steamed in banana leaves, which are available in African and Asian markets. However, if you cannot find them you can use large spring green leaves or several Savoy cabbage leaves instead.

Serves 6
45ml/3 tbsp Thai fish sauce
30ml/2 tbsp sesame oil
15ml/1 tbsp sugar
10ml/2 tsp five-spice powder
2 shallots, peeled and
    finely chopped
2 garlic cloves, crushed
750g/1lb 10oz/3¼ cups minced
    (ground) pork
25g/1oz/¼ cup potato starch
7.5ml/1½ tsp baking powder
1 banana leaf, trimmed into a
    strip 25cm/10in wide
vegetable oil, for brushing
salt and ground black pepper
Thai dipping sauce and a
    baguette or salad, to serve

1 In a bowl, beat the fish sauce and oil with the sugar and five-spice powder. Once the sugar has dissolved, stir in the shallots and garlic. Add the pork and seasoning, and knead well until thoroughly combined. Cover and chill for 2–3 hours.

2 Knead the mixture again, thumping it down into the bowl to remove any air. Add the potato starch and baking powder and knead until smooth and pasty. Mould the pork mixture into a fat sausage, about 18cm/7in long, and place it on an oiled dish.

3 Lay the banana leaf on a flat surface, brush it with a little vegetable oil, and place the pork sausage across it. Lift up the edge of the banana leaf nearest to you and fold it over the sausage mixture, tuck in the sides, and roll it up into a firm, tight bundle. Secure the bundle with a piece of string, so that it doesn't unravel during cooking.

4 Fill a wok one-third full with water. Balance a bamboo steamer, with its lid on, above the level of the water. Bring to the boil, lift the lid and place the banana leaf bundle on the rack, being careful not to burn yourself. Re-cover and steam for about 45 minutes. Leave the pâté to cool in the leaf, then open it up and cut it into slices. Drizzle with the sauce, and serve accompanied by a baguette or salad.

Herbed Liver Pâté Pie

Serve this highly flavoured pâté with a glass of Pilsner beer and some spicy dill pickles to complement the strong tastes.

Serves 10
675g/1½lb minced (ground) pork
350g/12oz pork liver
350g/12oz/2 cups diced
    cooked ham
1 small onion, finely chopped
30ml/2 tbsp chopped
    fresh parsley
5ml/1 tsp German mustard
30ml/2 tbsp Kirsch
5ml/1 tsp salt
beaten egg, for sealing and glazing
25g/1oz sachet aspic jelly
250ml/8fl oz/1 cup boiling water
ground black pepper
mustard, bread and dill pickles,
    to serve

For the pastry
450g/1lb/4 cups plain
    (all-purpose) flour
275g/10oz/1¼ cups butter
2 eggs plus 1 egg yolk
30ml/2 tbsp water

1 Preheat the oven to 200°C/400°F/Gas 6. For the pastry, sift the flour and salt and rub in the butter. Beat the eggs, egg yolk and water, and mix into the flour. Knead the pastry dough until it becomes smooth. Roll out two-thirds on a lightly floured surface and use to line a 10 × 25cm/4 × 10in hinged loaf tin (pan). Trim any excess pastry.

2 Process half the pork and all of the liver until fairly smooth. Stir in the remaining pork, ham, onion, parsley, mustard, Kirsch, salt and black pepper. Spoon into the tin and level the surface.

3 Roll out the remaining pastry and use it to top the pie. Seal the edges with egg. Decorate with pastry trimmings and glaze with egg. Make four holes in the top.

4 Bake for 40 minutes, then reduce the oven temperature down to 180°C/350°F/Gas 4 and cook for another hour. Cover with foil and leave to cool in the tin.

5 Dissolve the aspic jelly in the boiling water, then leave to cool slightly. Make a small hole near the pie edge and pour in the aspic. Chill for 2 hours. Serve the pie in slices, accompanied by mustard, bread and dill pickles.

Spiced Pork Pâté Energy 234kcal/978kJ; Protein 28g; Carbohydrate 8g, of which sugars 3g; Fat 10g, of which saturates 2g; Cholesterol 79mg; Calcium 46mg; Fibre 0.4g; Sodium 700mg.
Liver Pâté Pie Energy 576kcal/2407kJ; Protein 32.9g; Carbohydrate 36g, of which sugars 1.6g; Fat 33.7g, of which saturates 18.1g; Cholesterol 273mg; Calcium 87mg; Fibre 1.5g; Sodium 888mg.

Roasted Salmon with Honey and Mustard

Salmon is not only one of the most versatile fishes but is also one of the tastiest. This quick and easy way with salmon is sure to be popular with the whole family over the festive season. Serve with seasonal green vegetables for a delicious dinner dish.

Serves 4

30ml/2 tbsp olive oil
15ml/1 tbsp honey
30ml/2 tbsp wholegrain
    French mustard
grated rind ½ lemon
4 salmon fillets, each
    about 150g/5oz
salt and ground black pepper

1 To make the marinade, put the olive oil, honey, wholegrain mustard and lemon rind in a small bowl and mix together until well combined. Season the marinade with salt and ground black pepper to taste.

2 Put the salmon fillets in a shallow ovenproof dish or on a baking sheet lined with a sheet of baking parchment and spread the marinade over each fillet, rubbing it in with your fingers. Leave to marinate for 30 minutes.

3 Preheat the oven to 200°C/400°F/Gas 6. Roast the fish in the oven for 10–12 minutes, until the flesh flakes easily when tested with the tip of a knife. Serve immediately.

Cook's Tip
Choose the best salmon you can find to really elevate this dish. Look for wild salmon rather than the farmed variety.

Variation
This dish also tastes great using trout fillets, which come from the same family of fish as salmon. Rainbow trout is best but brown trout could also be used.

Salmon with Mixed Herb and Peppercorn Sauce

This wonderful sauce relies on absolutely fresh herbs (any combination will do) and good-quality olive oil for its fabulous flavour. The sauce is a perfect accompaniment to the rich fish. Cook the salmon simply to make the most of this sauce, which also works well with grilled beef or lamb steaks.

Serves 4–6

10ml/2 tsp cumin seeds
15ml/1 tbsp pink or green
    peppercorns in brine, drained
    and rinsed
25g/1oz/1 cup fresh mixed herbs,
    such as parsley, mint, chives
    and coriander (cilantro)
45ml/3 tbsp lemon-infused
    olive oil
4–6 salmon steaks

1 Crush the cumin seeds using a mortar and pestle. Alternatively, put the seeds in a small bowl and pound them with the end of a rolling pin. Add the pink or green peppercorns and pound a little to break them up slightly.

2 Remove any tough stalks from the herbs. Put the herbs in a food processor with the cumin seeds, peppercorns, oil and salt and process until the herbs are finely chopped, scraping the sauce down from the sides of the bowl if necessary.

3 Turn the sauce into a small serving dish, cover with clear film (plastic wrap) and chill until ready to serve.

4 Preheat the oven to 200°C/400°F/Gas 6. Roast the salmon steaks in the oven for 10–12 minutes, until the flesh flakes easily when tested with the tip of a knife.

5 Serve the salmon with the sauce drizzled over the top.

Cook's Tip
It is best to make the sauce a day in advance, to allow the flavours to mingle.

Roasted Salmon Energy 296kcal/1231kJ; Protein 25.9g; Carbohydrate 3.2g, of which sugars 3.2g; Fat 20g, of which saturates 3.2g; Cholesterol 63mg; Calcium 36mg; Fibre 0.4g; Sodium 178mg.
Salmon with Sauce nergy 526kcal/2180kJ; Protein 36.3g; Carbohydrate 2.9g, of which sugars 2.3g; Fat 40g, of which saturates 13.5g; Cholesterol 127mg; Calcium 63mg; Fibre 0.4g; Sodium 110mg.

Baked Salmon with Watercress Sauce

This is a great festive dish as the whole fish looks very impressive at the table.

Serves 6–8

2–3kg/4½–6¾lb salmon, cleaned, with head and tail left on
3–5 spring onions (scallions), thinly sliced
1 lemon, thinly sliced
1 cucumber, thinly sliced
fresh dill sprigs, to garnish
lemon wedges, to serve

For the watercress sauce
3 garlic cloves, chopped
200g/7oz watercress leaves, finely chopped
40g/1½oz fresh tarragon, finely chopped
300g/11oz mayonnaise
15–30ml/1–2 tbsp freshly squeezed lemon juice
200g/7oz/scant 1 cup unsalted butter, melted
salt and ground black pepper

1 Preheat the oven to 180°C/350°F/Gas 4. Rinse the salmon and lay it on a large piece of foil.

2 Stuff the fish with the sliced spring onions and layer the lemon slices inside and around the fish, then sprinkle with plenty of salt and ground black pepper. Loosely fold the foil around the fish and fold the edges over to seal. Bake for about 1 hour.

3 Remove the fish from the oven. Leave to stand, wrapped in the foil, for 15 minutes, then unwrap and leave to cool. When cool, lift it on to a large plate, still covered with lemon slices. Wrap in clear film (plastic wrap) and chill for several hours.

4 Before serving, discard the lemon slices around the fish. Using a blunt knife to lift up the edge of the skin, carefully peel the skin away from the flesh, avoiding tearing the flesh, and pull out any fins at the same time. Arrange the cucumber in overlapping rows along the length of the fish, to resemble large fish scales.

5 To make the sauce, put the garlic, watercress, tarragon, mayonnaise and lemon juice in a food processor or blender or a bowl, and process or mix to combine. Add the butter, a little at a time, processing or stirring, until the sauce is thick and smooth. Cover and chill before serving. Serve the fish, garnished with dill, with the sauce and lemon wedges.

Salmon with Cucumber Sauce

Salmon is a traditional choice during the festive season and is great to serve for dinner on Christmas Day. Cucumber and fresh dill are a perfect combination in this unusual hot sauce, which really complements the baked salmon.

Serves 6–8

1.8kg/4lb salmon, cleaned and scaled
melted butter, for brushing

3 fresh parsley or thyme sprigs
½ lemon, halved
orange slices and salad leaves, to serve

For the cucumber sauce
1 large cucumber, peeled
25g/1oz/2 tbsp butter
120ml/4fl oz/½ cup dry white wine
45ml/3 tbsp finely chopped fresh dill
60ml/4 tbsp sour cream
salt and ground black pepper

1 Preheat the oven to 220°C/425°F/Gas 7. Season the salmon with salt and ground black pepper. Brush it inside and out with melted butter. Place the herb sprigs and lemon in the cavity.

2 Wrap the salmon in foil, folding the edges together securely, then bake in the preheated oven for 15 minutes.

3 Remove the fish from the oven and leave in the foil for about 1 hour, then remove the skin from the salmon.

4 Meanwhile, halve the cucumber lengthways, scoop out the seeds, then finely dice the flesh.

5 Place the cucumber in a colander, toss lightly with salt and leave for about 30 minutes to drain. Rinse well under cold running water, drain again and pat dry with kitchen paper.

6 Heat the butter in a small pan, add the diced cucumber and cook for 2 minutes until translucent.

7 Add the wine to the pan and boil briskly until the cucumber is dry. Stir in the dill and sour cream and season to taste with salt and pepper. Fillet the salmon and serve with the cucumber sauce, orange slices and salad leaves.

Baked Salmon Energy 783kcal/3242kJ; Protein 38.7g; Carbohydrate 1g, of which sugars 0.9g; Fat 69.3g, of which saturates 21.3g; Cholesterol 173mg; Calcium 102mg; Fibre 0.5g; Sodium 418mg.
Salmon and Cucumber Energy 406kcal/1686kJ; Protein 34.9g; Carbohydrate 1.5g, of which sugars 1.5g; Fat 26.7g, of which saturates 8.3g; Cholesterol 107mg; Calcium 62mg; Fibre 0.3g; Sodium 123mg.

Fish Fillets in a Creamy Mustard Sauce

You can use any kind of fish that is good for pan-frying for this dish. The mustard sauce is made with grainy mustard to add texture to the dish. Fried potatoes with bacon and onions are a good accompaniment.

Serves 4

300ml/½ pint/1¼ cups fish stock
100ml/3½fl oz/scant ½ cup
  single (light) cream
10ml/2 tsp grainy mustard
1kg/2¼lb boiled potatoes,
  thinly sliced
150g/5oz bacon, diced into cubes
1 onion, finely chopped
small bunch chives, chopped
800g/1¾lb fish fillets (cod,
  salmon, trout, pike or perch)
juice of 1 lemon
oil, for frying
salt and ground white pepper
fresh dill, to garnish

1 Heat the fish stock in a pan and season it, if necessary, with salt and pepper. Add the cream and mustard and simmer over low heat for 5 minutes to make the sauce.

2 Heat some oil in a frying pan over high heat and fry the potato slices and the bacon until browned and crisp.

3 Add the onion to the pan and fry for another 5 minutes. Season with salt and pepper and stir in the chives.

4 Meanwhile, season the fish with lemon juice, salt and pepper. Heat some oil in another pan and fry the fillets, turning once, until golden on both sides.

5 Arrange the fried potatoes in the middle of a warmed serving plate with the fish round them, and pour the sauce around. Garnish with fresh dill and serve.

> **Cook's Tip**
> If the sauce seems too thin, thicken it with about 5ml/1 tsp cornflour (cornstarch) slaked in a little cold water.

Roast Cod Wrapped in Prosciutto

Wrapping chunky fillets of cod in wafer-thin slices of prosciutto keeps the fish succulent and moist, at the same time adding flavour and visual impact. Serve with baby new potatoes and a herb salad for a stylish supper at Christmas time.

Serves 4

2 thick skinless cod fillets, each
  weighing about 375g/13oz
75ml/5 tbsp extra virgin
  olive oil
75g/3oz prosciutto,
  thinly sliced
400g/14oz vine tomatoes
salt and ground black pepper

1 Preheat the oven to 220°C/425°F/Gas 7. Pat the fish dry on kitchen paper and remove any stray bones. Season lightly on both sides with salt and pepper.

2 Place one fillet in an ovenproof dish and drizzle 15ml/1 tbsp of the oil over it. Cover with the second fillet, laying the thick end on top of the thin end of the lower fillet.

3 Lay the ham over the fish, overlapping the slices to cover the fish in an even layer. Tuck the ends of the ham under the fish and tie it in place at intervals with fine string.

4 Using kitchen scissors, snip the tomato vines into four portions and add to the dish. Drizzle the tomatoes and ham with the remaining oil and season lightly.

5 Roast for 35 minutes, until the tomatoes are tender and the fish is cooked through. Test the fish by piercing one end of the parcel with the tip of a sharp knife to check that it flakes easily.

6 Slice the fish and transfer the portions to warm plates, adding the tomatoes. Spoon over the cooking juices from the dish and serve immediately.

> **Variation**
> You can use Serrano ham, or other air-dried ham, in place of the prosciutto, if you prefer.

Fish Fillets Energy 570kcal/2387kJ; Protein 47.9g; Carbohydrate 42.5g, of which sugars 5.1g; Fat 24.1g, of which saturates 6.9g; Cholesterol 126mg; Calcium 62mg; Fibre 2.7g; Sodium 738mg.
Roast Cod Energy 281kcal/1172kJ; Protein 32.8g; Carbohydrate 3.1g, of which sugars 3.1g; Fat 15.3g, of which saturates 2.3g; Cholesterol 81mg; Calcium 23mg; Fibre 1g; Sodium 116mg.

Hake au Poivre with Pepper Relish

This version of the classic steak au poivre can be made with monkfish or cod. It has a festive appearance thanks to the red pepper relish, green basil leaves and white fish.

Serves 4
30–45ml/2–3 tbsp mixed peppercorns (black, white, pink and green)
4 hake steaks, 175g/6oz each
30ml/2 tbsp olive oil

For the (bell) pepper relish
2 red (bell) peppers, halved, cored and seeded
15ml/1 tbsp olive oil
2 garlic cloves, chopped
4 ripe tomatoes, peeled, seeded and quartered
4 drained canned anchovy fillets, chopped
5ml/1 tsp capers
15ml/1 tbsp balsamic vinegar, plus extra for drizzling
12 fresh basil leaves, shredded, plus a few extra to garnish
salt and ground black pepper

1 Put the peppercorns in a mortar and crush them coarsely with a pestle. Season the hake fillets lightly with salt, then coat them on both sides with the crushed peppercorns. Set aside.

2 Make the relish. Cut the peppers into 1cm/½in-wide strips. Heat the oil in a frying pan that has a lid. Add the peppers and stir them for about 5 minutes, until they are slightly softened. Stir in the chopped garlic, tomatoes and the anchovies, then cover the pan and simmer the mixture very gently for about 20 minutes, until the peppers are very soft.

3 Transfer the contents of the pan into a food processor and process to a coarse purée. Transfer to a bowl and season to taste with salt and pepper. Stir in the capers, balsamic vinegar and basil. Keep the relish hot.

4 Heat the olive oil in a shallow pan, add the hake steaks and cook them, in batches if necessary, for 5 minutes on each side, turning them once or twice, until they are just cooked through.

5 Place the fish steaks on warmed plates and spoon some relish on to the side of each plate. Garnish with basil leaves and a little balsamic vinegar. Serve the rest of the relish separately.

Baked Cod Steaks with Herby Cream Sauce

Always versatile, cod is enjoyed throughout the year, but baked or poached whole fresh cod is a supreme dish to serve for dinner on New Year's Eve. The simple preparation shows off the lean, firm texture of the flavoursome white fish. Serve the fish with boiled potatoes, remoulade or mustard sauce and peas.

Serves 4–6
1.3kg/3lb cod steaks
15ml/1 tbsp salt
1 egg, beaten
50g/2oz/½ cup fine white breadcrumbs
40g/1½oz/3 tbsp butter, cut into small pieces
300ml/½ pint/1¼ cups single (light) cream
45ml/3 tbsp chopped fresh parsley, to garnish
8 lemon wedges, to garnish

1 Preheat the oven to 190°C/375°F/Gas 5. Pat the fish steaks dry and rub the salt over the skin.

2 Place in a lightly greased baking dish, brush with the egg, sprinkle with breadcrumbs and dot with butter. Pour the cream around the steaks.

3 Bake the fish for 15–20 minutes, depending on thickness, until the topping is browned and the flesh flakes easily with a fork. Serve garnished with the parsley and lemon wedges.

> **Cook's Tip**
> If you can find a whole cod, bake it in the oven for around 1 hour, adding the single (light) cream about 20 minutes before the end of the cooking time.

> **Variation**
> Haddock, hake or monkfish steaks are just as delicious as cod when cooked in this way.

Hake au Poivre Energy 283kcal/1186kJ; Protein 33.7g; Carbohydrate 8.2g, of which sugars 8g; Fat 13g, of which saturates 1.9g; Cholesterol 42mg; Calcium 47mg; Fibre 2.3g; Sodium 304mg.
Baked Cod Energy 355kcal/1484kJ; Protein 42.5g; Carbohydrate 8.9g, of which sugars 1.4g; Fat 16.7g, of which saturates 9.8g; Cholesterol 141mg; Calcium 78mg; Fibre 0.2g; Sodium 261mg.

Spicy Squid

This aromatically spiced squid dish is simple yet delicious. Squid can be bought ready-cleaned from fish stores, market stalls and the fish counters of large supermarkets, making this dish quick to prepare over the busy festive season.

Serves 3–4
675g/1½lb squid, cleaned
45ml/3 tbsp groundnut (peanut) oil
1 onion, finely chopped
2 garlic cloves, crushed
1 beefsteak tomato, peeled and chopped
15ml/1 tbsp dark soy sauce
2.5ml/½ tsp grated nutmeg
6 cloves
150ml/¼ pint/⅔ cup water
juice of ½ lemon or lime
salt and ground black pepper
fresh coriander (cilantro) leaves and shredded spring onions (scallions), to garnish

1 Rinse and drain the squid, then slice lengthways along one side and open it out flat. Score the inside of the squid in a lattice pattern, using the blunt side of a knife blade, then cut it crossways into long thin strips.

2 Heat a wok and add 15ml/1 tbsp of the oil. When hot, toss in the squid strips and stir-fry for 2–3 minutes, by which time the squid will have curled into attractive shapes or into firm rings. Lift out and set aside.

3 Wipe out the wok, add the remaining oil and heat it. Stir-fry the onion and garlic until soft and beginning to brown.

4 Stir in the tomato, soy sauce, nutmeg, cloves, water and lemon or lime juice. Bring to the boil, lower the heat and add the squid with salt and black pepper to taste.

5 Cook the mixture gently for a further 3–5 minutes, stirring occasionally to prevent it from sticking to the base of the pan. Take care not to overcook the squid.

6 Spoon the spicy squid on to warm plates. Garnish with fresh coriander leaves and shredded spring onions and serve. Boiled rice is an ideal accompaniment.

Seared Scallops with Chive Sauce

Scallops are partnered with a chive sauce and a pilaff of wild and white rice with leeks and carrots.

Serves 4
12–16 shelled scallops
45ml/3 tbsp olive oil
50g/2oz/⅓ cup wild rice
65g/2½oz/5 tbsp butter
4 carrots, cut into long thin strips
2 leeks, cut into diagonal slices
1 small onion, finely chopped
115g/4oz/⅔ cup long grain rice
1 fresh bay leaf
200ml/7fl oz/scant 1 cup white wine
450ml/¾ pint/scant 2 cups fish stock
60ml/4 tbsp double (heavy) cream
a little lemon juice
25ml/5 tsp chopped fresh chives
30ml/2 tbsp chervil sprigs
salt and ground black pepper

1 Lightly season the scallops, brush with 15ml/1 tbsp of the olive oil and set aside. Cook the wild rice in plenty of boiling water for about 30 minutes, until tender, then drain.

2 Melt half the butter in a frying pan and cook the carrots for 5 minutes. Add the leeks and fry for 2 minutes. Season and add 30–45ml/2–3 tbsp water, then cover and cook for a few minutes more. Uncover and cook until the liquid has reduced.

3 Melt half the rest of the butter with 15ml/1 tbsp of the remaining oil in a pan. Fry the onion for 3–4 minutes. Add the long grain rice and bay leaf and stir-fry for 3–4 minutes.

4 Pour in half the wine and half the stock. Season with salt and bring to the boil. Stir, then cover and simmer for 15 minutes, or until the liquid is absorbed and the rice is cooked and tender. Stir the carrots, leeks and wild rice into the long grain rice. Boil the remaining wine and stock in a pan until reduced by half.

5 Heat a frying pan over high heat. Add the remaining butter and oil. Sear the scallops for 1–2 minutes each side, then set aside. Pour the reduced stock and cream into the pan and boil until thick. Season and stir in the lemon juice, chives and scallops.

6 Stir the chervil into the rice and pile it on to plates. Arrange the scallops on top and spoon the sauce over the rice.

Spicy Squid Energy 310kcal/1301kJ; Protein 35.8g; Carbohydrate 8.6g, of which sugars 4.7g; Fat 15.1g, of which saturates 3g; Cholesterol 506mg; Calcium 46mg; Fibre 1.2g; Sodium 610mg.
Seared Scallops Energy 598kcal/2489kJ; Protein 30.8g; Carbohydrate 38.9g, of which sugars 6.3g; Fat 32g, of which saturates 15.3g; Cholesterol 108mg; Calcium 88mg; Fibre 3.1g; Sodium 321mg.

Lobster and Crab Steamed in Beer

This recipe is very easy to make and, although it may be expensive, it is a wonderful dish for a festive occasion.

Serves 4

4 uncooked lobsters, about
   450g/1lb each
4 uncooked crabs, about
   225g/8oz each
600ml/1 pint/2½ cups beer
4 spring onions (scallions),
   trimmed and chopped into
   long pieces

4cm/1½in fresh root ginger,
   peeled and finely sliced
2 green or red Thai chillies,
   seeded and finely sliced
3 lemon grass stalks, finely sliced
1 bunch fresh dill,
   fronds chopped
1 bunch each fresh basil and
   coriander (cilantro), stalks
   removed, leaves chopped
about 30ml/2 tbsp Thai fish
   sauce, plus extra for serving
juice of 1 lemon
salt and ground black pepper

1 Clean the lobsters and crabs thoroughly and rub them with salt and ground black pepper. Place them in a large steamer and pour the beer into the base.

2 Sprinkle half the spring onions, ginger, chillies, lemon grass and herbs over the lobsters and crabs, and steam for about 10 minutes, or until the lobsters turn red. Lift them on to a warmed serving dish.

3 Add the remaining flavouring ingredients to the beer with the fish sauce and lemon juice. Pour into a dipping bowl and serve immediately with the hot lobsters and crabs, with extra splashes of fish sauce, if you like.

> **Cook's Tip**
> *Whether you cook the lobsters and crabs at the same time depends on the number of people you are cooking for and the size of your steamer. However, they don't take long to cook so it is easy to steam them in batches. You can make this recipe for as many people as you like because the quantities are simple to adjust, so even if you are having a lot of guests over for a Christmas dinner party, this recipe can be made to suit.*

Lobster Noodles

This dish is in the luxury league so it is ideal for impressing your guests when entertaining over the festive season. Restaurants present this dish with great fanfare, with the lobster sitting in all its pink-shelled glory on top of the plate of cooked noodles, so why not follow their example?

Serves 4

1 large live or freshly cooked
   lobster, about 1kg/2¼lb
400g/14oz dried egg noodles
30ml/2 tbsp vegetable oil
15ml/1 tbsp crushed garlic
115g/4oz/½ cup beansprouts
200ml/7fl oz/scant 1 cup water
30ml/2 tbsp oyster sauce
5ml/1 tsp ground black pepper
30ml/2 tbsp sesame oil

1 If the lobster is live, place it in a plastic bag and put it in the freezer for 5–7 hours. Bring a large pan of water to the boil, add the comatose lobster and cook for 10 minutes or until the shell has turned scarlet. Remove and set aside to cool.

2 Heat a separate pan of water and cook the noodles according to the instructions on the packet. Drain and set aside.

3 When the lobster is cool enough to handle, use a sharp knife to cut off the head and the tip of the tail. Rinse and set aside for the garnish. Twist off the claws and set aside.

4 Using a sharp pair of poultry shears or strong scissors, cut down the shell from the top to the tail. Remove the lobster meat, and slice it into rounds. Remove the meat from the claws and legs. Set all the lobster meat aside.

5 Heat the oil in a wok or large frying pan, and fry the garlic for about 40 seconds. Add the beansprouts and cook over the heat for 2 minutes, stirring constantly.

6 Add the noodles, water, oyster sauce, black pepper and sesame oil to the pan and cook, stirring, for 2 minutes.

7 Add the lobster slices and toss lightly. Arrange on a large oval plate, making sure that the lobster pieces are fairly prominent. Decorate with the lobster head and tail.

Lobster and Crab Energy 264kcal/1112kJ; Protein 48g; Carbohydrate 4g, of which sugars 1g; Fat 7g, of which saturates 1g; Cholesterol 210mg; Calcium 185mg; Fibre 0.5g; Sodium 130mg.
Lobster Noodles Energy 501kcal/2110kJ; Protein 29.9g; Carbohydrate 56.9g, of which sugars 4g; Fat 18.8g, of which saturates 3.5g; Cholesterol 123mg; Calcium 83mg; Fibre 2.6g; Sodium 559mg.

Roast Chicken with Red Pears

This traditional recipe for a roast chicken is ideal for the festive season because it is easy to prepare.

Serves 4
butter, for greasing
1.2kg/2½lb free-range chicken
2 onions
a large bunch of lemon balm, plus
    extra leaves to garnish

800g/1¾lb waxy potatoes, sliced
100g/3¾oz/scant ⅔ cup diced
    lean smoked bacon
salt and ground black pepper

To serve
1kg/2¼lb red cooking pears
½ vanilla pod (bean)
45ml/3 tbsp sugar
dash of red wine
45ml/3 tbsp potato flour

1 First, make the accompaniments. Peel the pears, but leave them whole. Remove the calyx from the base, but leave the stalks. Place them in a heavy pan with the vanilla pod and sugar, add water almost to cover and bring to the boil. Lower the heat, cover and simmer for 1 hour. Add the wine, re-cover the pan and simmer for a further 2 hours.

2 Transfer the pears to a wide dish, standing them upright. Measure 500ml/17fl oz/generous 2 cups of the cooking liquid, pour into a clean pan and bring to the boil. Mix the potato flour with 90ml/6 tbsp cold water to a paste in a cup and stir into the liquid. Cook, stirring, until the liquid thickens, then remove from the heat. Pour the sauce over the pears and cool.

3 To cook the chicken, soak an unglazed clay pot in cold water for 15 minutes. Dry the inside and grease with butter. Stuff the chicken with the peeled, whole onion and the lemon balm. Rub with seasoning. Place the chicken in the pot, cover and place in a cold oven set to 240°C/475°F/Gas 9 for 30 minutes.

4 Chop the remaining onion and season the potato slices. Remove the pot from the oven and arrange the potato around the chicken. Sprinkle the bacon and chopped onion on top.

5 Bake for a further 45 minutes. Remove the lid and cook the chicken for 5–10 minutes more, until browned. Garnish with lemon balm leaves and serve immediately with the pears.

Coq au Vin

This rustic, one-pot casserole of chicken, slowly simmered in a rich red wine sauce, makes a delicious festive meal for the family.

Serves 6
45ml/3 tbsp light olive oil
12 shallots
225g/8oz rindless streaky (fatty)
    bacon rashers (strips), chopped
3 garlic cloves, finely chopped
225g/8oz button (white)
    mushrooms, halved
6 boneless chicken thighs
3 chicken breast fillets, halved

1 bottle red wine
salt and ground black pepper
45ml/3 tbsp chopped fresh
    parsley, to garnish
boiled potatoes, to serve

For the bouquet garni
3 sprigs each parsley, thyme
    and sage
1 bay leaf
4 peppercorns

For the beurre manié
25g/1oz/2 tbsp butter, softened
25g/1oz/¼ cup plain
    (all-purpose) flour

1 Heat the oil in a flameproof casserole and cook the shallots for 5 minutes until golden. Increase the heat, then add the bacon, garlic and mushrooms and cook, stirring, for 10 minutes.

2 Transfer the cooked ingredients to a plate, then brown the chicken pieces in the oil remaining in the pan, turning them until golden brown all over. Return the shallots, garlic, mushrooms and bacon to the casserole and pour in the red wine.

3 Tie the ingredients for the bouquet garni in a bundle in a piece of muslin (cheesecloth) and add to the casserole. Bring to the boil. Reduce the heat, cover and simmer for 30–40 minutes.

4 To make the beurre manié, cream the butter and flour together in a bowl using your fingers to make a smooth paste. Add small lumps of the paste to the casserole, stirring well until each piece has melted. When all the paste has been added, bring the casserole back to the boil and simmer for 5 minutes.

5 Season the casserole to taste with salt and pepper. Serve immediately, garnished with chopped fresh parsley and accompanied by boiled potatoes.

Roast Chicken Energy 829kcal/3466kJ; Protein 47.4g; Carbohydrate 79.2g, of which sugars 40.2g; Fat 37.3g, of which saturates 11.1g; Cholesterol 213mg; Calcium 69mg; Fibre 7.9g; Sodium 573mg.
Coq au Vin Energy 630kcal/2618kJ; Protein 42.8g; Carbohydrate 19.3g, of which sugars 7.4g; Fat 41g, of which saturates 17.3g; Cholesterol 209mg; Calcium 67mg; Fibre 2.6g; Sodium 480mg.

Chicken Casserole with Spiced Figs

This is a delicious dish that is perfect for an informal festive gathering or as a tasty alternative to the usual roast bird on Christmas Day itself. Joints of chicken are cooked with bacon in a beautifully spiced sauce, which goes perfectly with a glass or two of red wine.

Serves 4

50g/2oz bacon lardons or pancetta, diced
15ml/1 tbsp olive oil
1.3–1.6kg/3–3½lb free-range or corn-fed chicken, jointed into eight pieces
120ml/4fl oz/½ cup dry white wine
finely pared rind of ½ lemon
50ml/2fl oz/¼ cup chicken or vegetable stock
salt and ground black pepper
green salad, to serve

For the figs

150g/5oz/¾ cup sugar
120ml/4fl oz/½ cup white wine vinegar
1 lemon slice
1 cinnamon stick
120ml/4fl oz/½ cup water
450g/1lb fresh figs

1 Prepare the figs. In a heavy pan, simmer the sugar, vinegar, lemon and cinnamon with the water for about 5 minutes. Add the figs and cook for a further 10 minutes. Remove the pan from the heat and leave to stand for 3 hours.

2 Heat a large frying pan without any oil. Fry the bacon or pancetta, stirring frequently, for 6–8 minutes until golden. Transfer to an ovenproof dish.

3 Add the olive oil to the pan. Season the chicken, then add to the pan and quickly brown on both sides. Transfer the joints to the ovenproof dish.

4 Preheat the oven to 180°C/350°F/Gas 4. Drain the figs. Add the wine and lemon rind to the pan and boil until the wine has reduced and is syrupy. Pour over the chicken.

5 Cook the chicken in the oven, uncovered, for 20 minutes, then add the figs and chicken stock. Cover and return to the oven for a further 10 minutes. Serve with a green salad.

Chicken Fricassée

This creamy mix of tender chicken and fresh vegetables is a sophisticated dish for festive entertaining. Served with rice it is irresistible, and is a popular meal with diners of all ages. Try different herbs such as lemon thyme, chives or chervil; you can also substitute different seasonal vegetables.

Serves 4

1 chicken (approximately 1.6kg/3½lb)
2 bay leaves
3 allspice berries
30ml/2 tbsp oil
200g/7oz mushrooms, quartered
2 small onions, sliced
400g/14oz white asparagus, peeled and cut into small pieces
200g/7oz frozen peas
200ml/7fl oz/scant 1 cup single (light) cream
juice of 1 lemon
25g/1oz/2 tbsp butter, mixed with 25g/1oz/¼ cup flour to make a beurre manié
oil, for frying
salt, ground white pepper and sugar
chopped parsley, to garnish
steamed or boiled rice, to serve

1 Put the chicken in a large pot and cover with water. Bring to the boil and skim. Add the spices and a pinch of salt and simmer for 60–90 minutes, until the chicken is tender.

2 Lift out the chicken and leave to cool. Strain and reserve the stock. When the chicken is cold, pick the meat off the bones and cut it into bitesize pieces.

3 Heat the oil in a large pan and fry the mushrooms for 2–3 minutes over medium heat. Add the onions, asparagus and peas and fry gently for 2 minutes until softened.

4 Pour in 500ml/17fl oz/generous 2 cups of the reserved stock and bring it to the boil. Stir in the cream and lemon juice and season to taste with salt, pepper and sugar. Whisk knobs of the beurre manié into the bubbling sauce to thicken it.

5 Finally, return the chicken to the sauce and cook gently until heated through. Garnish with the chopped parsley and serve with steamed or boiled rice.

Chicken Casserole Energy 811kcal/3396kJ; Protein 44g; Carbohydrate 69.8g, of which sugars 69.8g; Fat 39.2g, of which saturates 10.9g; Cholesterol 215mg; Calcium 183mg; Fibre 4.3g; Sodium 394mg.
Chicken Fricassée Energy 926kcal/3832kJ; Protein 55.1g; Carbohydrate 16g, of which sugars 6.1g; Fat 71.5g, of which saturates 22.6g; Cholesterol 282mg; Calcium 118mg; Fibre 5g; Sodium 264mg.

Classic Roast Turkey

It is hard to imagine the festive season without eating this classic roast and stuffing at least once.

Serves 8
4.5kg/10lb oven-ready turkey, with giblets
1 large onion, peeled and studded with 6 whole cloves
50g/2oz/4 tbsp butter, softened
10 chipolata sausages
salt and ground black pepper

For the stuffing
225g/8oz rindless streaky (fatty) bacon rashers (strips), chopped
1 large onion, finely chopped
450g/1lb pork sausage meat (bulk sausage)
25g/1oz/⅓ cup rolled oats
30ml/2 tbsp chopped fresh parsley
10ml/2 tsp dried mixed herbs
1 large (US extra large) egg, beaten
115g/4oz ready-to-eat dried apricots, finely chopped

For the gravy
25g/1oz/2 tbsp plain (all-purpose) flour
450ml/¾ pint/scant 2 cups giblet stock

1 Preheat the oven to 200°C/400°F/ Gas 6. For the stuffing, cook the bacon and onion in a frying pan until done. Mix with the other ingredients and season well.

2 Stuff the neck-end of the turkey and secure with a small skewer. Shape the remaining stuffing into balls. Put the onion in the body cavity. Weigh the stuffed bird and calculate the cooking time; allow 15 minutes per 450g/1lb plus 15 minutes.

3 Place the bird in a large roasting pan. Spread with butter and season well. Cover with foil and cook for 30 minutes. Lower the oven to 180°C/350°F/Gas 4. Baste every 30 minutes. Remove the foil for the last hour. Put the stuffing balls and sausages into ovenproof dishes in the oven and bake for the last 20 minutes.

4 Transfer the turkey to a serving plate, cover with foil and leave to stand for 15 minutes. To make the gravy, spoon off the fat from the roasting pan, leaving the meat juices. Blend in the flour and cook for 2 minutes. Stir in the stock, bring to the boil and transfer to a gravy jug (pitcher). To serve, carve the turkey and surround with sausages and stuffing balls.

Roast Turkey with Fruit and Nut Stuffing

The sausage meat inside this bird is black morcilla, and prunes and raisins make it even more sweet and fruity. The sauce is flavoured with grape juice and a splash of anis. It is the ideal way to spruce up a festive roast.

Serves 8
3kg/6½lb bronze or black turkey, weighed without the giblets
60ml/4 tbsp oil
200g/7oz rashers (strips) streaky (fatty) bacon

50g/2oz/½ cup Muscatel raisins, soaked in 45ml/3 tbsp anis spirit, and chopped
115g/4oz ready-to-eat pitted prunes, chopped
50g/2oz/½ cup almonds, chopped
1.5ml/¼ tsp dried thyme
finely grated rind of 1 lemon
freshly grated nutmeg
60ml/4 tbsp chopped fresh parsley
1 large (US extra large) egg, beaten
60ml/4 tbsp cooked rice or stale breadcrumbs
salt and ground black pepper

For the stuffing
45ml/3 tbsp olive oil
1 onion, chopped
2 garlic cloves, finely chopped
115g/4oz fatty bacon lardons
150g/5oz morcilla or black pudding (blood sausage), diced
1 turkey liver, diced

For the sauce
45ml/3 tbsp plain (all-purpose) flour
350ml/12fl oz/1½ cups turkey giblet stock, warmed
350ml/12fl oz/1½ cups red grape juice
30ml/2 tbsp anis spirit
salt and ground black pepper

1 Make the stuffing. Heat 30ml/2 tbsp oil in a pan and fry the onion, garlic and bacon for 6–8 minutes. Transfer to a large bowl. Fry the morcilla or black pudding in the remaining oil for about 3–4 minutes and the liver for 2–3 minutes.

2 Add the soaked raisins, prunes, almonds, thyme, lemon rind, nutmeg, seasoning and parsley to the pan. Stir in the beaten egg and rice or breadcrumbs.

3 About 3 hours before serving, preheat the oven, with a low shelf, to 200°C/400°F/Gas 6. Remove the turkey's wishbone, running fingernails up the two sides of the neck to find it, then pull it out. Season the turkey inside with salt and pepper, then fill the cavity with the stuffing and retruss the bird. Season.

4 Heat a roasting pan in the oven with 60ml/4 tbsp oil. Put in the turkey and baste the outside. Lay the bacon over the breast and legs. Reduce the temperature to 180°C/350°F/Gas 4 and roast for 2¼–2½ hours, basting once or twice. To test, insert a skewer into the thickest part of the inside leg. The juices should run clear. Remove the trussing thread and transfer the turkey to a heated serving plate. Keep warm.

5 Make the sauce. Skim as much fat as possible from the roasting pan. Sprinkle in the flour and cook gently for a few minutes, stirring constantly.

6 Stir the warm turkey stock into the pan and bring to simmering point. Add the grape juice and anis, and bring back to simmering point. Taste for seasoning and pour into a jug (pitcher). Carve the turkey and serve with the sauce.

Classic Roast Energy 828kcal/3452kJ; Protein 73.1g; Carbohydrate 19.4g, of which sugars 7g; Fat 51.3g, of which saturates 18.1g; Cholesterol 292mg; Calcium 77mg; Fibre 1.8g; Sodium 1267mg.
Roast Turkey Energy 662kcal/2772kJ; Protein 66.3g; Carbohydrate 27.9g, of which sugars 15.5g; Fat 31.5g, of which saturates 8.1g; Cholesterol 274mg; Calcium 104mg; Fibre 2.2g; Sodium 658mg.

Roast Turkey with Herby Liver Stuffing

In this festive recipe the roast turkey is packed with a rich herb and liver stuffing.

Serves 6
1 turkey, about
    4.5–5.5kg/10–12lb, washed and
    patted dry
25g/1oz/2 tbsp butter, melted
salt and ground black pepper
cranberry jelly, to serve

For the stuffing
200g/7oz/3½ cups fresh white
    breadcrumbs
175ml/6fl oz/¾ cup milk
25g/1oz/2 tbsp butter
1 egg, separated
1 calf's liver, about 600g/1lb 6oz,
    finely chopped
2 onions, finely chopped
90ml/6 tbsp chopped fresh dill
10ml/2 tsp clear honey
    salt and ground black pepper

1 For the stuffing, soak the breadcrumbs in the milk until soft. Melt the butter and mix 5ml/1 tsp with the egg yolk. Heat the remaining butter in a frying pan and add the liver and onions. Fry gently for 5 minutes, until the onions are golden brown. Remove from the heat and leave to cool.

2 Preheat the oven to 180°C/350°F/Gas 4. Add the cooled liver mixture to the soaked breadcrumbs and add the butter and egg yolk mixture, with the dill, honey and seasoning.

3 Whisk the egg white to soft peaks, then fold into the mixture, stirring gently to combine thoroughly.

4 Season the turkey and fill the cavity with the stuffing, then weigh to calculate the cooking time. Allow 20 minutes per 500g/1¼lb, plus an extra 20 minutes. Tuck the legs inside the cavity and tie the end shut with string. Brush with melted butter and transfer to a roasting pan. Roast for the calculated time.

5 Baste the turkey regularly, and cover with foil for the final 30 minutes. To test whether it is cooked, pierce the thickest part of the thigh with a knife; the juices should run clear. Leave to rest for 15 minutes. Carve into slices, spoon over the juices and serve with the stuffing and cranberry jelly.

Roast Turkey with Mushrooms

One sure way to boost the flavour and succulence of the festive turkey is to stuff it with the season's wild mushrooms. The gravy, too, can be flavoured with all kinds of mushrooms.

Serves 6–8
4.5kg/10lb fresh turkey
butter, for basting
watercress, to garnish

For the mushroom stuffing
60ml/4 tbsp unsalted butter
1 medium onion, chopped
225g/8oz/3 cups wild mushrooms

75g/3oz/1½ cups fresh white,
    brown, or mixed breadcrumbs
115g/4oz pork sausages, skinned
1 small fresh truffle, sliced (optional)
5 drops truffle oil (optional)
salt and ground black pepper

For the gravy
75ml/5 tbsp medium sherry
400ml/14fl oz/1⅔ cups
    chicken stock
15g/½oz/¼ cup dried ceps, soaked
20ml/4 tsp cornflour (cornstarch)
5ml/1 tsp Dijon mustard
2.5ml/½ tsp wine vinegar
salt and ground black pepper
butter pat

1 Preheat the oven to 220°C/425°F/Gas 7. For the stuffing, melt the butter in a pan and cook the onion for 4–6 minutes. Add the mushrooms and cook for 5 minutes. Remove from the heat, add the breadcrumbs, skinned sausages, and the truffle and truffle oil if using, season and stir well to combine. Spoon the stuffing into the neck cavity of the turkey and enclose.

2 Rub the skin of the turkey with butter, place in a large roasting pan and roast uncovered in the oven for 50 minutes. Lower the temperature to 180°C/350°F/Gas 4, cover with foil and cook for another 2 hours and 30 minutes.

3 To make the gravy, transfer the turkey to a board, and keep warm. Spoon off the fat from the roasting pan and discard. Heat the remaining liquid until reduced to half. Add the sherry and stir to loosen the residue. Stir in the stock and drained ceps.

4 Blend the cornflour and mustard with 10ml/2 tsp water and the wine vinegar. Stir this into the juices in the pan and simmer to thicken. Season and then stir in a pat of butter. Garnish the turkey with watercress. Serve the gravy separately.

Roast Turkey Energy 828kcal/3452kJ; Protein 73.1g; Carbohydrate 19.4g, of which sugars 7g; Fat 51.3g, of which saturates 18.1g; Cholesterol 292mg; Calcium 77mg; Fibre 1.8g; Sodium 1267mg.
Stuffed Turkey Energy 740kcal/3126kJ; Protein 112.3g; Carbohydrate 35.9g, of which sugars 7.3g; Fat 13.5g, of which saturates 6.6g; Cholesterol 507mg; Calcium 122mg; Fibre 1.7g; Sodium 517mg.

Duck with Orange Sauce

The classic partnering of duck with orange sauce makes for a tasty festive dish.

Serves 2–3
2kg/4½lb duck 2 oranges
90g/3½oz/½ cup caster
  (superfine) sugar
90ml/6 tbsp white wine vinegar
  or cider vinegar
120ml/4fl oz/½ cup Grand
  Marnier or other orange
  flavoured liqueur
salt and ground black pepper
watercress and orange slices,
  to garnish

1 Preheat the oven to 150°C/300°F/Gas 2. Trim off all the excess fat and skin from the duck and prick the skin all over with a fork. Generously season the duck inside and out, and tie the legs together with string to hold them in place.

2 Place the duck on a rack in a large roasting pan. Cover tightly with foil and cook in the preheated oven for 1½ hours. Remove the rind in wide strips from the oranges, then stack up two or three strips at a time and slice into very thin julienne strips. Squeeze the juice from the oranges and set it aside.

3 Place the sugar and vinegar in a pan and stir to dissolve the sugar. Boil over high heat, without stirring, until the mixture is a rich caramel colour. Remove the pan from the heat and carefully add the orange juice, pouring it down the side of the pan. Swirl the pan to blend, then bring back to the boil and add the orange rind and liqueur. Simmer for 2–3 minutes.

4 Remove the duck from the oven and pour off all the fat from the pan. Raise the oven temperature to 200°C/400°F/Gas 6. Roast the duck, uncovered, for 25–30 minutes, basting three or four times with the caramel mixture, until the duck is golden brown and the juices run clear when the thigh is pierced.

5 Pour the juices from the cavity into the casserole and transfer the duck to a carving board. Cover loosely with foil and leave to stand for 10–15 minutes. Pour the roasting juices into the pan with the rest of the caramel mixture, skim off the fat and simmer gently. Serve the duck with the orange sauce, garnished with sprigs of watercress and orange slices.

Duck Legs with Spiced Red Cabbage

This Christmas dish is traditionally served with red cabbage.

Serves 4
8 duck legs or 4 goose legs
15ml/1 tbsp oil
10ml/2 tsp tomato purée (paste)
200l/7fl oz/scant 1 cup red wine
salt and ground white pepper
chopped parsley, to garnish
mashed potato, to serve, optional

For the red cabbage
3 onions
60g/2½oz lard
1 red cabbage, finely sliced
100ml/3½fl oz/scant ½ cup red
  wine vinegar
15ml/1 tbsp sugar
2 bay leaves
3 pieces star anise
1 cinnamon stick
250ml/8fl oz/ 1 cup apple juice
2 apples, chopped
30ml/2 tbsp redcurrant jelly
5ml/1 tsp cornflour (cornstarch)

1 For the cabbage, chop two of the onions, melt the lard in a large pan and fry the onion for 2 minutes. Add the cabbage, vinegar, sugar, spices and apple juice, bring to the boil, cover and simmer for 30 minutes.

2 Stir the apples and redcurrant jelly into the pan and cook for a further 45 minutes, adding more apple juice if necessary. Towards the end of the cooking time, blend the cornflour with water in a cup and stir into the cabbage. Preheat the oven to 200°C/400°F/Gas 6.

3 While the cabbage is cooking, place the duck legs in a roasting pan, season, add a cup of water and roast in the oven for 20 minutes, then reduce the oven to 160°C/325°F/Gas 3 and cook for a further 40 minutes, basting from time to time.

4 Keep the legs warm. Add the remaining onion, chopped, and the tomato purée to the pan and fry for 3–4 minutes. Deglaze the pan with the wine and cook for another 2 minutes.

5 Serve the duck legs with the sauce poured over, garnished with fresh parsley and accompanied by the red cabbage.

Duck with Orange Energy 280kcal/1181kJ; Protein 30.8g; Carbohydrate 23.8g, of which sugars 23.8g; Fat 10g, of which saturates 1.9g; Cholesterol 165mg; Calcium 48mg; Fibre 0.4g; Sodium 195mg.
Duck Legs Energy 958kcal/3961kJ; Protein 20.7g; Carbohydrate 32.7g, of which sugars 28.5g; Fat 79.8g, of which saturates 22.8g; Cholesterol 12mg; Calcium 122mg; Fibre 5.1g; Sodium 146mg.

Roast Pheasant with Sherry and Mustard Sauce

Roast pheasant makes a pleasant change from the traditional turkey or chicken at Christmas time. Look out for them hanging in the window of butchers' stores in the run-up to the festive season.

Serves 4
2 young oven-ready pheasants
50g/2oz/¼ cup softened butter
200ml/7fl oz/scant 1 cup sherry
15ml/1 tbsp Dijon mustard
salt and ground black pepper

1 Preheat the oven to 200°C/400°F/Gas 6. Put the pheasants in a roasting pan and spread the butter all over both birds. Season with salt and pepper.

2 Roast the pheasants in the preheated oven for 50 minutes, basting often to stop the birds from drying out.

3 When the pheasants are cooked, take them out of the pan and leave to rest on a chopping board, loosely covered with a sheet of foil, for about 10–15 minutes.

4 Meanwhile, place the roasting pan over medium heat. Add the sherry and season with salt and pepper.

5 Simmer for 5 minutes, until the sherry has slightly reduced, then stir in the mustard. Carve the pheasants and serve with the sherry and mustard sauce.

Cook's Tips
• *Serve with potatoes braised in wine with garlic and onions, Brussels sprouts and bread sauce.*
• *Use only young pheasants for roasting in this recipe – older birds are too tough for roasting and are only suitable for long, slow cooking in a casserole.*
• *Like many gamebirds – including grouse, guinea fowl and partridge – pheasants are at their best over the festive season.*

Marinated Pheasant with Port

This warming dish is delicious served with mashed root vegetables and shredded cabbage or leeks. Marinating the pheasant in port is a good way of moistening and tenderizing pheasant, especially the legs, which can be a little tough.

Red wine can be substituted for the port, if you prefer.

Serves 4
2 pheasants, cut into portions
300ml/½ pint/1¼ cups port
50g/2oz/¼ cup butter
300g/11oz brown cap (cremini)
  mushrooms, halved if large

1 Place the pheasant portions in a large bowl and pour over the port. Cover and marinate for at least 3–4 hours or overnight, turning occasionally.

2 Drain the meat portions thoroughly, reserving the marinade. Pat the portions dry on kitchen paper and season lightly with salt and ground black pepper.

3 Melt three-quarters of the butter in a frying pan and cook the pheasant portions on all sides for about 5 minutes, until deep golden. Drain well, transfer to a plate, then cook the mushrooms in the fat remaining in the pan for 3 minutes.

4 Return the pheasant to the pan and pour in the reserved marinade with 200ml/7fl oz/scant 1 cup water. Bring to the boil, reduce the heat and cover, then simmer gently for about 45 minutes, until the pheasant is tender.

5 Using a slotted spoon, carefully remove the pheasant portions and mushrooms from the frying pan and set aside to keep warm. Bring the cooking juices to the boil and boil vigorously for about 5 minutes, until they are reduced and have thickened slightly.

6 Strain the juices through a fine sieve (strainer) and return them to the pan. Whisk in the remaining butter over gentle heat until it has melted. Season to taste with salt and ground black pepper, then pour the juices over the pheasant and mushrooms and serve immediately.

Roast Pheasant Energy 692kcal/2897kJ; Protein 81.7g; Carbohydrate 1.2g, of which sugars 1.1g; Fat 34.2g, of which saturates 14.5g; Cholesterol 27mg; Calcium 132mg; Fibre 0g; Sodium 456mg.
Marinated Pheasant Energy 457kcal/1910kJ; Protein 46.2g; Carbohydrate 6.4g, of which sugars 4.5g; Fat 23.1g, of which saturates 6.1g; Cholesterol 9mg; Calcium 102mg; Fibre 2g; Sodium 483mg.

Gammon with Cumberland Sauce

A gammon joint is a traditional addition to the kitchen at Christmas time. Serve this dish and sauce either hot as a festive main course or cold in a buffet.

Serves 8–10
2.25kg/5lb smoked or unsmoked
  gammon (smoked or cured
  ham) joint
1 onion
1 carrot
1 celery stick
bouquet garni sachet
6 peppercorns

For the glaze
whole cloves
50g/2oz/4 tbsp soft light brown
  or demerara (raw) sugar
30ml/2 tbsp golden
  (light corn) syrup
5ml/1 tsp English (hot)
  mustard powder

For the cumberland sauce
juice and shredded rind of
  1 orange
30ml/2 tbsp lemon juice
120ml/4fl oz/½ cup port or
  red wine
60ml/4 tbsp redcurrant jelly

1 Soak the gammon overnight in a cool place in enough cold water to cover. Discard this water. Put the joint into a large pan and cover it with more cold water. Bring the water to the boil slowly and skim off any scum that rises to the surface. Add the vegetables and seasonings, cover and simmer gently for 2 hours.

2 Leave the meat to cool in the liquid for 30 minutes. Remove it from the liquid and strip off the skin neatly. Score the fat in diamonds with a sharp knife and stick a clove in the centre of each diamond.

3 Preheat the oven to 180°C/350°F/Gas 4. Put the sugar, golden syrup and mustard powder in a small pan and heat gently to melt them. Place the gammon in a roasting pan and spoon over the glaze. Bake until golden brown, about 20 minutes. Put it under a hot grill (broiler), if necessary, to get a good colour. Stand in a warm place for 15 minutes before carving.

4 For the sauce, put the orange and lemon juice into a pan with the port or red wine and jelly, and heat to melt the jelly. Pour boiling water on to the orange rind, drain, and add to the sauce. Cook for 2 minutes. Serve in a sauce boat.

Cider-glazed Ham

This wonderful ham glazed with cider is traditionally served with cranberry sauce and is ideal for Christmas.

1.3 litres/2¼ pints/5⅔ cups
  medium-dry cider
45ml/3 tbsp soft light brown sugar
flat leaf parsley, to garnish

Serves 8–10
2kg/4½lb middle gammon
  (smoked or cured ham) joint
1 large or 2 small onions
about 30 whole cloves
3 bay leaves
10 black peppercorns

For the cranberry sauce
350g/12oz/3 cups cranberries
175g/6oz/¾ cup soft light
  brown sugar
grated rind and juice of
  2 clementines
30ml/2 tbsp port

1 Weigh the ham and calculate the cooking time at 20 minutes per 450g/1lb, then place it in a large casserole or pan. Stud the onion or onions with 5–10 of the cloves and add to the casserole or pan with the bay leaves and peppercorns.

2 Add 1.2 litres/2 pints/5 cups of the cider and enough water just to cover the ham. Heat until simmering, and then skim off the scum that rises to the surface. Start timing the cooking from the moment the stock simmers. Cover with a lid or foil and simmer gently for the calculated time. Towards the end of the cooking time, preheat the oven to 220°C/425°F/Gas 7.

3 Heat the sugar and remaining cider in a pan until the sugar has dissolved. Simmer for 5 minutes to make a dark, sticky glaze. Leave to cool for 5 minutes.

4 Lift the ham out of the casserole or pan. Carefully and evenly, cut the rind off, then score the fat into a neat diamond pattern. Place the ham in a roasting pan or ovenproof dish. Press a clove into the centre of each diamond, then carefully spoon over the glaze. Bake for about 20–25 minutes, or until the fat is brown, glistening and crisp.

5 Simmer all the cranberry sauce ingredients in a heavy pan for 15–20 minutes, stirring often. Transfer to a sauce boat. Serve the ham hot or cold, garnished with parsley and with the sauce.

Gammon Energy 524kcal/2212kJ; Protein 66.5g; Carbohydrate 34.7g, of which sugars 32.9g; Fat 12.4g, of which saturates 4.7g; Cholesterol 45mg; Calcium 29mg; Fibre 0g; Sodium 2512mg.
Cider-glazed Ham Energy 368kcal/1541kJ; Protein 39.6g; Carbohydrate 15.2g, of which sugars 15.2g; Fat 16.9g, of which saturates 5.6g; Cholesterol 52mg; Calcium 25mg; Fibre 0.6g; Sodium 1982mg.

Roast Pork with Sage Stuffing

Sage and onion make a festive stuffing for roast pork.

Serves 6–8
1.6kg/3½lb boneless loin of pork
60ml/4 tbsp fine, dry breadcrumbs
10ml/2 tsp chopped fresh sage
25ml/1½ tbsp plain
 (all-purpose) flour
300ml/½ pint/1¼ cups cider
150ml/¼ pint/⅔ cup water
5–10ml/1–2 tsp crab apple or
 redcurrant jelly

salt and ground black pepper
sprigs of thyme, to garnish

For the stuffing
25g/1oz/2 tbsp butter
50g/2oz bacon, finely chopped
2 large onions, finely chopped
75g/3oz/1½ cups fresh
 white breadcrumbs
30ml/2 tbsp chopped fresh sage
5ml/1 tsp chopped fresh thyme
10ml/2 tsp grated lemon rind
1 small egg, beaten

1 Preheat the oven to 220°C/425°F/Gas 7. For the stuffing, melt the butter in a frying pan. Cook the bacon until it browns, then add the onions and cook until they soften. Mix with the breadcrumbs, sage, thyme, lemon rind, egg and salt and pepper.

2 Cut the rind off the joint of pork in one piece and score it well. Place the pork fat side down and season. Add a layer of stuffing, then roll up and tie. Lay the rind over the pork and rub in 5ml/1 tsp salt. Roast for 2–2½ hours, basting once or twice. Reduce the temperature to 190°C/375°F/Gas 5 after 20 minutes.

3 Shape the remaining stuffing into balls and add to the pan for the last 30 minutes. When the pork is done, remove the rind, increase the oven to 220°C/425°F/Gas 7 and roast the rind for about 20–25 minutes, until crisp.

4 Mix the dry breadcrumbs and sage and press them into the fat on the pork. Cook the pork for 10 minutes, then cover and set aside in a warm place for 15–20 minutes.

5 For the gravy, remove all but 30–45ml/2–3 tbsp of the fat from the roasting pan and place it on the stove. Stir in the flour, followed by the cider and water. Simmer for 10 minutes. Strain into a pan and add the jelly. Season and cook for 5 minutes. Serve with slices of pork and crackling, garnished with thyme.

Porchetta

This is a simplified version of a traditional Italian festive dish. Make sure the piece of belly pork has a good amount of crackling – because this is the best part, which guests will just love. Serve with plenty of creamy mashed potatoes and a seasonal green vegetable.

Serves 8
2kg/4½lb boned belly pork
45ml/3 tbsp fresh rosemary
 leaves, roughly chopped
50g/2oz/⅔ cup freshly grated
 Parmesan cheese
15ml/1 tbsp olive oil
salt and ground black pepper

1 Preheat the oven to 180°C/350°F/Gas 4. Lay the belly pork skin side down on a chopping board.

2 Spread the chopped rosemary leaves over the meat, pushing it in a little with your hand, and sprinkle with the grated Parmesan cheese. Season with salt and plenty of ground black pepper and drizzle over the olive oil.

3 Starting from one end, roll the pork up firmly and tie string around it at 2.5cm/1in intervals, to secure. Transfer the rolled pork to a roasting pan and cook for about 3 hours, or until cooked through and tender.

4 Transfer the pork to a chopping board and leave it to rest for about 10 minutes, this will improve the texture and flavour of the meat after the heating process. Carve the pork into thick slices and serve immediately.

Cook's Tip
To help ensure that you have crisp crackling on the pork you should dry and score the skin. Pat the outside of the pork with kitchen paper or a clean dish towel to dry it. The skin will already have a few cuts in it but it does not hurt to add a few more. Use a very sharp paring knife or use a craft knife with a sharp, clean blade and score the skin in a few places, ensuring that you have cut just through to the fat beneath the skin.

Porchetta Energy 773kcal/3216kJ; Protein 65.2g; Carbohydrate 0g, of which sugars 0g; Fat 56.9g, of which saturates 20g; Cholesterol 219mg; Calcium 98mg; Fibre 0g; Sodium 293mg.
Roast Pork Energy 390kcal/1637kJ; Protein 47.9g; Carbohydrate 21.6g, of which sugars 4.8g; Fat 12.9g, of which saturates 5.2g; Cholesterol 164mg; Calcium 62mg; Fibre 1.3g; Sodium 434mg.

Braised Pork and Chickpea Stew

Slow cooking allows the meat to become tender and juicy on the inside and crisp on the outside, and is the secret of many flavourful dishes. It also allows the fat in the meat to dry a little and release flavour. The chickpea stew, which can be a meal in itself, combines well with the pork, and with other meat, such as game – making it suitable for many festive favourites.

Serves 4
1kg/2¼lb pork loin, preferably
    from black pork
15ml/1 tbsp sweet paprika
15ml/1 tbsp chopped fresh thyme

3 garlic cloves, finely chopped
105ml/7 tbsp white wine
105ml/7 tbsp olive oil
sea salt and ground black pepper

For the stew
50ml/2fl oz/¼ cup olive oil
1 onion, finely chopped
50g/2oz/⅓ cup bacon,
    finely diced
100g/3¾oz wild mushrooms,
    such as ceps and horn of
    plenty, chopped
300g/11oz/scant 2 cups cooked
    chickpeas, plus 100ml/3½fl oz/
    scant ½ cup cooking liquid
100g/3¾oz day-old white bread,
    crust removed, cut into cubes
1 small bunch of fresh parsley,
    finely chopped

1 Trim off any excess fat from the pork and cut the meat into pieces weighing 125g/4¼oz. Place them in a shallow, ovenproof dish. Mix together the paprika, thyme, garlic, wine and olive oil in a jug (pitcher), and season with salt and pepper. Pour the mixture over the meat, cover and leave to marinate for 4 hours.

2 Preheat the oven to 140°C/275°F/Gas 1. Place the dish in the oven with the marinade and braise for 2 hours.

3 Towards the end of the cooking time, prepare the chickpea stew. Heat the oil in a pan. Add the onion and bacon and cook over low heat, stirring occasionally, for 5–8 minutes, until the onion has softened and the bacon is lightly coloured.

4 Add the mushrooms and cook for 5 minutes. Add the chickpeas, the reserved cooking liquid and the bread. Cook, stirring, until the bread has disintegrated, then add the parsley. Serve the pork immediately, with the chickpea stew.

Fried Pork and Apples

This is a very simple dish that turns an inexpensive cut of meat into a most enjoyable meal. It is ideal for a quick supper dish over the festive period.

Serves 4
600g/1¼lb lightly salted or
    fresh belly of pork, cut into
    thin slices

500g/1¼lb crisp eating apples
30ml/2 tbsp soft light brown sugar
salt and ground black pepper
chopped fresh parsley or chives,
    to garnish

To serve
boiled potatoes
a seasonal green vegetable,
    such as cabbage, Brussels
    sprouts or kale

1 Heat a large frying pan, without any oil or fat, until hot. Add the salted or fresh belly pork slices and fry over low heat for about 3–4 minutes each side, until golden brown. Season the pork slices with salt and pepper. Transfer to a warmed serving dish and keep warm.

2 Core the apples but do not peel, then cut the apples into rings. Add the apple rings to the frying pan and fry gently in the pork fat for about 3–4 minutes each side, until just beginning to turn golden and translucent.

3 Sprinkle the slices with the sugar and turn once more for a couple of minutes until the sugar side starts to caramelize.

4 Serve the pork slices with the apple rings. Accompany the pork with plain boiled potatoes and a green seasonal vegetable, garnished with fresh parsley.

Cook's Tips
• This is a great dish to make the most of seasonal apples, which are at their best in the run-up to Christmas. Cut the rings to a depth of 5mm/¼in across the apple. Most apples will make about four rings for this dish.
• Other seasonal vegetables that would go well with this dish include beetroot (beets), carrots, cauliflower or leeks.

Fried Pork and Apples Energy 645kcal/2676kJ; Protein 23.4g; Carbohydrate 19g, of which sugars 19g; Fat 53.4g, of which saturates 19.7g; Cholesterol 108mg; Calcium 21mg; Fibre 2g; Sodium 113mg.
Braised Pork Energy 756kcal/3155kJ; Protein 64.1g; Carbohydrate 26g, of which sugars 1.2g; Fat 42.8g, of which saturates 8.5g; Cholesterol 164mg; Calcium 89mg; Fibre 3.7g; Sodium 666mg.

Rack of Lamb with Herb Crust

This dish is very popular for special occasions so is ideal for an elegant Christmas dinner party. Serve with creamy potato gratin, baby carrots and vegetables such as mangetouts or green beans. Offer mint jelly separately.

Serves 6–8

2 racks of lamb (fair end), chined and trimmed by the butcher

salt, ground black pepper and a pinch of cayenne pepper

For the herb crust

115g/4oz/½ cup butter
10ml/2 tsp mustard powder
175g/6oz/3 cups fresh white breadcrumbs
2 garlic cloves, finely chopped
30ml/2 tbsp chopped fresh parsley
5ml/1 tsp very finely chopped fresh rosemary

1 Preheat the oven to 200°C/400°F/Gas 6. Remove any meat and fat from the top 4–5cm/1½–2in of the bones and scrape the bones clean, then wrap the bones in foil to prevent burning. Remove almost all the fat from the lamb and score the thin layer remaining to make a lattice pattern.

2 Season the lamb with salt, pepper and cayenne pepper, and cook the racks in the preheated oven for 20 minutes. Remove from the oven and cool to room temperature.

3 Next make the herb crust: when the lamb is cold, blend 75g/3oz/6 tbsp of the butter with the mustard to make a smooth paste, and spread it over the fatty sides of the lamb.

4 Mix the breadcrumbs, garlic, parsley and rosemary together in a bowl. Melt the remaining butter, and stir it into the bowl. Divide the herb mixture between the two racks, laying it on top of the butter paste and pressing it well on to the lamb. Set aside and keep at room temperature until ready to finish cooking.

5 When ready to cook the meat, preheat the oven to 200°C/400°F/Gas 6, and roast for a final 20 minutes. To serve, remove the foil from the bones; finish them with paper cutlet frills, if you wish. Carve into cutlets, allowing two or three per person, and replace any of the crust that falls off.

Roast Lamb with Potatoes and Garlic

The meat and vegetables for this dish are cooked together, making a festive meal that is moist and flavourful.

Serves 6–8

1 whole leg of lamb, about 2kg/4½lb
3 garlic cloves, quartered lengthways, plus 6–8 whole, unpeeled garlic cloves, or 1 or 2 heads of garlic, halved

900g/2lb potatoes, peeled and quartered lengthways
juice of 1 lemon
45ml/3 tbsp extra virgin olive oil
450ml/¾ pint/scant 2 cups hot water
5ml/1 tsp dried oregano
2.5ml/½ tsp dried thyme or 5ml/1 tsp chopped fresh thyme
salt and ground black pepper
a few sprigs of fresh thyme, to garnish

1 Preheat the oven to 220°C/425°F/Gas 7. Place the lamb in a large roasting pan. Make several incisions in the meat, pressing the point of a sharp knife deep into the flesh, and insert one or two quartered pieces of peeled garlic into each one.

2 Arrange the quartered potatoes and whole garlic cloves or halved heads of garlic around the meat. Pour over the lemon juice and extra virgin olive oil. Add half the water to the dish, pouring it around the lamb rather than over it. Sprinkle over half the dried oregano and thyme. Season with salt and pepper.

3 Roast the lamb for 15 minutes on the high heat, then reduce the oven temperature to 190°C/375°F/Gas 5. Roast for 1 hour, basting the meat occasionally.

4 After an hour, turn the meat over so that the other side browns as well, sprinkle over the rest of the herbs and season with salt and pepper. Turn the potatoes over gently. Add the remaining hot water to the pan and continue to cook for another 25–30 minutes, basting occasionally with the pan juices.

5 Cover the meat with a clean dish towel or piece of foil and set it aside to rest for 10–15 minutes before carving and serving. The cloves of garlic can be popped out of their skins and eaten with the meat; they make a deliciously creamy accompaniment to the taste of the lamb.

Rack of Lamb Energy 455kcal/1899kJ; Protein 26.4g; Carbohydrate 22.7g, of which sugars 0.9g; Fat 29.4g, of which saturates 16.1g; Cholesterol 130mg; Calcium 51mg; Fibre 0.7g; Sodium 438mg.
Roast Lamb Energy 750kcal/3,132kJ; Protein 73.4g; Carbohydrate 24.3g, of which sugars 2.1g; Fat 40.4g, of which saturates 17.3g; Cholesterol 273mg; Calcium 37mg; Fibre 1.8g; Sodium 175mg.

Rib of Beef with Yorkshire Puddings

Roast beef has always been traditional fare at Christmas.

Serves 6–8
rib of beef joint, weighing
   about 3kg/6½lb
oil, for brushing
salt and ground black pepper

For the Yorkshire puddings
115g/4oz/1 cup plain
   (all-purpose) flour
1.5ml/¼ tsp salt
1 egg
200ml/7fl oz/scant 1 cup milk
olive oil or beef dripping, to grease

For the gravy
600ml/1 pint/2½ cups beef stock

1 Preheat the oven to 220°C/425°F/Gas 7. Weigh the joint and calculate the cooking time required as follows: 10–15 minutes per 500g/1¼lb for rare beef, 15–20 minutes for medium and 20–25 minutes for well done.

2 Put the joint into a large roasting pan. Brush with oil and season with salt and pepper. Put into the hot oven and cook for 30 minutes, until the beef is browned. Lower the oven temperature to 160°C/325°F/Gas 3 and cook for the calculated time, basting the meat occasionally during cooking.

3 For the Yorkshire puddings, sift the flour and salt into a bowl and add the egg. Make the milk up to 300ml/½ pint/1¼ cups with water. Blend into the flour to make a batter. Set aside while the beef cooks. Grease eight Yorkshire pudding tins (muffin pans).

4 At the end of its cooking time, remove the beef from the oven, cover with foil and leave to stand for 30–40 minutes.

5 Increase the oven temperature to 220°C/425°F/Gas 7 and put the prepared tins on the top shelf for 5 minutes until very hot. Pour in the batter and cook for about 15 minutes until well risen, crisp and golden brown.

6 For the gravy, transfer the beef to a serving plate. Pour off the fat, leaving the meat juices. Add the stock, bring to the boil and reduce by half. Season. Carve the beef and serve with the gravy, Yorkshire puddings and roast potatoes.

Roast Sirloin with Sweet Peppers

This substantial and warming dish makes an ideal dinner for cold winter nights during the Christmas period. It is also good enough to serve as the main course on Christmas Day.

Serves 8
1.3–1.6kg/3–3½lb piece of sirloin
15ml/1 tbsp olive oil
450g/1lb small red (bell) peppers

115g/4oz/¾ cup mushrooms
175g/6oz thick-sliced
   pancetta, cubed
50g/2oz/2 tbsp plain
   (all-purpose) flour
150ml/¼ pint/⅔ cup full-bodied
   red wine
300ml/½ pint/1¼ cups
   beef stock
30ml/2 tbsp Marsala
10ml/2 tsp mixed dried herbs
salt and ground black pepper

1 Preheat the oven to 190°C/375°F/Gas 5. Season the meat. Heat the oil in a pan, then brown the meat. Place in a roasting pan and cook for 1¼ hours.

2 Put the red peppers in the oven to roast for 20 minutes (or roast for 45 minutes if using larger peppers).

3 Near the end of the meat's cooking time, prepare the gravy. Roughly chop the mushroom caps and stems.

4 Heat the pan again and add the pancetta. Cook until the fat runs from the meat. Add the flour to the pan and cook for a few minutes until browned.

5 Stir in the red wine and stock and bring to the boil. Lower the heat and add the Marsala, herbs and seasoning.

6 Add the mushrooms and heat through. Remove the sirloin from the oven and leave to stand for 10 minutes. Serve with the roasted peppers and hot gravy.

Cook's Tip
To serve this beef joint on Christmas Day, simply accompany it with all the usual festive trimmings.

Rib of Beef Energy 1037kcal/4338kJ; Protein 129g; Carbohydrate 15.1g, of which sugars 4.1g; Fat 51.5g, of which saturates 24.3g; Cholesterol 352mg; Calcium 123mg; Fibre 0.5g; Sodium 249mg.
Roast Sirloin Energy 490kcal/2043kJ; Protein 35.7g; Carbohydrate 19.5g, of which sugars 5.2g; Fat 30.4g, of which saturates 7.5g; Cholesterol 99mg; Calcium 29mg; Fibre 2.2g; Sodium 109mg.

Steak with Mustard Sauce

This steak recipe is quite delicious, with plenty of sauce in which the potatoes can be submerged. The mustard used should not be overly spicy, but rather slightly sweet.

Serves 4

25g/1oz/2 tbsp butter
30ml/2 tbsp olive oil
4 fillet steaks (beef tenderloin), weighing about 175g/6oz each
30ml/2 tbsp mild mustard (preferably Savora)
105ml/7 tbsp single (light) cream
105ml/7 tbsp milk
juice of 1/2 lemon
sea salt and ground black pepper
chips (French fries) or fried potatoes, to serve

1 Melt the butter with the oil in a large frying pan. Season the steaks with salt and black pepper, add to the pan and cook until done to your liking: about 2 minutes each side for rare and 3 minutes each side for medium.

2 Remove the steaks from the pan and set aside to keep warm. Spoon off and discard the fat from the pan, reserving any juices left over from cooking the steaks.

3 Put the mustard, cream, milk and lemon juice in the pan. Return the steaks to the pan and heat gently, shaking the pan to blend everything together. Serve hot with chips.

Cook's Tip
Savora is the kind of mustard traditionally used for this dish. It is slightly sweet and a little spicy.

Variation
A fillet steak (beef tenderloin) is a fine cut of meat and is special enough to serve for a festive meal. If doing this, serve with roast potatoes rather than chips (French fries) and the traditional vegetables such as Brussels sprouts, roasted parsnips and carrots. Let diners help themselves to horseradish cream.

Collops of Beef with Shallots

In this recipe, the beef is paired with the sweetness of onions – a combination you will find time and again in traditional cooking. Here, shallots are being used, left whole to impart a wonderful texture and flavour to the meal.

Serves 4

4 fillet steaks (beef tenderloin)
15ml/1 tbsp olive oil
50g/2oz/1/4 cup butter
20 shallots, peeled
5ml/1 tsp caster (superfine) sugar
150ml/1/4 pint/2/3 cup beef stock
salt and ground black pepper

1 Take the steaks out of the refrigerator well before you need them and dry with kitchen paper. Heat the oil and butter in a large frying pan, then cook the steaks as you like them.

2 Once cooked, remove the steaks from the pan and keep warm. Put the shallots in the pan and brown lightly in the meat juices, stirring occasionally.

3 Add the sugar and then the stock. Reduce the heat to low and allow the liquid to evaporate, shaking the pan from time to time. The shallots will end up slightly soft, browned and caramelized with a shiny glaze. Season with salt and pepper.

4 Serve the steaks on warmed plates and spoon over the caramelized shallots and juices from the pan.

Cook's Tip
Experienced cooks can tell if the steak is ready by pressing it down with their fingers and feeling how springy the meat inside is. If you are unsure of this technique, then simply cut into the steak to ensure it is cooked to your liking.

Variation
This recipe can be used for other cuts of beef such as sirloin or rump (round) steak, or even with slices of roasted beef joint.

Collops of Beef Energy 424kcal/1767kJ; Protein 43.2g; Carbohydrate 6.1g, of which sugars 4.6g; Fat 25.4g, of which saturates 12.5g; Cholesterol 149mg; Calcium 27mg; Fibre 0.9g; Sodium 166mg.
Steak with Mustard Energy 475kcal/1976kJ; Protein 42.1g; Carbohydrate 2.6g, of which sugars 2.4g; Fat 33g, of which saturates 14.2g; Cholesterol 131mg; Calcium 70mg; Fibre 0g; Sodium 390mg.

Baked Polenta with Tomato Sauce

Polenta, or cornmeal, is a tasty and healthy choice for festive entertaining. It is cooked like a sort of porridge, and eaten soft, or set, cut into shapes then baked or grilled.

Serves 4
5ml/1 tsp salt
250g/9oz/2¼ cups quick
  cook polenta
5ml/1 tsp paprika
2.5ml/½ tsp freshly
  grated nutmeg
10ml/2 tsp olive oil
1 large onion, finely chopped
2 garlic cloves, crushed
2 × 400g/14oz cans
  chopped tomatoes
15ml/1 tbsp tomato purée (paste)
5ml/1 tsp sugar
salt and ground black pepper

1 Lightly grease an ovenproof dish and set aside. Line a 28 x 18cm/11 x 7in baking tin (pan) with clear film (plastic wrap). In a large, heavy pan, bring 1 litre/1¾ pints/4 cups water to the boil with the salt.

2 Pour in the polenta in a steady stream and cook, stirring constantly, for 5 minutes.

3 Beat the paprika and nutmeg into the polenta, then pour the mixture into the prepared baking tin and smooth the surface with a knife. Leave to cool.

4 Heat the oil in a non-stick pan and cook the onion and garlic until soft. Add the tomatoes, tomato purée and sugar. Season with salt and pepper. Bring to the boil, then reduce the heat and simmer for 20 minutes.

5 Meanwhile, preheat the oven to 200°C/400°F/Gas 6. Turn out the cooled polenta on to a clean chopping board, and cut into 5cm/2in squares.

6 Place half the polenta squares in the prepared dish. Spoon over half the tomato sauce, and sprinkle with half the cheese. Repeat the layers. Bake in the oven for about 25 minutes, or until golden. Serve immediately.

Festive Lentil and Nut Roast

An excellent celebration mould which can be served with all the trimmings, including vegetarian gravy. Garnish it with fresh cranberries and parsley for a really festive effect.

Serves 6–8
115g/4oz/½ cup red lentils
115g/4oz/1 cup hazelnuts
115g/4oz/1 cup walnuts
1 large carrot
2 celery sticks
1 large onion
115g/4oz mushrooms
50g/2oz/4 tbsp butter
10ml/2 tsp mild curry powder
30ml/2 tbsp tomato ketchup
30ml/2 tbsp vegetarian
  Worcestershire sauce
1 egg, beaten
10ml/2 tsp salt
60ml/4 tbsp fresh flat leaf
  parsley, chopped
150ml/¼ pint/⅔ cup water

1 Soak the lentils for 1 hour in cold water, then drain well. Grind the nuts in a food processor until quite fine but not too smooth. Set the nuts aside.

2 Chop the carrot, celery, onion and mushrooms into small chunks, then process them in a food processor or blender until they are quite finely chopped.

3 Fry the vegetables gently in the butter for 5 minutes, then stir in the curry powder and cook for a minute. Cool.

4 Mix the soaked lentils with the nuts, vegetables, ketchup, Worcestershire sauce, egg, salt, parsley and water.

5 Grease and line the base and sides of a long 1kg/2lb loaf tin (pan) with baking parchment or a sheet of foil. Press the mixture into the tin. Preheat the oven to 190°C/375°F/Gas 5.

6 Bake in the preheated oven for about 1–1¼ hours until just firm, covering the top with baking parchment or foil if it starts to brown too quickly.

7 Allow the roast to stand for about 15 minutes before you turn it out and peel off the paper or foil. It will be fairly soft when cut as it is a moist loaf.

Baked Polenta Energy 380kcal/1590kJ; Protein 15.2g; Carbohydrate 55.8g, of which sugars 9.5g; Fat 10.4g, of which saturates 4.3g; Cholesterol 19mg; Calcium 250mg; Fibre 3.9g; Sodium 724mg.
Nut Roast Energy 386kcal/1604kJ; Protein 11.7g; Carbohydrate 23.1g, of which sugars 5.4g; Fat 28.1g, of which saturates 6.4g; Cholesterol 44mg; Calcium 205mg; Fibre 3.2g; Sodium 281mg.

Mushroom, Nut and Prune Jalousie

The pie has a rich, nutty filling and, served with crisp roast potatoes and steamed vegetables, makes a great alternative to a festive roast.

Serves 6
75g/3oz/⅓ cup green lentils, rinsed
5ml/1 tsp vegetable
   bouillon powder
15ml/1 tbsp sunflower oil
2 large leeks, sliced
2 garlic cloves, chopped
200g/7oz/3 cups field (portabello)
   mushrooms, finely chopped
10ml/2 tsp dried mixed herbs
75g/3oz/¾ cup chopped
   mixed nuts
15ml/1 tbsp pine nuts (optional)
75g/3oz/⅓ cup pitted prunes
25g/1oz/½ cup fresh breadcrumbs
2 eggs, beaten
2 sheets ready-rolled puff pastry,
   total weight about 425g/15oz
flour, for dusting
salt and ground black pepper

1 Put the lentils in a pan and cover with water. Bring to the boil, then reduce the heat and add the bouillon powder. Partly cover and simmer for 20 minutes until the lentils are tender. Set aside.

2 Heat the oil in a frying pan, and cook the leeks and garlic for 5 minutes or until softened. Add the mushrooms and herbs and cook for 5 minutes. Transfer the mixture to a bowl. Stir in the nuts, pine nuts, if using, prunes, breadcrumbs and lentils.

3 Preheat the oven to 220°C/425°F/Gas 7. Add two-thirds of the beaten egg to the mixture and season. Set aside to cool.

4 Meanwhile, unroll one of the pastry sheets. Cut off 2.5cm/1in from its width and length, then lay it on a dampened baking sheet. Unroll the second pastry sheet, dust with flour, then fold in half lengthways. Make a series of cuts across the fold, 1cm/½in apart, leaving a 2.5cm/1in border around the edge of the pastry.

5 Spoon the filling over the pastry base, leaving a 2.5cm/1in border. Dampen the edges with water. Open out the folded piece and carefully lay it over the top. Trim the edges, then press the edges of the pastry together to seal and crimp.

6 Brush the top of the pastry with the remaining beaten egg and bake for 25–30 minutes until golden. Serve hot.

Spicy Potato Strudel

Wrap up a tasty mixture of vegetables in a spicy, creamy sauce with crisp filo pastry for a festive centrepiece. Serve with a good selection of chutneys or a yogurt sauce, or as a side dish with the Christmas Day meal.

Serves 4
1 onion, chopped
2 carrots, coarsely grated
1 courgette (zucchini), chopped
350g/12oz firm potatoes, diced
65g/2½ oz/5 tbsp butter
10ml/2 tsp mild curry paste
2.5ml/½ tsp dried thyme
150ml/¼ pint/⅔ cup water
1 egg, beaten
30ml/2 tbsp single (light) cream
50g/2oz/½ cup grated
   Cheddar cheese
8 sheets filo pastry, thawed
   if frozen
sesame seeds, for sprinkling
salt and ground black pepper

1 In a large frying pan, cook the onion, carrots, courgette and potatoes in 25g/1oz/2 tbsp of the butter for 5 minutes, tossing frequently so they cook evenly. Add the curry paste and stir in. Continue to cook the vegetables for a further minute or so.

2 Add the thyme and water to the pan, and season with salt and pepper. Bring to the boil, then reduce the heat and simmer for 10 minutes, until tender, stirring occasionally.

3 Remove from the heat and leave to cool. Transfer the mixture into a large bowl and then mix in the egg, cream and cheese. Chill until ready to fill the filo pastry.

4 Melt the remaining butter in a pan and lay out four sheets of filo pastry on a chopping board, slightly overlapping them to form a fairly large rectangle. Brush with some melted butter and fit the other sheets on top. Brush again.

5 Preheat the oven to 190°C/375°F/Gas 5. Spoon the filling along one long side, then roll up the pastry. Form it into a circle and set on a baking sheet. Brush again with the last of the butter and sprinkle over the sesame seeds.

6 Bake the strudel in the oven for about 25 minutes until golden and crisp. Stand for 5 minutes before cutting.

Potato Strudel Energy 362kcal/1512kJ; Protein 9.8g; Carbohydrate 34.8g, of which sugars 6.5g; Fat 21.1g, of which saturates 12.7g; Cholesterol 98mg; Calcium 169mg; Fibre 3g; Sodium 227mg.
Mushroom Jalousie Energy 480kcal/2004kJ; Protein 13.5g; Carbohydrate 42.3g, of which sugars 7.3g; Fat 30.5g, of which saturates 1.6g; Cholesterol 63mg; Calcium 99mg; Fibre 4.2g; Sodium 281mg.

Filo Vegetable Pie

This stunning pie makes a delicious main course for vegetarians, or serve as part of a festive party buffet with left-over turkey or ham.

Serves 6–8
225g/8oz leeks
165g/5½oz/11 tbsp butter
225g/8oz carrots, cubed
225g/8oz/3 cups sliced mushrooms
225g/8oz Brussels sprouts, cut
   into quarters

2 garlic cloves, crushed
115g/4oz/½ cup cream cheese
115g/4oz/½ cup Roquefort or
   Stilton cheese
150ml/¼ pint/⅔ cup double
   (heavy) cream
2 eggs, beaten
225g/8oz cooking apples
225g/8oz/1 cup cashew nuts or
   pine nuts, toasted
350g/12oz frozen filo
   pastry, defrosted
salt and ground black pepper

1 Preheat the oven to 180°C/350°F/Gas 4. Cut the leeks in half through the root and wash them, separating the layers slightly to check they are clean. Slice into 1cm/½in pieces, drain and dry.

2 Heat 40g/1½oz/3 tbsp of the butter in a large pan and cook the leeks and carrots, covered, over medium heat for 5 minutes. Add the mushrooms, sprouts and garlic and cook for another 2 minutes. Turn the vegetables into a bowl and let them cool.

3 Whisk the cream cheese and blue cheese, cream, eggs and seasoning together in a bowl. Pour them over the vegetables. Peel and core the apples and cut into 1cm/½in cubes. Stir them into the vegetables. Lastly, add the toasted cashew or pine nuts.

4 Melt the remaining butter. Brush all over the inside of a 23cm/9in loose-based springform cake tin (pan) with melted butter. Brush two-thirds of the filo pastry sheets with butter, one sheet at a time, and use them to line the base and sides of the tin, overlapping the layers so that there are no gaps.

5 Spoon in the filling and fold over the excess pastry to cover. Brush the remaining sheets with butter and cut into 2.5cm/1in strips. Cover the top of the pie with the strips, in a rough mound. Bake for 40 minutes until golden brown. Leave to stand for 5 minutes, and then gently remove the tin and serve.

Cheese and Spinach Flan

This flan freezes well and can be reheated. It makes an excellent addition to a festive buffet party.

Serves 8
115g/4oz/½ cup butter
225g/8oz/2 cups plain
   (all-purpose) flour
2.5ml/½ tsp English (hot)
   mustard powder
2.5ml/½ tsp paprika
large pinch of salt
115g/4oz/1 cup grated
   Cheddar cheese

45–60ml/3–4 tbsp cold water
1 egg, beaten, to glaze

For the filling
450g/1lb frozen spinach
1 onion, chopped
pinch of grated nutmeg
225g/8oz/1 cup cottage cheese
2 large (US extra large)
   eggs, beaten
50g/2oz/½ cup Parmesan
   cheese, grated
150ml/¼ pint/⅔ cup single
   (light) cream
salt and ground black pepper

1 Using your fingertips, rub the butter into the flour until it resembles fine breadcrumbs. Mix in the next four ingredients. Alternatively, process in a food processor. Bind to a dough with the cold water. Knead until smooth and pliable, wrap in clear film (plastic wrap) and chill for about 30 minutes.

2 Put the spinach and onion in a pan, cover, and cook slowly. Increase the heat to drive off any water. Season with salt, pepper and nutmeg. Turn the spinach into a bowl, and leave to cool slightly. Add the remaining filling ingredients.

3 Preheat the oven to 200°C/400°F/Gas 6. Put a baking tray in the oven to preheat. Cut one-third off the pastry for the lid. Roll out the remaining pastry and line a 23cm/9in loose-based flan tin (pan). Press the pastry into the edges and make a lip around the top edge. Remove any excess pastry. Carefully pour the filling into the flan case.

4 Roll out the remaining pastry, cut it with a lattice pastry cutter and open it out. Using a rolling pin, lay it over the flan. Brush the joins with egg glaze. Press the edges together and trim off any excess. Brush the lattice with egg glaze and bake for 40 minutes, until golden brown. Serve hot or cold.

Filo Pie Energy 748kcal/3102kJ; Protein 16.1g; Carbohydrate 34.8g, of which sugars 7.4g; Fat 62.4g, of which saturates 26.5g; Cholesterol 178mg; Calcium 160mg; Fibre 4.7g; Sodium 379mg.
Cheese Flan Energy 401kcal/1674kJ; Protein 17.5g; Carbohydrate 24.1g, of which sugars 2.4g; Fat 26.4g, of which saturates 15.6g; Cholesterol 147mg; Calcium 374mg; Fibre 2.2g; Sodium 389mg.

Chestnut and Mushroom Loaf

You can prepare this festive dish ahead, freezing it unbaked. Thaw overnight before baking.

Serves 8
45ml/3 tbsp olive oil, plus extra for brushing
2 medium onions, chopped
2 cloves garlic, chopped
75g/3oz/1¼ cups chopped button (white) mushrooms
100ml/4fl oz/½ cup red wine
225g/8oz can unsweetened chestnut purée
50g/2oz/1 cup fresh wholemeal (whole-wheat) breadcrumbs
75g/3oz/¾ cup fresh cranberries, plus extra to decorate
450g/1lb pastry
flour, for dusting
1 small egg, beaten, to glaze
salt and ground black pepper

1 Preheat the oven to 190°C/375°F/Gas 5. Heat the oil in a pan and fry the onions over medium heat until translucent. Add the garlic and mushrooms and fry for 3 minutes. Pour in the wine, stir well and simmer until it has evaporated, stirring occasionally. Remove from the heat, stir in the chestnut purée and breadcrumbs and season with salt and pepper. Set aside.

2 Simmer the cranberries in a little water for 5 minutes until they start to pop, then drain and leave to cool. Lightly brush a 600ml/1 pint/2½ cup loaf tin (pan) with oil.

3 On a lightly floured surface, roll out the pastry to a thickness of 3mm/⅛in. Cut rectangles to fit the base and sides of the tin and press them in place. Press the edges together to seal them. Cut a piece of pastry to fit the top of the tin and set it aside.

4 Spoon half the chestnut mixture into the tin and level the surface. Sprinkle on a layer of the cranberries and cover with the remaining chestnut mixture. Cover with the pastry lid and pinch the edges to the sides. Cut festive shapes from the pastry trimmings to use as decorations.

5 Brush the pastry top and the decorative shapes with the beaten egg glaze and arrange the shapes in a pattern on top. Bake in the oven for 35 minutes, or until golden brown. Decorate the top with fresh cranberries. Serve hot.

Pumpkin Gnocchi

A chanterelle sauce provides both richness and flavour to this tasty, wintery dish.

Serves 4
50g/1lb floury potatoes, peeled
450g/1lb peeled pumpkin, chopped
2 egg yolks
200g/7oz/1¾ cups plain (all-purpose) flour
pinch of ground allspice
1.5ml/¼ tsp ground cinnamon
pinch of grated nutmeg
finely grated rind of ½ orange
salt and ground black pepper

For the sauce
30ml/2 tbsp olive oil
1 shallot
175g/6oz chanterelles, sliced
10ml/2 tsp almond butter
150ml/¼ pint/⅔ cup crème fraîche
a little milk or water
75ml/5 tbsp chopped fresh parsley
50g/2oz/½ cup grated Parmesan cheese

1 Cover the potatoes with cold salted water, bring to the boil and cook for 20 minutes. Drain and set aside. Wrap the pumpkin in foil and bake at 180°C/350°F/Gas 4 for 30 minutes. Drain well, then add to the potato and process briefly in a food processor or blender. Transfer to a bowl, add the egg yolks, flour, spices, rind and seasoning and mix well to make a soft dough.

2 Bring a large pan of salted water to the boil, then dredge a work surface with flour. Spoon the gnocchi mixture into a piping (pastry) bag fitted with a 1cm/½in nozzle. Pipe on to the floured surface to make a 15cm/6in sausage shape. Roll in flour and cut into 2.5cm/1in pieces. Repeat the process, making more sausage shapes, until the dough is used up. Mark each gnocchi lightly with a fork and cook for 3–4 minutes in the boiling water.

3 Meanwhile, make the sauce. Heat the oil in a non-stick frying pan. Add the shallot and fry until soft without colouring. Add the chanterelles and cook briefly, then add the almond butter. Stir to melt, and stir in the crème fraîche. Simmer briefly and adjust the consistency with milk or water. Add the parsley and season to taste with salt and pepper.

4 Lift the gnocchi out of the water with a slotted spoon, turn into warmed bowls and spoon the sauce over the top. Sprinkle with the grated Parmesan cheese and serve immediately.

Chestnut Loaf Energy 428kcal/1785kJ; Protein 5.3g; Carbohydrate 46.3g, of which sugars 6.3g; Fat 25g, of which saturates 7g; Cholesterol 21mg; Calcium 83mg; Fibre 3.3g; Sodium 285mg.
Pumpkin Gnocchi Energy 576kcal/2411kJ; Protein 16g; Carbohydrate 62.1g, of which sugars 6.2g; Fat 31g, of which saturates 16g; Cholesterol 161mg; Calcium 325mg; Fibre 5.1g; Sodium 185mg.

Spicy Chickpea Curry

This is a popular spicy dish. It makes the most of the wonderful combination of vegetables, tomatoes and exotic spices.

Serves 4

3 large aubergines (eggplants), cut into cubes
200g/7oz/1 cup chickpeas, soaked for 8 hours or overnight
60ml/4 tbsp olive oil
3 garlic cloves, chopped
2 large onions, chopped
2.5ml/½ tsp ground cumin
2.5ml/½ tsp ground cinnamon
2.5ml/½ tsp ground coriander
3 × 400g/14oz cans chopped tomatoes
200g/7oz fresh tomatoes, chopped
salt and ground black pepper
cooked rice, to serve

For the garnish
30ml/2 tbsp olive oil
1 onion, sliced
1 garlic clove, sliced
fresh coriander (cilantro) sprigs

1 Place the aubergines in a colander and sprinkle with salt. Leave for 30 minutes, to allow any bitter juices to escape. Rinse with cold water and dry on kitchen paper. Drain the chickpeas and put in a pan with enough water to cover. Bring to the boil and simmer for about 1 hour, or until tender. Drain.

2 Heat the oil in a large pan. Add the garlic and onions and cook gently, until soft. Add the spices and cook, stirring, for a few seconds. Stir in the aubergines and stir to coat with the spices and onions. Cook for 5 minutes. Add the tomatoes and chickpeas and season. Cover and simmer for 20 minutes.

3 To make the garnish, heat the oil in a frying pan and, when very hot, add the sliced onion and garlic. Cook until golden and crisp. Serve the stew with rice, topped with the onion and garlic, and garnished with coriander.

Cook's Tip
If you are in a hurry during the festivities, substitute two cans of chickpeas for the dried variety. Rinse and drain before adding to the tomato mixture, and cook for about 15 minutes.

Baked Vegetable Lasagne

Vegetable lasagne is made extra special by using fresh pasta and tasty wild mushrooms, and is great for serving to friends for an informal Christmas meal.

Serves 8

30ml/2 tbsp olive oil
1 medium onion, finely chopped
500g/1¼lb tomatoes, chopped
75g/3oz/6 tbsp butter
675g/1½lb/8 cups wild mushrooms, sliced
2 garlic cloves, finely chopped
juice of ½ lemon
12–16 fresh lasagne sheets, precooked if necessary
175g/6oz/2 cups freshly grated Parmesan cheese
salt and ground black pepper

For the white sauce
50g/2oz/¼ cup butter
50g/2oz/½ cup plain (all-purpose) flour
900ml/1½ pints/3¾ cups hot milk

1 Preheat the oven to 200°C/400°F/Gas 6. Heat the oil in a pan and sauté the onion until translucent. Add the tomatoes and cook for 6–8 minutes, stirring often. Season and set aside.

2 Heat half the butter in a frying pan and cook the mushrooms until the juices run. Add the garlic, lemon juice and seasoning. Cook until the liquid has almost completely evaporated and the mushrooms are starting to brown. Set aside.

3 Make the white sauce. Melt the butter in a pan, add the flour and cook, stirring, for 1–2 minutes. Gradually add the hot milk, stirring until the sauce boils and thickens.

4 Spread a spoonful of the white sauce over the base of an ovenproof dish and cover it with 3–4 sheets of lasagne. Add a thin layer of mushrooms, then one of white sauce. Sprinkle with a little Parmesan. Make another layer of pasta, spread with a thin layer of the tomato mixture, then add a layer of white sauce. Sprinkle with cheese. Repeat the layers, ending with a layer of pasta coated with white sauce, saving some cheese.

5 Sprinkle with the remaining Parmesan cheese, dot with the remaining butter and bake in the oven for 20 minutes, until the cheese is bubbling and golden. Serve immediately.

Spicy Stew Energy 334kcal/1410kJ; Protein 16.9g; Carbohydrate 48.7g, of which sugars 21.1g; Fat 9.5g, of which saturates 1.2g; Cholesterol 0mg; Calcium 169mg; Fibre 12.9g; Sodium 144mg.
Vegetable Lasagne Energy 466kcal/1943kJ; Protein 19.2g; Carbohydrate 34.8g, of which sugars 9.8g; Fat 28.7g, of which saturates 13g; Cholesterol 50mg; Calcium 456mg; Fibre 2.6g; Sodium 787mg.

Stuffed Pasta Shells

This tasty baked gratin makes a perfect light lunch or supper. Serve with a green or mixed salad on the side.

Serves 4
20 large pasta shells for stuffing
25g/1oz/2 tbsp butter
1 small onion, finely chopped
275g/10oz fresh spinach leaves, trimmed, washed and shredded
1 garlic clove, crushed
1 sachet of saffron powder
nutmeg
250g/9oz ricotta cheese
1 egg
600ml/1 pint/2½ cups passata (bottled strained tomatoes)
about 150ml/¼ pint/⅔ cup dry white wine or vegetable stock
100ml/3½fl oz/scant ½ cup double (heavy) cream
50g/2oz/⅔ cup freshly grated Parmesan cheese
salt and ground black pepper

1 Preheat the oven to 190°C/375°F/Gas 5. Bring a pan of salted water to the boil. Cook the pasta for 10 minutes. Drain the shells, half fill the pan with cold water and add the shells.

2 Melt the butter in a pan, add the onion and cook gently, stirring, for 5 minutes until softened. Add the spinach, garlic and saffron, then grate in plenty of nutmeg and season to taste. Stir well, increase the heat to medium and cook for 5–8 minutes, stirring frequently, until the spinach is wilted and tender.

3 Increase the heat and stir until the water evaporates. Place the spinach in a bowl, add the ricotta and beat well to mix. Taste for seasoning, then add the egg and beat well again.

4 Pour the passata into a measuring jug and make it up to 750ml/1¼ pints/3 cups with wine, stock or water. Add the double cream, stir well to mix and taste for seasoning.

5 Spread about half the sauce over the bottom of four individual gratin dishes. Drain the pasta shells and fill with the spinach and ricotta mixture using a teaspoon. Arrange five shells in the centre of each dish, spoon the remaining sauce over them, then cover with the grated Parmesan. Bake for 10–12 minutes or until heated through. Leave to stand for about 5 minutes before serving.

Cheesy Baked Eggs and Leeks

This delicious dish of potatoes, leeks, eggs and cheese sauce is a traditional favourite. A nice variation is to add a little freshly grated nutmeg to the cheese sauce.

Serves 4
500g/1lb 2oz potatoes, peeled
3 leeks, sliced
6 eggs
600ml/1 pint/2½ cups milk
50g/2oz/3 tbsp butter, cut into small pieces
50g/2oz/½ cup plain (all-purpose) flour
100g/3½oz/1 cup Caerphilly cheese, grated
salt and ground black pepper

1 Cook the potatoes in boiling, lightly salted water for about 15 minutes or until soft. Meanwhile, cook the leeks in a little water for about 10 minutes until soft. Boil the eggs for 10 minutes, drain and put under cold running water to cool them.

2 Preheat the oven to 200°C/400°F/Gas 6. Drain the potatoes thoroughly and mash them with a potato masher. Drain the leeks and stir into the potatoes with plenty of black pepper to taste. Remove the shells from the hard-boiled eggs and cut each in half or into quarters lengthways.

3 Pour the milk into a pan and add the butter and flour. Stirring constantly, bring slowly to the boil and bubble gently for 2 minutes, until thickened and smooth. Remove from the heat, stir in half the cheese and season to taste.

4 Arrange the eggs in four shallow ovenproof dishes (or use one large one). Spoon the potato and leek mixture around the edge of the dishes. Pour the cheese sauce over and top with the remaining cheese. Place into the hot oven and cook for about 15–20 minutes, until bubbling and golden brown.

Cook's Tip
To save time, the leeks could just as easily be cooked in the microwave in a covered dish: there is no need to add water. Stir once or twice during cooking.

Stuffed Pasta Shells Energy 358kcal/1505kJ; Protein 11.6g; Carbohydrate 43.3g, of which sugars 7.7g; Fat 16.7g, of which saturates 5.6g; Cholesterol 20mg; Calcium 56mg; Fibre 2.9g; Sodium 542mg.
Baked Eggs Energy 540kcal/2259kJ; Protein 26.6g; Carbohydrate 41.3g, of which sugars 12.3g; Fat 30.6g, of which saturates 16.2g; Cholesterol 345mg; Calcium 471mg; Fibre 5g; Sodium 443mg.

Savoury Potato Cakes

Make these crisp cakes of grated potato any size.

Serves 4
50g/1lb potatoes, grated, rinsed, drained and dried
1 small onion, grated
3 rashers (slices) streaky (fatty) bacon, finely chopped
30ml/2 tbsp self-raising (self-rising) flour
2 eggs, beaten
vegetable oil, for frying
salt and ground black pepper

1 Mix the potatoes with the onion, bacon, flour, eggs and seasoning. Heat 1cm/½in oil in a frying pan, add about 15ml/1 tbsp of the mixture and spread it with the back of the spoon.

2 Add a few more spoonfuls, leaving space between them, and cook for 4–5 minutes, until golden underneath. Turn the cakes over and cook for 3–4 minutes until golden brown and cooked through. Keep warm while you cook the remaining mixture.

Sweet and Sour Red Cabbage

Serve with goose, pork or strong-flavoured game dishes.

Serves 8
900g/2lb red cabbage
30ml/2 tbsp olive oil
2 large onions, sliced
2 large cooking apples, peeled, cored and sliced
30ml/2 tbsp cider vinegar
30ml/2 tbsp soft light brown sugar
225g/8oz rindless streaky (fatty) bacon, chopped (optional)
salt and ground black pepper

1 Preheat the oven to 180°C/350°F/Gas 4. Cut the cabbage into quarters and shred it finely with a sharp knife. Heat the oil in a large flameproof casserole. Cook the onion over a gentle heat for 2 minutes.

2 Stir the cabbage, apples, vinegar, sugar and seasoning into the casserole. Cover and cook in the oven for 1 hour, until tender. Stir halfway through cooking. Fry the bacon, if using, until crisp. Stir it into the cabbage before serving.

Parsnip and Chestnut Croquettes

This is a tasty way to serve Christmas vegetables.

Serves 10–12
450g/1lb parsnips, cut roughly into small pieces
115g/4oz frozen chestnuts
25g/1oz/2 tbsp butter
1 garlic clove, crushed
15ml/1 tbsp chopped fresh coriander (cilantro)
1 egg, beaten
40–50g/1½–2oz/½ cup fresh white breadcrumbs
vegetable oil, for frying
salt and ground black pepper
sprig of coriander (cilantro), to garnish

1 Cook the parsnips in simmering water for about 15–20 minutes, until tender. Drain. Cook the chestnuts in the same way for 8–10 minutes, until tender. Drain, then mash roughly.

2 Cook the garlic in the butter for 30 seconds. Mash the parsnips with the garlic butter. Add the chestnuts, coriander and seasoning.

3 Form into croquettes, 7.5cm/3in long. Dip into the beaten egg, then roll in breadcrumbs. Fry for 3–4 minutes until golden. Drain and serve, garnished with coriander.

Thyme-roasted Onions

These slow-roasted onions are ideal served with festive roast meats.

Serves 4
75ml/5 tbsp olive oil
50g/2oz/4 tbsp unsalted butter
900g/2lb small onions, skinned
30ml/2 tbsp chopped fresh thyme
salt and ground black pepper

1 Preheat the oven to 220°C/425°F/ Gas 7. Heat the oil and butter in a roasting pan. Add the onions and toss them over medium heat until they are very lightly sautéed.

2 Add the thyme and seasoning to the pan and roast for about 45 minutes, basting regularly.

Savoury Potato Cakes Energy 186kcal/776kJ; Protein 6g; Carbohydrate 12.3g, of which sugars 1.2g; Fat 12.6g, of which saturates 4.2g; Cholesterol 38mg; Calcium 126mg; Fibre 1g; Sodium 246mg.
Sweet and Sour Cabbage Energy 148kcal/620kJ; Protein 2.2g; Carbohydrate 23.8g, of which sugars 22.2g; Fat 4g, of which saturates 0.4g; Cholesterol 0mg; Calcium 60mg; Fibre 2.9g; Sodium 19mg.
Parsnip Croquettes Energy 107kcal/445kJ; Protein 1.8g; Carbohydrate 10.8g, of which sugars 2.9g; Fat 6.6g, of which saturates 1.8g; Cholesterol 21mg; Calcium 27mg; Fibre 2.2g; Sodium 52mg.
Thyme-roasted Onions Energy 297kcal/1225kJ; Protein 2.8g; Carbohydrate 17.8g, of which sugars 12.6g; Fat 24.4g, of which saturates 8.7g; Cholesterol 29mg; Calcium 58mg; Fibre 3.2g; Sodium 101mg.

Roast Potatoes

For crisp roasties with fluffy interiors, cook them in a single layer. Cooking potatoes in goose fat may seem decadent, but the results will be well worth the expense.

Serves 4
1.3kg/3lb floury potatoes
90ml/6 tbsp oil, lard, white cooking fat or goose fat
salt

1 Preheat the oven to 200°C/400°F/Gas 6. Peel the potatoes and cut into chunks. Boil in salted water for 5 minutes, drain, return to the pan, and shake them to roughen the surfaces.

2 Put the fat into a large roasting pan and put into the hot oven to heat the fat. Add the potatoes, coating them in the fat. Return to the oven and roast for 40–50 minutes, turning once or twice, until crisp, golden and cooked through.

Creamy Potato and Cabbage

This accompaniment will enhance any meat dish.

Serves 4
450g/1lb potatoes, peeled and chopped
50g/2oz/¼ cup butter
50ml/2fl oz/¼ cup milk
450g/1lb cabbage, washed and finely shredded
30ml/2 tbsp olive oil
50ml/2fl oz/¼ cup double (heavy) cream
salt and ground black pepper

1 Place the potatoes in boiling water and boil for 15–20 minutes. Drain, replace on the heat for a few minutes, then mash. Heat the butter and milk in a small pan and then mix into the mashed potatoes. Season to taste.

2 Heat the olive oil in a large frying pan, add the shredded cabbage and fry for a few minutes. Season to taste with salt and ground black pepper. Add the mashed potato, mix well, then stir in the cream. Serve immediately.

Hasselback Potatoes

This dish is named after the Stockholm restaurant that created it, and is a method of cooking rather than a recipe. Choose similar-sized potatoes so that they cook uniformly, and the essential thing is to cut the potatoes most of the way, but not completely, through. It is a good idea to thread a skewer through the potato three-quarters of the way down before cutting, so that your knife travels just to the point you want it to reach and no farther.

Serves 4
4 large potatoes
75g/3oz/6 tbsp butter
45ml/3 tbsp olive oil
50g/2oz/1 cup fine fresh breadcrumbs
50g/2oz/⅔ cup grated Parmesan cheese
salt and ground black pepper

1 Preheat the oven to 200°C/400°F/Gas 6. Peel the potatoes, then – and this is the crucial part – cut them widthways, not lengthways, down to three-quarters of their depth at 3mm/⅛in intervals, preferably at a slight angle.

2 Wash the potatoes in cold water, then arrange, cut sides uppermost, in a deep, ovenproof dish.

3 Melt the butter in a small pan, then add the olive oil and mix together. Brush the mixture over the potatoes, then season well with salt and black pepper. Sprinkle over the breadcrumbs and the grated cheese.

4 Roast the potatoes in the preheated oven for about 1 hour, depending on their size, until golden brown and fanned apart along the cut lines. Serve hot.

> **Cook's Tip**
> If the potatoes are to be served as an accompaniment to a roast joint of meat, you can use the cooking juices from the meat to baste them during cooking. Don't move them around while they roast, because they won't crisp up properly.

Roast Potatoes Energy 163kcal/681kJ; Protein 3.4g; Carbohydrate 26.4g, of which sugars 5g; Fat 5.5g, of which saturates 3.3g; Cholesterol 13mg; Calcium 26mg; Fibre 2.6g; Sodium 49mg.
Creamy Potato Energy 183kcal/766kJ; Protein 3.9g; Carbohydrate 24g, of which sugars 7.3g; Fat 8.5g, of which saturates 2.4g; Cholesterol 7mg; Calcium 73mg; Fibre 3.5g; Sodium 24mg.
Hasselback Potatoes Energy 380kcal/1593kJ; Protein 9.9g; Carbohydrate 42g, of which sugars 3.1g; Fat 20.4g, of which saturates 12.5g; Cholesterol 52mg; Calcium 182mg; Fibre 2.3g; Sodium 367mg.

Stir-fried Brussels Sprouts

This recipe makes the most of the sprouts' flavour and has an Asian twist.

Serves 4
450g/1lb Brussels sprouts
15ml/1 tbsp sunflower oil
6–8 spring onions (scallions), cut into 2.5cm/1in lengths
2 slices fresh root ginger
40g/1½oz/⅓ cup slivered almonds
150–175ml/4–6fl oz/⅔–¾ cup vegetable or chicken stock

1 Remove any large outer leaves and trim the bases of the Brussels sprouts. Cut into slices about 1cm/½in thick.

2 Heat the oil in a wok or heavy frying pan, and fry the spring onions and ginger for 2–3 minutes, stirring often. Add the almonds and stir-fry until the onions and almonds brown.

3 Discard the ginger, reduce the heat and stir in the sprouts. Stir-fry for a few minutes and then add the stock and gently cook for 5–6 minutes, or until the sprouts are nearly tender. Increase the heat to boil off the excess liquid. Spoon the sprouts into a warmed serving dish and serve.

Festive Brussels Sprouts

Peeling chestnuts can be fiddly but is worth the effort.

Serves 8
450g/1lb fresh chestnuts
450ml/¾ pint/1⅞ cups stock
450g/1lb Brussels sprouts, trimmed
450g/1lb carrots, sliced
25g/1oz/2 tbsp butter
salt and ground black pepper

1 Drop the chestnuts into boiling water for a few minutes, and remove with a slotted spoon. The skins should slip off easily. Put them in a pan with the stock. Simmer for 10 minutes, then drain. Boil the sprouts in salted water for 5 minutes. Drain.

2 Cook the carrots for 6 minutes. Drain. Melt the butter in a pan, add the chestnuts, sprouts and carrots and season. Serve.

Creamed Leeks

This dish is a real festive favourite, delicious with the full roast meal, or even on its own. It is very important to have good firm leeks without a core in the middle. Christmas is one time of year when leeks are at their best.

Serves 4
2 leeks, tops trimmed and roots removed
50g/2oz/¼ cup butter
200ml/7fl oz/scant 1 cup double (heavy) cream
salt and ground black pepper

1 Split the leeks down the middle, then cut across so you make pieces approximately 2cm/¾in square. Wash thoroughly and drain in a colander.

2 Melt the butter in a large pan and when quite hot throw in the leeks, stirring to coat them in the butter, and heat through. They will wilt but should not exude water. Keep the heat high but don't allow them to colour. You need to create a balance between keeping the temperature high so the water steams out of the vegetable, keeping it bright green, while taking care not to burn or brown the leeks too much.

3 Keeping the heat high, pour in the cream, mix in thoroughly and allow to bubble and reduce. Season with salt and ground black pepper. When the texture is smooth, thick and creamy the leeks are ready to serve.

> **Cook's Tip**
> *When buying leeks, choose smaller and less bendy ones as they are more tender than the larger specimens.*

> **Variation**
> *Although these leeks have a wonderful taste themselves, you may like to add extra flavourings, such as a little chopped garlic or some chopped fresh tarragon or thyme.*

Stir-fried Sprouts Energy 341kcal/1426kJ; Protein 11.1g; Carbohydrate 34.7g, of which sugars 10.2g; Fat 18.5g, of which saturates 8.8g; Cholesterol 40mg; Calcium 78mg; Fibre 9.3g; Sodium 485mg.
Festive Sprouts Energy 341kcal/1426kJ; Protein 11.1g; Carbohydrate 34.7g, of which sugars 10.2g; Fat 18.5g, of which saturates 8.8g; Cholesterol 40mg; Calcium 78mg; Fibre 9.3g; Sodium 485mg.
Creamed Leeks Energy 363kcal/1496kJ; Protein 2.5g; Carbohydrate 3.8g, of which sugars 3.1g; Fat 37.6g, of which saturates 23.3g; Cholesterol 95mg; Calcium 51mg; Fibre 2.2g; Sodium 89mg.

Roast Parsnips with Honey and Nutmeg

Parsnips are at their best in winter, so they are always popular at Christmas. They are delicious when roasted around a festive joint of beef or a roast turkey. Their sweetness mingles well with the spice and honey.

Serves 4–6

4 medium parsnips
30ml/2 tbsp plain (all-purpose) flour seasoned with salt and pepper
60ml/4 tbsp vegetable oil
15–30ml/1–2 tbsp clear honey
freshly grated nutmeg

1 Preheat the oven to 200°C/400°F/Gas 6. Peel the parsnips and cut each one lengthways into rough quarters, removing and discarding any tough woody cores.

2 Place the parsnips into a pan of boiling water and cook for 5 minutes until slightly softened.

3 Drain the parsnips thoroughly, then toss in the seasoned flour, shaking off any excess.

4 Pour the oil into a roasting pan and put into the oven until hot. Add the parsnips, tossing them in the oil and arranging them in a single layer.

5 Return the pan to the oven and cook the parsnips for about 30 minutes, turning occasionally, until crisp, golden brown and tender.

6 Drizzle with the honey and sprinkle with a little grated nutmeg. Return the parsnips to the oven for 5 minutes to warm through before serving.

Cook's Tip
The Romans considered parsnips to be a culinary luxury, at which time they were credited with a variety of medicinal and aphrodisiac qualities.

Celeriac Purée

Celeriac is a versatile vegetable that is good grated raw or cooked.

Serves 4

1 celeriac bulb, cut into chunks
1 lemon, halved
2 potatoes, cut into chunks
300ml/½ pint/1¼ cups double (heavy) cream
salt and ground black pepper
chopped fresh chives, to garnish

1 Place the celeriac in a pan. Add the lemon halves. Add the potatoes to the pan and just cover with cold water. Cover the pan, boil, then simmer until tender, about 20 minutes.

2 Remove the lemon and drain the vegetables. Return to the pan and steam dry for a few minutes over low heat.

3 Purée in a food processor. Bring the cream to the boil. Add the celeriac mixture and mix. Season, top with chives and serve.

Parsnip Chips

These chips are particularly good served with game meats at Christmas time.

Serves 4

vegetable oil, for deep-frying
2 large parsnips, peeled
30ml/2 tbsp plain (all-purpose) flour
salt
good pinch of mild curry powder (optional)

1 Heat the oil to about 180°C/350°F. Season the flour with salt and curry powder, if using.

2 Using a potato peeler, cut lengthways strips from the parsnips. Put them into a pan, cover with water and bring to the boil. Drain and dry, then toss the strips in the flour.

3 Fry the strips, in batches, in the oil until crisp and golden outside and soft inside. Drain on kitchen paper. Sprinkle with a little salt and curry powder (if using) to serve.

Roast Parsnips Energy 144kcal/600kJ; Protein 2g; Carbohydrate 16.2g, of which sugars 6.7g; Fat 8.3g, of which saturates 1g; Cholesterol 0mg; Calcium 41mg; Fibre 4g; Sodium 9mg.
Celeriac Purée Energy 403kcal/1661kJ; Protein 2.2g; Carbohydrate 7.9g, of which sugars 2.3g; Fat 40.5g, of which saturates 25.1g; Cholesterol 103mg; Calcium 65mg; Fibre 1.1g; Sodium 58mg.
Parsnip Chips Energy 230kcal/956kJ; Protein 2.3g; Carbohydrate 16.8g, of which sugars 5.1g; Fat 17.6g, of which saturates 2.1g; Cholesterol 0mg; Calcium 47mg; Fibre 4.3g; Sodium 9mg.

Young Vegetables with Tarragon

The vegetables here are just lightly cooked to bring out their flavours. It is a great addition to the festive feast.

Serves 4
5 spring onions (scallions)
50g/2oz/¼ cup butter
1 garlic clove, crushed
115g/4oz asparagus tips
115g/4oz mangetouts (snowpeas), trimmed
115g/4oz broad (fava) beans
2 Little Gem (Bibb) lettuces
5ml/1 tsp chopped fresh tarragon
salt and ground black pepper

1 Cut the spring onions into quarters lengthways and fry gently over medium-low heat in half the butter with the garlic.

2 Add the asparagus tips, mangetouts and broad beans. Mix in, covering all the pieces with oil. Just cover the base of the pan with water, season, and allow to simmer for a few minutes.

3 Cut the lettuces into quarters and add to the pan. Cook for 3 minutes then, off the heat, swirl in the remaining butter and the tarragon, and serve immediately.

Crispy Cabbage

This quick side dish makes a crunchy base for slices of ham or left-over turkey. Savoy cabbage is especially pretty cooked this way.

Serves 4–6
1 medium green or small white cabbage
30ml/2 tbsp vegetable oil
salt and ground black pepper

1 Remove any coarse outside leaves from the cabbage and also the central rib from the larger remaining leaves. Shred the leaves finely. Wash well under cold running water, shake well and blot on kitchen paper to dry.

2 Heat a wok or wide-based flameproof casserole over a fairly high heat. Heat the oil and add the cabbage. Stir-fry for about 2–3 minutes, or until it is just cooked but still crunchy. Season with salt and pepper and serve.

Cabbage with Bacon

Bacon, especially if smoked, makes all the difference to the flavour of the cabbage, turning it into a delicious vegetable accompaniment to serve with a festive turkey or even with roast beef or grilled chicken.

Serves 4
30ml/2 tbsp vegetable oil
1 onion, finely chopped
115g/4oz smoked bacon, finely chopped
500g/1¼lb cabbage (red, white or Savoy)
salt and ground black pepper

1 Heat the oil in a large pan over medium heat, add the chopped onion and the smoked bacon and cook for about 7 minutes, stirring occasionally.

2 Remove and discard any tough outer leaves from the cabbage and wash the leaves. Shred the leaves quite finely, discarding the core and any tough spines.

3 Add the cabbage to the pan and season with salt and ground black pepper. Stir for a few minutes until the cabbage begins to lose volume.

4 Continue to cook the cabbage, stirring frequently, for about 8–10 minutes until it is tender but still crisp. Serve immediately.

Cook's Tip
If you prefer softer cabbage, then cover the pan for part of the cooking time in step 4.

Variations
• This dish is equally delicious if you use spring greens (collards) instead of cabbage. You could also use curly kale, which is in season over the Christmas period.
• To make a more substantial dish to serve for lunch or supper, add more bacon, some chopped button (white) mushrooms and skinned, seeded and chopped tomatoes.

Vegetables with Tarragon Energy 149kcal/619kJ; Protein 4.7g; Carbohydrate 6.1g, of which sugars 3g; Fat 12g, of which saturates 7.3g; Cholesterol 29mg; Calcium 55mg; Fibre 3.5g; Sodium 89mg.
Crispy Cabbage Energy 54kcal/224kJ; Protein 1.9g; Carbohydrate 4.6g, of which sugars 4.5g; Fat 3.2g, of which saturates 0.5g; Cholesterol 0mg; Calcium 59mg; Fibre 2.7g; Sodium 6mg.
Cabbage with Bacon Energy 151kcal/623kJ; Protein 6.7g; Carbohydrate 7.4g, of which sugars 7g; Fat 10.5g, of which saturates 2.6g; Cholesterol 15mg; Calcium 67mg; Fibre 2.8g; Sodium 452mg.

Peas and Carrots with Bacon

Sweet and tender peas, accompanied by young carrots, pearl onions, lettuce and salty bacon or cured ham make a delicious side dish. It is especially good served with roast pork or beef for a traditional celebratory meal.

Serves 4–6
8 young carrots, thinly sliced
1.6kg/3½lb fresh peas in pods or 575g/1¼lb/5 cups frozen peas
40g/1½oz/3 tbsp butter
115g/4oz rindless smoked bacon, cut into fine strips
100g/3¾oz/⅔ cup baby or small pearl onions, peeled and left whole
100ml/3½fl oz/scant ½ cup chicken stock
1 small lettuce, cut in thin strips
pinch of sugar and grated nutmeg
salt and ground black pepper
chopped fresh parsley, to garnish, optional

1 Bring a pan of salted water to the boil. Add the carrots and cook for 3 minutes until just tender. Remove with a slotted spoon and set aside.

2 Pod the peas if they are fresh, and add them to the pan of boiling water. Cook for 2 minutes, then drain and add the peas to a bowl of iced water to stop them from cooking any further. Drain and set aside.

3 Melt 25g/1oz/2 tbsp of the butter in a large frying pan. Add the bacon and sauté for 3 minutes, then add the onions and sauté for 4 minutes.

4 When the onions are translucent, add the carrots and sauté for 3 minutes until they are glazed.

5 Pour in the stock, cover and cook for 10–15 minutes, or until all the liquid has been absorbed. Add the lettuce and cook for 3–5 minutes until the strips have wilted.

6 Add the peas, with the remaining butter. Simmer for 2–3 minutes until the peas are just tender. Add the sugar and nutmeg, season and stir to mix. Spoon into a warmed bowl, garnish with parsley, if using, and serve.

Kale with Mustard Dressing

This is a classic winter side dish – ideal for Christmas. Use curly kale if you can't get sea kale. You will need to boil it for a few minutes before chilling and serving.

Serves 4
250g/9oz sea kale or curly kale
45ml/3 tbsp light olive oil
5ml/1 tsp wholegrain mustard
15ml/1 tbsp white wine vinegar
pinch of caster (superfine) sugar
salt and ground black pepper

1 Wash the sea kale, drain thoroughly, then trim it and cut in two. Whisk the oil and mustard in a bowl. Whisk in the white wine vinegar. It should begin to thicken.

2 Season the mustard dressing to taste with sugar, salt and pepper. Toss the sea kale in the dressing and serve immediately.

Roast Beetroot with Horseradish

Beetroot is enhanced by horseradish and vinegar. Serve with a festive roast.

Serves 4–6
10–12 small whole
beetroot (beets)
30ml/2 tbsp vegetable oil
45ml/3 tbsp grated fresh horseradish
15ml/1 tbsp white wine vinegar
10ml/2 tsp caster (superfine) sugar
150ml/¼ pint/⅔ cup double

1 Preheat the oven to 180°C/350°F/Gas 4. Wash the beetroot without breaking their skins. Trim the stalks short but do not remove them completely. Toss the beetroot in the oil and season with salt. Spread them in a roasting pan and cover with foil and roast for 1½ hours. Leave to cool, covered, for 10 minutes.

2 Meanwhile, make the horseradish sauce. Mix the horseradish, vinegar and sugar in a bowl. Whip the cream and fold into the horseradish mixture. Cover and chill until required.

3 When the beetroot are cool enough to handle, slip off the skins and serve with the sauce.

Peas and Carrots Energy 141kcal/585kJ; Protein 9.8g; Carbohydrate 15.5g, of which sugars 7.4g; Fat 4.9g, of which saturates 1.5g; Cholesterol 10mg; Calcium 49mg; Fibre 5.8g; Sodium 311mg.
Kale with Mustard Dressing Energy 99kcal/409kJ; Protein 2.1g; Carbohydrate 1.9g, of which sugars 1.9g; Fat 9.3g, of which saturates 1.3g; Cholesterol 0mg; Calcium 82mg; Fibre 2g; Sodium 27mg.
Roast Beetroot Energy 254kcal/1052kJ; Protein 2.1g; Carbohydrate 10g, of which sugars 9.1g; Fat 22.2g, of which saturates 3.2g; Cholesterol 1mg; Calcium 26mg; Fibre 2.3g; Sodium 143mg.

Christmas Pudding

This can be made up to a month before Christmas and stored in a cool, dry place.

Serves 8

115g/4oz/1/2 cup butter
225g/8oz/1 cup soft dark
  brown sugar
50g/2oz/1/2 cup self-raising
  (self-rising) flour
5ml/1 tsp mixed (apple pie) spice
1.5ml/1/4 tsp grated nutmeg
2.5ml/1/2 tsp ground cinnamon
2 eggs
115g/4oz/2 cups fresh white
  breadcrumbs

175g/6oz/1 1/4 cups sultanas
  (golden raisins)
175g/6oz/1 1/4 cup raisins
115g/4oz/1/2 cup currants
25g/1oz/3 tbsp mixed (candied)
  peel, chopped finely
25g/1oz/1/4 cup chopped almonds
1 small cooking apple, peeled,
  cored and coarsely grated
finely grated rind of 1 orange
  or lemon
juice of 1 orange or lemon, made
  up to 150ml/1/4 pint/2/3 cup
  with brandy, rum or sherry

1 Cut a disc of baking parchment to fit the base of a 1.2-litre /2-pint/5-cup heatproof bowl and butter the disc and bowl.

2 Whisk the butter and sugar together in a mixing bowl until soft. Beat in the flour, spices and eggs. Add the rest of the ingredients and mix well. The mixture should have a soft dropping consistency.

3 Transfer to the greased bowl and level the top. Cover with another disc of buttered baking parchment.

4 Make a pleat across the centre of a large piece of baking parchment and cover the bowl with it, tying it in place with string under the rim. Cut off the excess paper.

5 Cover with pleated foil in the same way, tucking it around the bowl, and tie with string to form a handle.

6 Steam the pudding over simmering water for 6 hours. Leave to cool, then replace the foil and paper with clean pieces. Clean the bowl and replace the pudding. To reheat for serving, steam for about 2 hours.

Rum Butter

No Christmas Dinner would be complete without the traditional Christmas pudding to round it off. This rich and luscious rum butter is the perfect accompaniment.

Serves 8

225g/8oz/1 cup unsalted butter
  at room temperature
225g/8oz/1 cup soft light
  brown sugar
90ml/6 tbsp dark rum, or to taste

1 Beat the butter and sugar until the mixture is soft, creamy and pale in colour. Gradually add the rum, almost drop by drop, beating to incorporate each addition before adding more. If you are too hasty in adding the rum, the mixture may curdle.

2 When all the rum has been added, spoon the mixture into a covered container and chill for at least 1 hour. The butter will keep well in the refrigerator for about 4 weeks.

Brandy Butter

This alcohol-spiked butter is traditionally served with Christmas pudding and mince pies, but a good spoonful over a hot oven-baked apple is equally delicious.

Serves 6

115g/4oz/1/2 cup butter
115g/4oz/1/2 cup icing
  (confectioners'), caster
  (superfine) or soft light
  brown sugar
45ml/3 tbsp brandy

1 Cream the butter in a mixing bowl until very pale and soft. Beat in the sugar gradually.

2 Add the brandy to the sugared butter, a few drops at a time, beating constantly. Add enough for a good flavour but take care it does not curdle.

3 Pile the brandy butter into a small serving dish and set aside to harden. Alternatively, spread it out on to aluminium foil and chill in the refrigerator until firm. Cut the butter into festive shapes with small fancy cutters.

Christmas Pudding Energy 448kcal/1902kJ; Protein 2.4g; Carbohydrate 99.8g, of which sugars 92.5g; Fat 7.1g, of which saturates 3.6g; Cholesterol 20mg; Calcium 67mg; Fibre 0.9g; Sodium 123mg.
Rum Butter Energy 213kcal/888kJ; Protein 4.1g; Carbohydrate 9.6g, of which sugars 9.6g; Fat 7.2g, of which saturates 4.5g; Cholesterol 20mg; Calcium 146mg; Fibre 0g; Sodium 89mg.
Brandy Butter Energy 204kcal/851kJ; Protein 0.2g; Carbohydrate 17.4g, of which sugars 17.4g; Fat 13.6g, of which saturates 9g; Cholesterol 38mg; Calcium 11mg; Fibre 0g; Sodium 126mg.

Crème Anglaise

Here is the classic English custard; it is light and creamy without the harsh flavours or gaudy colouring of its poorer package relations. Serve hot or cold with your festive dessert.

Serves 4
1 vanilla pod (bean)
450ml/³⁄₄ pint/scant 2 cups milk
40g/1¹⁄₂oz/¹⁄₃ cup icing (confectioners') sugar
4 egg yolks

1 Put the vanilla pod in a pan with the milk. Bring slowly to the boil. Remove from the heat and steep for 10 minutes before removing the pod.

2 In a heatproof mixing bowl, beat together the sugar and egg yolks until the mixture is thick, light and creamy.

3 Slowly pour the warm milk on to the egg mixture in the mixing bowl, stirring constantly.

4 Place the bowl over a pan of hot water. Stir the mixture frequently over low heat for 10 minutes or until it has thickened and coats the back of the spoon.

5 Strain the custard into a jug (pitcher) if serving hot or, if serving cold, strain into a bowl and cover the surface with buttered baking parchment or clear film (plastic wrap).

Cook's Tip
Crème anglaise can curdle if left to simmer too long, so once the custard has thickened in step 4, ensure that the bowl is removed from the heat immediately.

Variation
If you prefer a fruit-flavoured crème anglaise, you can steep a few strips of thinly pared lemon or orange rind with the milk, instead of the vanilla pod (bean).

Apple Pudding

This delicious pudding is a real treat on a wintry night during the festive season. It is sure to be popular with the whole family.

Serves 4
4 crisp eating apples
a little lemon juice

300ml/¹⁄₂ pint/1¹⁄₄ cups milk
40g/1¹⁄₂oz/3 tbsp butter
40g/1¹⁄₂oz/¹⁄₃ cup plain (all-purpose) flour
25g/1oz/2 tbsp caster (superfine) sugar
2.5ml/¹⁄₂ tsp vanilla extract
2 eggs, separated

1 Preheat the oven to 200°C/400°F/Gas 6. Butter an ovenproof dish measuring 20–23cm/8–9in in diameter and 5cm/2in deep. Peel, core and slice the apples and put in the dish. Sprinkle with lemon juice and toss to coat.

2 Put the milk, butter and flour in a pan. Cook over medium heat, whisking constantly, until it thickens and comes to the boil.

3 Let it bubble for 1–2 minutes, stirring well to make sure it does not stick and burn on the bottom. Pour into a bowl, add the sugar and vanilla extract, and then stir in the egg yolks.

4 In a separate bowl, whisk the egg whites until stiff peaks form. With a large, metal spoon fold the egg whites into the custard. Pour the custard mixture over the apples in the dish.

5 Put into the hot oven and cook for about 40 minutes until puffed up, deep golden brown and firm to the touch.

6 Serve the pudding straight out of the oven, before the soufflé-like topping begins to fall.

Variation
Stewed fruit, such as cooking apples, plums, rhubarb or gooseberries sweetened with honey or sugar, would also make a good base for this pudding, as would fresh summer berries (blackberries, raspberries, redcurrants and blackcurrants).

Crème Anglaise Energy 152kcal/640kJ; Protein 6.7g; Carbohydrate 16.1g, of which sugars 16.1g; Fat 7.4g, of which saturates 2.7g; Cholesterol 208mg; Calcium 164mg; Fibre 0g; Sodium 72mg.
Apple Pudding Energy 240kcal/1006kJ; Protein 7g; Carbohydrate 26.8g, of which sugars 19.2g; Fat 12.5g, of which saturates 6.8g; Cholesterol 121mg; Calcium 127mg; Fibre 1.9g; Sodium 131mg.

Mince Pies with Orange Pastry

Home-made mince pies are so much nicer at Christmas time than those bought from a store, especially with this flavoursome pastry.

Makes 18
225g/8oz/2 cups plain (all-purpose) flour
40g/1½oz/⅓ cup icing (confectioners') sugar
10ml/2 tsp ground cinnamon
150g/5oz/generous 1 cup cold butter, diced
grated rind of 1 orange
about 60ml/4 tbsp iced water
225g/8oz/⅔ cup mincemeat
1 egg, beaten, to glaze
icing (confectioners') sugar, for dusting

1 Sift together the flour, icing sugar and cinnamon in a large mixing bowl. Rub in the butter with your fingertips until it resembles fine breadcrumbs. Stir in the grated orange rind.

2 Mix to a firm dough with the water. Knead lightly, then roll out on a lightly floured surface to a 5mm/¼in thickness. Using a 6cm/2½in round pastry (cookie) cutter, stamp out 18 circles, then stamp out 18 smaller 5cm/2in circles.

3 Line two bun trays with the larger circles. Place a small spoonful of mincemeat into each pastry case (pie shell) and top with the smaller pastry circles, pressing the edges to seal.

4 Brush the tops with egg glaze and leave in the refrigerator for 30 minutes. Preheat the oven to 200°C/400°F/Gas 6.

5 Bake for 15–20 minutes, or until golden brown. Remove to cool on wire racks. Serve just warm, dusted with icing sugar.

> **Cook's Tip**
> *This sweet and spicy pastry works for all kinds of sweet pies and tarts. This quantity will line a 23cm/9in flan tin (pan) as well as leaving enough for a lattice or cut-out pastry shapes to decorate the top. It is particularly suitable for autumn fruit pies made with apples, plums or pears.*

Bakewell Tart

This is a modern version of the Bakewell pudding, which is made with puff pastry and has a custard-like almond filling. It is said to be the result of a 19th-century kitchen accident and is still baked in the original shop in Bakewell, Derbyshire, UK. This popular, tart-like version is simpler to make and is sure to become a favourite dessert. It is easy and quick to make and would be a delicious pudding to eat during the festive season as a change from spicier, richer desserts.

Serve 4
For the pastry
115g/4oz/1 cup plain (all-purpose) flour
pinch of salt
50g/2oz/4 tbsp butter, diced

For the filling
30ml/2 tbsp raspberry or apricot jam
2 whole eggs and 2 extra yolks
115g/4oz/generous ½ cup caster (superfine) sugar
115g/4oz/½ cup butter, melted
55g/2oz/⅔ cup ground almonds
few drops of almond extract
icing (confectioners') sugar, to dust

1 Sift the flour and salt and rub in the butter until the mixture resembles fine breadcrumbs. Stir in about 20ml/2 tbsp cold water and gather into a smooth ball of dough. Wrap the dough in clear film and chill for 30 minutes. Preheat the oven to 200°C/400°F/Gas 6.

2 Roll out the pastry and use to line an 18cm/7in loose-based flan tin (pan). Spread the jam over the pastry.

3 Whisk the eggs, egg yolks and sugar together in a large bowl until the mixture is thick and pale.

4 Gently stir in the melted butter, ground almonds and the almond extract.

5 Pour the mixture over the jam in the pastry case (pie shell). Put the tart into the hot oven and cook for 30 minutes until just set and browned. Sift a little icing sugar over the top before serving warm.

Bakewell Tart Energy 700kcal/2919kJ; Protein 10.8g; Carbohydrate 57.1g, of which sugars 36.7g; Fat 49.9g, of which saturates 17.1g; Cholesterol 257mg; Calcium 110mg; Fibre 0.9g; Sodium 394mg.
Mince Pies with Orange Pastry Energy 145kcal/610kJ; Protein 1.3g; Carbohydrate 19.3g, of which sugars 9.7g; Fat 7.6g, of which saturates 4.4g; Cholesterol 18mg; Calcium 24mg; Fibre 0.6g; Sodium 53mg.

Christmas Stars

These pretty pastries are a delicious twist on the usual mince pies, although the prune filling is less sweet than mincemeat and does not include any alcohol.

Makes 9
200g/7oz/1¾ cups plain
  (all-purpose) flour

5ml/1 tsp baking powder
130g/4½oz/½ cup butter,
  softened
150ml/¼ pint/⅔ cup cold water,
  or enough to bind
200g/7oz/scant 1 cup
  ready-to-eat prunes
1 egg, beaten, to glaze

1 Preheat the oven to 200°C/400°F/Gas 6. Sift the flour and baking powder into a large bowl.

2 Cut the butter into small pieces, add to the flour and rub in until the mixture resembles fine breadcrumbs. Alternatively, put the flour and baking powder in a food processor, add the butter and, using a pulsating action, blend to form fine breadcrumbs. Gradually add cold water and mix until it forms a dough.

3 On a lightly floured surface, roll out the pastry to a square about 3mm/⅛in thick, then cut the square into a further nine equal squares. Make a diagonal cut from each corner of the squares towards the centre.

4 Chop the prunes into small pieces. Put a spoonful of the chopped prunes in the centre of each square of pastry, then lift each corner of the pastry and fold it over to the centre to form a rough star shape.

5 Place the stars on a baking sheet and brush with beaten egg. Bake in the preheated oven for about 15 minutes, or until golden brown. Serve warm.

> **Cook's Tip**
> A little brandy, mixed into the prunes, adds an extra delicious dimension to these tasty treats.

American Pumpkin Pie

This spicy sweet pie is traditionally served at Thanksgiving, or at Halloween, but it also makes a delicious dessert at Christmas time.

Serves 8
200g/7oz/1¾ cups plain
  (all-purpose) flour
2.5ml/½ tsp salt
90g/3½oz/7 tbsp
  unsalted butter
1 egg yolk

For the filling
900g/2lb piece of pumpkin
2 large (US extra large) eggs
75g/3oz/6 tbsp soft light
  brown sugar
60ml/4 tbsp golden
  (light corn) syrup
250ml/8fl oz/1 cup double
  (heavy) cream
15ml/1 tbsp mixed
  (pumpkin pie) spice
2.5ml/½ tsp salt
icing (confectioners') sugar,
  for dusting

1 Sift the flour and salt into a mixing bowl. Rub in the butter until the mixture resembles breadcrumbs, then mix in the egg yolk and enough iced water (about 15ml/1 tbsp) to make a dough. Roll the dough into a ball, wrap it up in clear film (plastic wrap) and chill it for at least 30 minutes.

2 Make the filling. Peel the pumpkin and remove the seeds. Cut the flesh into cubes. Place in a heavy pan, add water to cover and boil for 20 minutes or until tender. Mash until smooth, then leave in a sieve (strainer) set over a bowl to drain thoroughly.

3 Roll out the pastry on a lightly floured surface and line a 23–25cm/9–10in loose-bottomed flan tin (pan). Prick the base and line with baking parchment and baking beans. Chill for 15 minutes. Preheat the oven to 200°C/400°F/Gas 6.

4 Bake the pastry case (pie shell) for 10 minutes, remove the parchment and baking beans, return the pastry case to the oven and bake for 5 minutes more.

5 Lower the oven temperature to 190°C/375°F/Gas 5. Put the pumpkin in a bowl. Beat in the eggs, sugar, syrup, cream, mixed spice and salt. Pour into the pastry case. Bake for 40 minutes or until the filling is set. Dust with icing sugar and serve.

Christmas Stars Energy 140kcal/583kJ; Protein 1.3g; Carbohydrate 13g, of which sugars 6g; Fat 9.5g, of which saturates 5.9g; Cholesterol 24mg; Calcium 21mg; Fibre 1.3g; Sodium 70mg.
Pumpkin Pie Energy 416kcal/1736kJ; Protein 5.3g; Carbohydrate 38.2g, of which sugars 18.6g; Fat 28g, of which saturates 16.9g; Cholesterol 114mg; Calcium 98mg; Fibre 1.9g; Sodium 360mg.

Fresh Cherry and Hazelnut Strudel

Serve this wonderful treat as a warm dessert with custard after a festive meal, or allow it to cool and offer it as a scrumptious cake with afternoon tea or coffee to warm the soul on a cold winter's day.

Serves 6–8
75g/3oz/6 tbsp butter
90ml/6 tbsp light muscovado (brown) sugar
3 egg yolks
grated rind of 1 lemon
1.5ml/¼ tsp grated nutmeg
250g/9oz/generous 1 cup ricotta cheese
8 large sheets filo pastry, thawed if frozen
75g/3oz ratafias, crushed
450g/1lb/2½ cups cherries, pitted
30ml/2 tbsp chopped hazelnuts
icing (confectioners') sugar, for dusting
crème fraîche, to serve

1 Preheat the oven to 190°C/375°F/Gas 5. Soften 15g/½oz/1 tbsp of the butter. Place it in a bowl and beat in the sugar and egg yolks until light and fluffy. Beat in the lemon rind, nutmeg and ricotta, then set aside.

2 Melt the remaining butter in a small pan. Working quickly, place a sheet of filo on a clean dish towel and brush it generously with melted butter. Place a second sheet on top and repeat the process. Continue until all the filo has been layered and buttered, reserving some of the melted butter.

3 Sprinkle the crushed ratafias over the top, leaving a 5cm/2in border around the outside. Spoon the ricotta mixture over the biscuits, spread it lightly to cover, then sprinkle over the cherries.

4 Fold in the filo pastry border and use the dish towel to carefully roll up the strudel, Swiss-roll (jelly-roll) style, beginning from one of the long sides of the pastry. Grease a baking sheet with the remaining melted butter.

5 Place the strudel on the baking sheet and sprinkle the hazelnuts over the surface. Bake for 35–40 minutes or until the strudel is golden and crisp. Dust with icing sugar and serve with a dollop of crème fraîche.

Figs and Pears in Honey

A stunningly simple dessert using fresh figs and pears scented with the warm fragrances of cinnamon and cardamom and drenched in a lemon and honey syrup. Pears are at their best around Christmas time and this dessert really makes the most of them.

Serves 4
1 lemon
90ml/6 tbsp clear honey
1 cinnamon stick
1 cardamom pod
2 pears
8 fresh figs, halved

1 Pare the rind from the lemon using a zester. Alternatively, use a vegetable peeler and then cut the peeled rind into very thin strips, no bigger than the size of a matchstick.

2 Place the lemon rind, honey, cinnamon stick, cardamom pod and 350ml/12fl oz/1½ cups water in a heavy pan and bring to the boil. Continue to boil, uncovered, for about 10 minutes until reduced by about half.

3 Cut the pears into eighths, discarding the cores. Place the pieces in the syrup, add the figs and simmer for about 5 minutes, or until the fruit is tender.

4 Transfer the fruit to a serving bowl. Continue cooking the liquid until syrupy, then discard the cinnamon stick and pour over the figs and pears. Serve.

Cook's Tips
• *You can leave the peel on the pears or discard, depending on your preference.*
• *Figs vary in colour from pale green and yellow to dark purple. When buying them, look for firm fruit that is free from bruises or blemishes on the skin. A ripe fig will yield gently in your hand without pressing.*
• *It is best to use pale green or light beige cardamom pods,*

Fresh Cherry Strudel Energy 317kcal/1326kJ; Protein 6.5g; Carbohydrate 34.2g, of which sugars 22.9g; Fat 18.1g, of which saturates 9.1g; Cholesterol 109mg; Calcium 54mg; Fibre 1.2g; Sodium 93mg.
Figs and Pears in Honey Energy 143kcal/606kJ; Protein 1.7g; Carbohydrate 34.4g, of which sugars 34.4g; Fat 0.7g, of which saturates 0g; Cholesterol 0mg; Calcium 109mg; Fibre 4.7g; Sodium 28mg.

Oranges in Hot Coffee Syrup

This recipe makes a lovely dessert and also works well with most citrus fruits.

Serves 6
6 medium oranges
200g/7oz/1 cup sugar

50ml/2fl oz/¼ cup cold water
100ml/3½fl oz/scant ½ cup
    boiling water
100ml/3½fl oz/scant ½ cup
    fresh strong brewed coffee
50g/2oz/⅓ cup pistachio nuts,
    chopped (optional)

1 Finely pare the rind from one orange, shred and reserve the rind. Peel the remaining oranges.

2 Cut each orange crossways into slices, then re-form into the original spherical shape and hold in place with a cocktail stick (toothpick) through the centre.

3 Put the sugar and cold water in a pan. Heat gently, stirring constantly, until the sugar dissolves, then bring to the boil and cook until the syrup turns pale gold.

4 Remove from the heat and carefully pour the boiling water into the pan. Return to the heat until the syrup has dissolved in the water. Stir in the coffee.

5 Add the oranges and the shredded rind to the coffee syrup. Simmer for 15–20 minutes, turning the oranges once during cooking. Sprinkle with pistachio nuts, if using, and serve hot.

Cook's Tip
When making this dessert, use a pan in which the oranges will just fit in a single layer.

Variation
Try the sweet clementines or tangerines that are in abundance over the Christmas period as an alternative to the oranges in this recipe, if you prefer.

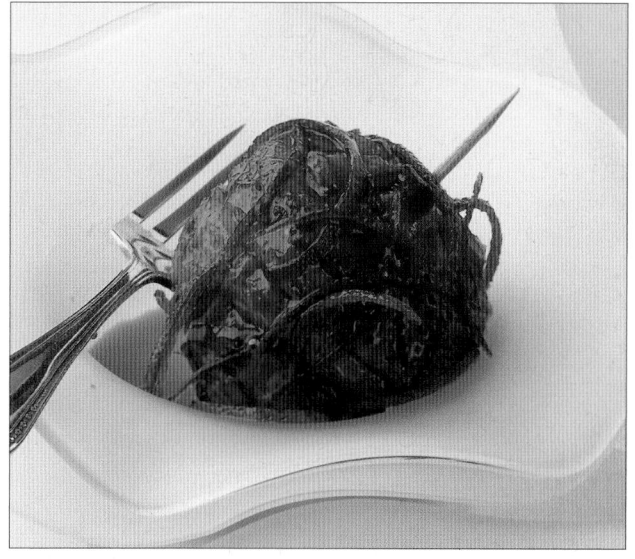

Toffee Bananas

This can be a bit tricky to master. You need to work fast, especially when dipping the fruit in the caramel. The luscious results, however, are worth the effort and will delight your festive guests.

Serves 4
4 firm bananas
75g/3oz/⅔ cup plain
    (all-purpose) flour

50g/2oz/½ cup cornflour
    (cornstarch)
10ml/2 tsp baking powder
175ml/6fl oz/¾ cup water
5ml/1 tsp sesame oil
groundnut (peanut), sunflower or
    corn oil, for deep-frying

For the caramel
225g/8oz/1 cup sugar
30ml/2 tbsp sesame seeds
60ml/4 tbsp water

1 Peel the bananas, then cut them diagonally into thick slices. Sift the flours and baking powder into a large bowl. Beat in the water and sesame oil. Stir in the bananas until coated.

2 Heat the groundnut, sunflower or corn oil in a deep pan until it registers 180°C/350°F or until a cube of bread, added to the oil, turns pale brown in 45 seconds. Using a fork, remove a piece of banana from the batter, allowing the excess batter to drain back into the bowl. Gently lower the piece of banana into the hot oil. Add more pieces in the same way but do not overcrowd the pan. Fry for about 2 minutes until golden.

3 As they are cooked, remove the banana fritters from the oil with a slotted spoon and place on kitchen paper to drain. Cook the rest of the battered bananas in the same way.

4 Make the caramel. Mix the sugar, sesame seeds and water in a pan. Heat gently, stirring occasionally, until the sugar has dissolved. Raise the heat and continue cooking, without stirring, until the syrup becomes a light caramel. Remove from the heat.

5 Have ready a bowl of iced water. Working quickly, drop one fritter at a time into the caramel. Flip over with a fork, remove immediately and plunge the piece into the water. Remove from the water quickly (carefully using your fingers for speed) and drain on a wire rack while coating the rest. Serve immediately.

Toffee Bananas Energy 551kcal/2324kJ; Protein 4.7g; Carbohydrate 101.6g, of which sugars 73.5g; Fat 16.7g, of which saturates 2.2g; Cholesterol 0mg; Calcium 111mg; Fibre 2.3g; Sodium 13mg.
Oranges in Coffee Syrup Energy 183kcal/782kJ; Protein 2g; Carbohydrate 46.4g, of which sugars 46.3g; Fat 0.1g, of which saturates 0g; Cholesterol 0mg; Calcium 84mg; Fibre 2.3g; Sodium 10mg.

Passion Fruit Crème Caramels

Christmas is a time when passion fruit are at their best. The fruit has an aromatic flavour that really permeates these crème caramels. Use some of the caramel for dipping the physalis in, to create a unique decoration for these pretty festive treats.

Serves 4

185g/6½oz/scant 1 cup caster (superfine) sugar
75ml/5 tbsp water
4 passion fruit
4 physalis
3 eggs plus 1 egg yolk
150ml/¼ pint/⅔ cup double (heavy) cream
150ml/¼ pint/⅔ cup creamy milk

1 Place 150g/5oz/⅔ cup of the caster sugar in a heavy pan. Add the water and heat the mixture gently until the sugar has dissolved. Increase the heat and boil until the syrup turns a dark golden colour.

2 Meanwhile, cut each passion fruit in half. Scoop out the seeds from the passion fruit into a sieve (strainer) set over a bowl. Press the seeds against the sieve to extract all their juice. Spoon a few of the seeds into each of four 150ml/¼ pint/⅔ cup ramekins. Set the juice aside.

3 Peel back the papery casing from each physalis and dip the orange berries into the caramel. Place on a sheet of non-stick baking parchment and set aside. Pour the remaining caramel carefully into the ramekins.

4 Preheat the oven to 150°C/300°F/Gas 2. Whisk the eggs, egg yolk and remaining sugar in a bowl. Whisk in the cream and milk, then the passion fruit juice. Strain through a sieve into each ramekin, then place the ramekins in a baking tin (pan). Pour in hot water to come halfway up the sides of the dishes; bake for 40–45 minutes or until just set.

5 Remove the custards from the tin and leave to cool, then cover and chill them for 4 hours before serving. Run a knife between the edge of each ramekin and the custard and invert each in turn on to a dessert plate. Shake the ramekins firmly to release the custards. Decorate each with a dipped physalis.

Whisky Trifle

This luxuriously rich trifle is made the traditional way, with real sponge cake, fresh fruit and rich egg custard, but with whisky rather than the usual sherry. If you like, you can decorate the top with glacé (candied) cherries and angelica, to add Christmas colours. A good egg custard is essential, so don't be tempted to use a convenient alternative.

Serves 6–8

1 × 15–18cm/6–7in sponge cake
225g/8oz raspberry jam
150ml/¼ pint/⅔ cup whisky
450g/1lb ripe fruit, such as pears and bananas
300ml/½ pint/1¼ cups whipping cream
flaked (sliced) almonds, toasted to decorate (optional)

For the custard

450ml/¾ pint/scant 2 cups full cream (whole) milk
1 vanilla pod (bean) or a few drops of vanilla extract
3 eggs
25g/1oz/2 tbsp caster (superfine) sugar

1 To make the custard, put the milk into a pan with the vanilla pod, if using, and bring almost to the boil. Remove the pan from the heat. Whisk the eggs and sugar together lightly. Remove the pod. Gradually whisk the milk into the egg mixture.

2 Rinse out the pan with cold water, return the mixture to it and stir over low heat until it thickens enough to coat the back of a spoon; do not allow it to boil. Alternatively, for a very slow method of cooking, use a double boiler, or a bowl over a pan of boiling water. Turn the custard into a bowl and add the vanilla extract, if using. Cover and set aside until needed.

3 Halve the sponge cake horizontally, spread with the jam and make a sandwich. Cut it into slices and use them to line the bottom and lower sides of a large glass serving bowl.

4 Sprinkle with the whisky. Peel and slice the fruit, then spread it out over the sponge in a layer. Pour the custard on top, cover with clear film (plastic wrap), and leave to cool and set. Chill until required. Before serving, whip the cream and spread it over the custard. Decorate with the toasted flaked almonds, if using.

Passion Fruit Caramels 318kcal/1336kJ; Protein 9.8g; Carbohydrate 36.6g, of which sugars 36.6g; Fat 16g, of which saturates 8.2g; Cholesterol 221mg; Calcium 150mg; Fibre 0g; Sodium 108mg.
Whisky Trifle Energy 710kcal/2959kJ; Protein 12.1g; Carbohydrate 58g, of which sugars 42.6g; Fat 43.2g, of which saturates 14.4g; Cholesterol 171mg; Calcium 194mg; Fibre 2.3g; Sodium 336mg.

Zabaglione

Light as air and wonderfully alcoholic, this egg custard is a much-loved Italian pudding. Though this delicious dessert is traditionally made with Marsala, the fortified wine can be replaced by sweet sherry if you wish. This dessert can be served either warm or cold.

Serves 8
4 egg yolks
50g/2oz/¼ cup caster (superfine) sugar
60ml/4 tbsp Marsala, Madeira or sweet sherry
amaretti, to serve

1 Place the egg yolks and sugar in a large heatproof bowl, and whisk with an electric beater until the mixture is pale and thick.

2 Gradually add the Marsala, Madeira or sherry to the egg mixture, 15ml/1 tbsp at a time, whisking well after each addition.

3 Place the bowl over a pan of gently simmering water and continue to whisk for 5–7 minutes, until the mixture becomes thick; when the beaters are lifted they should leave a thick trail on the surface of the mixture. Do not be tempted to underbeat the mixture, or the zabaglione will remain too runny and will be likely to separate.

4 Pour into four warmed, stemmed glasses and serve immediately, with amaretti for dipping.

> **Variations**
> *Ring the changes with different flavours: for a cappuccino zabaglione. After beating the mixture, fold in 30ml/2tbsp strong coffee, or for an added kick, add 30ml/2tbsp coffee liqueur such as Kahlúa or Tia Maria. If you prefer a fruity flavour, blend or liquidize about 22g/8oz strawberries or raspberries with 5ml/1 tsp lemon juice until puréed. Sieve and add icing sugar (confectioner's sugar) to taste. Fold into the zabaglione.*

Whisky Mac Cream

The warming tipple whisky mac is a combination of whisky and ginger wine. This recipe turns the drink into a rich, smooth, creamy dessert – very decadent and a suitable end to a festive feast.

Serves 4
4 egg yolks
15ml/1 tbsp caster (superfine) sugar, plus 50g/2oz/¼ cup
600ml/1 pint/2½ cups double (heavy) cream
15ml/1 tbsp whisky
green ginger wine, to serve

1 In a large bowl, whisk the egg yolks thoroughly with the first, smaller amount of the caster sugar. Whisk briskly until the egg yolks are light and pale.

2 Pour the double cream into a heavy pan with the whisky and the remainder of the caster sugar. Bring the mixture to scalding point but do not let it boil.

3 Pour the mixture from the pan on to the egg yolks, whisking continually. Return to the pan and, over low heat, stir until the custard has thickened slightly.

4 Pour the mixture into individual ramekin dishes, cover each with a piece of clear film (plastic wrap) and set aside for a few hours or overnight to set.

5 To serve, pour just enough green ginger wine over the top of each ramekin to cover the cream.

> **Cook's Tip**
> *Green ginger wine is made by two main companies in the UK – Stone's and Crabbie's. To make a simple Whisky Mac as a drink, mix equal parts Scotch whisky (it should traditionally be this variety but not a single malt) with equal parts ginger wine – or a little more whisky to ginger wine if you like it less sweet. Whether or not you add ice to the drink is a matter of preference although it will often be decided by how cold the festive weather is outside.*

Whisky Mac Cream Energy 892kcal/3682kJ; Protein 5.4g; Carbohydrate 19.7g, of which sugars 19.7g; Fat 86.1g, of which saturates 51.7g; Cholesterol 407mg; Calcium 107mg; Fibre 0g; Sodium 44mg.
Zabaglione Energy 134kcal/561kJ; Protein 3g; Carbohydrate 14.9g, of which sugars 14.9g; Fat 5.5g, of which saturates 1.6g; Cholesterol 202mg; Calcium 31mg; Fibre 0g; Sodium 10mg.

Tiramisù in Chocolate Cups

Give in to the temptation of tiramisù at Christmas, with its magical mocha flavour.

Serves 6
1 egg yolk
30ml/2 tbsp caster
    (superfine) sugar
2.5ml/½ tsp vanilla extract
250g/9oz/generous 1 cup
    mascarpone
120ml/4fl oz/½ cup strong
    black coffee

15ml/1 tbsp unsweetened
    cocoa powder
30ml/2 tbsp coffee liqueur
16 amaretti
unsweetened cocoa powder,
    for dusting

For the chocolate cups
175g/6oz good quality plain
    (semisweet) chocolate, broken
    into squares
25g/1oz/2 tbsp unsalted butter

1 Make the chocolate cups. Cut out six 15cm/6in rounds of baking parchment. Melt the chocolate and butter in a heatproof bowl over barely simmering water. Stir until smooth, then spread a spoonful over each circle, to within 2cm/¾in of the edge.

2 Carefully lift each paper round and drape it over an upturned teacup or ramekin so that the edges curve into frills. Leave until completely set, then carefully lift off and peel away the paper to reveal the chocolate cups.

3 To make the filling, beat the egg yolk and sugar in a bowl until smooth, then stir in the vanilla extract and mascarpone. Mix until smooth and creamy. In another bowl, mix the coffee, cocoa and liqueur. Break up the biscuits and stir into the mixture.

4 Divide half the biscuit mixture among the chocolate cups, then spoon over half the mascarpone mixture. Spoon over the remaining biscuit mixture, top with the rest of the mascarpone mixture and dust with cocoa. Serve as soon as possible.

> **Cook's Tip**
> When spreading the chocolate for the cups, don't aim for perfectly regular edges; uneven edges will give a prettier effect.

Mocha Velvet Cream Pots

These dainty pots of chocolate heaven are a fabulous way to round off a special festive meal.

Serves 8
15ml/1 tbsp instant
    coffee powder
475ml/16fl oz/2 cups milk
75g/3oz/6 tbsp caster
    (superfine) sugar

225g/8oz plain (semisweet)
    chocolate, chopped into
    small pieces
10ml/2 tsp vanilla extract
30ml/2 tbsp coffee-flavoured
    liqueur (optional)
7 egg yolks
whipped double (heavy) cream
    and crystallized mimosa balls,
    to decorate (optional)

1 Preheat the oven to 160°C/325°F/Gas 3. Place eight 120ml/4fl oz/½ cup custard cups or ramekins in a roasting pan. Set aside.

2 Put the instant coffee in a pan. Stir in the milk, then add the sugar and place the pan over medium heat. Bring to the boil, stirring constantly, until both the coffee and the sugar have dissolved completely.

3 Remove the pan from the heat and add the chocolate. Stir until it has melted and the sauce is smooth. Stir in the vanilla extract and coffee liqueur, if using.

4 In a bowl, whisk the egg yolks to blend them lightly. Slowly whisk in the chocolate mixture until well combined, then strain the mixture into a large jug (pitcher) and divide it equally among the cups or ramekins.

5 Pour enough boiling water into the roasting pan to come halfway up the sides of the cups or ramekins. Carefully place the roasting pan in the oven.

6 Bake in the oven for 30–35 minutes, until the custard is just set and a knife inserted into the custard comes out clean. Remove the cups or ramekins from the roasting pan and allow to cool completely. Place on a baking sheet, cover and chill. Decorate the pots with whipped cream and crystallized mimosa balls, if you wish.

Tiramisù Energy 351kcal/1469kJ; Protein 6.9g; Carbohydrate 34.5g, of which sugars 29.6g; Fat 20.4g, of which saturates 12.1g; Cholesterol 62mg; Calcium 33mg; Fibre 1.2g; Sodium 86mg.
Mocha Velvet Cream Pots Energy 261kcal/1095kJ; Protein 6g; Carbohydrate 30.5g, of which sugars 30.2g; Fat 13.7g, of which saturates 6.7g; Cholesterol 182mg; Calcium 106mg; Fibre 0.7g; Sodium 36mg.

Chocolate and Chestnut Pots

The chestnut purée adds substance and a festive flavour to these mousses. Crisp, delicate cookies, such as langues-de-chat, provide a good foil to the richness.

Serves 6
250g/9oz plain (semisweet)
  chocolate
60ml/4 tbsp Madeira
25g/1oz/2 tbsp butter, diced
2 eggs, separated
225g/8oz/scant 1 cup
  unsweetened chestnut purée
crème fraîche or whipped double
  (heavy) cream, to decorate

1 Make a few chocolate curls for decoration by rubbing a grater along the length of the bar of chocolate. Break the rest of the chocolate into squares and melt it in a pan with the Madeira over very low heat.

2 Remove the pan from the heat and add the butter, a few pieces at a time, stirring until melted and smooth.

3 Beat the egg yolks quickly into the mixture, then beat in the chestnut purée, mixing until smooth.

4 Whisk the egg whites in a clean, grease-free bowl until stiff. Stir about 15ml/1 tbsp of the whites into the chestnut mixture to lighten it, then fold in the rest smoothly and evenly.

5 Spoon the mixture into six small ramekin dishes and chill in the refrigerator until it is set.

6 Remove the pots from the refrigerator 30 minutes before serving. Serve the pots topped with a spoonful of crème fraîche or whipped cream and decorated with chocolate curls.

Cook's Tips
• If Madeira is not available, use brandy or rum instead.
• These pots can be frozen successfully for up to 2 months, making them ideal for a prepare-ahead Christmas dessert.

Chocolate Amaretto Marquise

This wickedly rich chocolate dessert is truly extravagant – perfect for a festive treat.

Serves 10–12
15ml/1 tbsp flavourless vegetable oil, such as groundnut (peanut) or sunflower
75g/3oz/7–8 amaretti, finely crushed
25g/1oz/¼ cup unblanched almonds, toasted and finely chopped
450g/1lb plain (semisweet) or dark (bittersweet) chocolate, chopped into small pieces
75ml/5 tbsp Amaretto Disaronno liqueur
75ml/5 tbsp golden (light corn) syrup
475ml/16fl oz/2 cups double (heavy) cream
unsweetened cocoa powder, for dusting

For the amaretto cream
350ml/12fl oz/1½ cups whipping cream or double (heavy) cream
30–45ml/2–3 tbsp Amaretto Disaronno liqueur

1 Lightly oil a 23cm/9in heart-shaped or springform cake tin (pan). Line the bottom with baking parchment, then oil the paper. In a small bowl, combine the crushed amaretti and the chopped almonds. Sprinkle evenly on to the base of the tin.

2 Place the chocolate, Amaretto liqueur and golden syrup in a medium pan over a very low heat. Stir frequently until the chocolate has melted and the mixture is smooth. Remove from the heat and allow it to cool for about 6–8 minutes, until the mixture feels just warm to the touch.

3 Whip the cream until it just begins to hold its shape. Stir a large spoonful into the chocolate mixture, to lighten it, then quickly add the remaining cream and gently fold in. Pour into the prepared tin, on top of the amaretti mixture. Level the surface. Cover with clear film (plastic wrap) and chill overnight.

4 To unmould, run a slightly warmed, thin-bladed sharp knife around the edge of the dessert, then unmould. Carefully peel off the paper, replacing any crust that sticks to it, and dust with cocoa. In a bowl, whip the cream and Amaretto liqueur to soft peaks. Serve separately.

Chocolate Pots Energy 348kcal/1455kJ; Protein 5g; Carbohydrate 41.4g, of which sugars 29.9g; Fat 18g, of which saturates 9.9g; Cholesterol 75mg; Calcium 42mg; Fibre 2.6g; Sodium 56mg.
Chocolate Marquise Energy 589kcal/2444kJ; Protein 3.9g; Carbohydrate 38.2g, of which sugars 35.1g; Fat 46.4g, of which saturates 27.5g; Cholesterol 87mg; Calcium 63mg; Fibre 1.2g; Sodium 57mg.

Clementines in Cinnamon Caramel

The combination of sweet, yet sharp clementines and caramel sauce with a hint of spice is divine. Served with Greek-style yogurt or crème fraîche, this makes a deliciously light dessert for a festive occasion.

Serves 4–6
8–12 clementines
225g/8oz/generous 1 cup
   granulated sugar
2 cinnamon sticks
30ml/2 tbsp orange-flavoured
   liqueur
25g/1oz/¼ cup shelled
   pistachio nuts

1 Pare the rind from two clementines using a vegetable peeler and cut it into fine strips. Set aside.

2 Peel the clementines, and take care to remove all of the pith while keeping each fruit intact.

3 Put the peeled clementines in a serving bowl and set aside.

4 Pour the sugar in to a heavy-based pan. Heat very gently until it melts and changes to a rich golden brown. Immediately turn off the heat.

5 Cover your hand with a dish towel and pour in 300ml/ ½ pint/1¼ cups warm water (the mixture will bubble and splutter). Bring the mixture slowly to the boil, stirring until the caramel has completely dissolved.

6 Add the shredded peel and cinnamon sticks, then simmer for about 5 minutes. Stir in the orange- flavoured liqueur.

7 Leave the syrup to cool for about 10 minutes, then pour over the clementines. Cover the bowl and chill for several hours or overnight.

8 Blanch the pistachio nuts in boiling water. Drain, cool and remove the dark outer skins by rubbing the nuts gently in a clean dish towel. Scatter the nuts over the clementines and serve at once. Arrange the cinnamon sticks over the clementines as decoration.

Poached Pears in Red Wine

When cooked in an aromatic mixure of red wine, vanilla, honey and spices, whole pears take on a lovely colour and taste. They make a delightful dessert after a rich main course.

Serves 4
1 bottle red wine
150g/5oz/¾ cup caster sugar
45ml/3 tbsp honey
juice of ½ lemon
1 cinnamon stick
1 vanilla pod, split open
   lengthways
5cm/2in piece of orange rind
1 clove
1 black peppercorn
4 firm, ripe pears
whipped cream or soured cream,
   to serve

1 Place the wine, sugar, honey, lemon juice, cinnamon stick, vanilla pod, orange rind, clove and peppercorn in a saucepan just large enough to hold the pears standing upright.

2 Heat the mixture gently, stirring occasionally until the sugar has completely dissolved.

3 Meanwhile, peel the pears, leaving the stem intact. Take a thin slice off the base of each pear so that it will stand square and upright in the pan.

4 Place the pears in the wine mixture, then simmer, uncovered, for 20–35 minutes depending on size and ripeness, until the pears are just tender; be careful not to overcook.

5 Carefully transfer the pears to a bowl using a slotted spoon. Continue to boil the poaching liquid until reduced by about half. Leave to cool.

6 Strain the cooled liquid over the pears and chill for at least 3 hours.

7 Place the pears in four individual serving dishes and spoon over a little of the red wine syrup.

8 Serve the pears with whipped cream or soured cream.

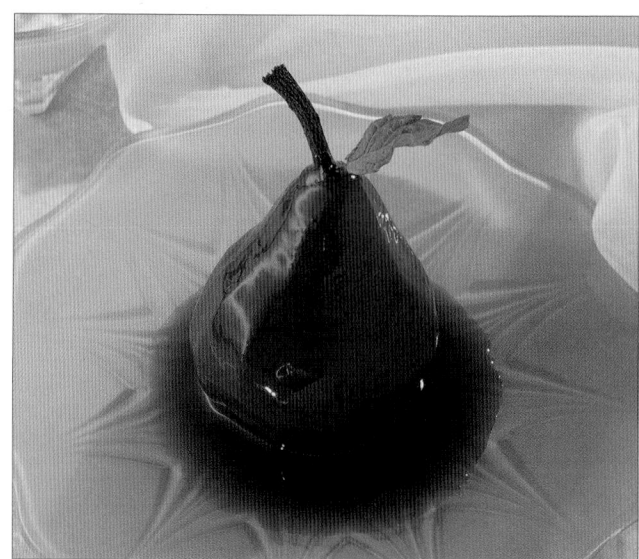

Clementines Energy 149kcal/632kJ; Protein 0.9g; Carbohydrate 24.7g, of which sugars 24.7g; Fat 0.1g, of which saturates 0g; Cholesterol 0mg; Calcium 40mg; Fibre 1g; Sodium 12mg.
Poached pears 374kcal/1597kJ; Protein 1.8g; Carbohydrate 95.7g, of which sugars 95.7g; Fat 0.9g, of which saturates 0g; Cholesterol 0mg; Calcium 82mg; Fibre 9.9g; Sodium 24mg.

Fig, Port and Clementine Sundaes

These sundaes are an ideal finale to a fine festive meal. The figs and clementines contrast beautifully with the warm spices and port.

Serves 6
6 clementines
30ml/2 tbsp clear honey

1 cinnamon stick, halved
15ml/1 tbsp light muscovado (brown) sugar
60ml/4 tbsp port
6 fresh figs
about 500ml/17fl oz/2¼ cups orange sorbet

1 Finely grate the rind from two clementines and put it in a small, heavy pan. Cut the peel off the clementines, then slice the flesh thinly. Add the honey, cinnamon, sugar and port to the rind. Heat gently until the sugar has dissolved, to make a syrup.

2 Put the clementine slices in a heatproof bowl and pour over the syrup. Cool completely, then chill.

3 Slice the figs thinly and add to the clementines and syrup, tossing the ingredients together gently. Leave to stand for 10 minutes, then discard the cinnamon stick.

4 Arrange half the fig and clementine slices around the sides of six serving glasses. Half fill the glasses with scoops of orange sorbet. Arrange the remaining fruit slices around the sides of the glasses, then pile more sorbet into the centre. Pour over the port syrup and serve immediately.

> **Cook's Tip**
> *A variety of different types of fresh figs are available. Dark purple skinned figs have a deep red flesh; the yellow-green figs have a pink flesh and green skinned figs have an amber coloured flesh. All types can be eaten, complete with the skin, simply as they are or baked and served with Greek (US strained plain) yogurt and honey for a quick dessert. When they are ripe, you can split them open with your fingers to reveal the soft, sweet flesh full of edible seeds.*

Fragrant Fruit Salad

A medley of colourful and exotic fruit, this fresh-tasting salad is the perfect dessert for a festive dinner party.

Serves 6
130g/4½oz/scant ¾ cup sugar
thinly pared rind and juice of 1 lime
150ml/¼ pint/⅔ cup water

60ml/4 tbsp brandy
5ml/1 tsp instant coffee granules or powder dissolved in 30ml/2 tbsp boiling water
1 small pineapple
1 papaya
2 pomegranates
1 mango
2 passion fruit or kiwi fruit
strips of lime rind, to decorate

1 Put the sugar and lime rind in a small pan with the water. Heat gently until the sugar dissolves, then bring to the boil and simmer for 5 minutes. Leave to cool, then strain into a large serving bowl, discarding the lime rind. Stir in the lime juice, brandy and dissolved coffee.

2 Using a sharp knife, cut the plume and stalk ends from the pineapple. Cut off the peel, then remove the central core and discard. Slice the flesh into bitesize pieces and add to the bowl.

3 Halve the papaya and scoop out the seeds. Cut away the skin, then slice the papaya. Halve the pomegranates and scoop out the seeds. Add to the bowl.

4 Cut the mango lengthwise into three pieces, along each side of the stone (pit). Peel the skin off the flesh. Cut the flesh into chunks and add to the bowl.

5 Halve the passion fruit and scoop out the flesh using a teaspoon, or peel and chop the kiwi fruit. Add to the bowl and serve, decorated with lime rind.

> **Cook's Tip**
> *Allow the salad to stand at room temperature for 1 hour before serving so that the many fruit flavours have plenty of time to blend together.*

Fig Sundaes Energy 282kcal/1205kJ; Protein 3.7g; Carbohydrate 66.5g, of which sugars 66.5g; Fat 0.9g, of which saturates 0g; Cholesterol 0mg; Calcium 173mg; Fibre 5.4g; Sodium 50mg.
Fragrant Fruit Salad Energy 146kcal/620kJ; Protein 1g; Carbohydrate 33.2g, of which sugars 33.2g; Fat 0.3g, of which saturates 0g; Cholesterol 0mg; Calcium 40mg; Fibre 2.9g; Sodium 7mg.

Christmas Spice Cakes

Mincemeat and brandy liven up these delicious celebration cupcakes. The decorations will require a small snowflake or other Christmas themed cutter.

Makes 14
2 eggs
115g/4oz/¹/₂ cup golden caster (superfine) sugar
50ml/2fl oz/¹/₄ cup double (heavy) cream
grated rind of 1 clementine
115g/4oz/¹/₃ cup mincemeat
115g/4oz/1 cup self-raising (self-rising) flour

2.5ml/¹/₂ tsp baking powder
5ml/1 tsp mixed (apple pie) spice
10ml/2 tsp brandy
50g/2oz/4 tbsp butter, melted

For the icing
350g/12oz/3 cups icing (confectioners') sugar, sifted
15ml/1 tbsp hot water
red food colouring

To decorate
175g/6oz ready-to-roll fondant
red paste food colouring (or use 115g/4oz red and 50g/2oz white ready-to-roll fondant)

1 Preheat the oven to 180°C/350°F/ Gas 4. Line the cups of a bun tin (pan) with paper cases.

2 Lightly beat the eggs with the sugar. Beat the cream into the egg mixture for about 1 minute, then add the grated clementine rind. Fold in the mincemeat. Sift in the flour, baking powder and mixed spice and fold in. Finally add the brandy and the melted butter and stir to combine.

3 Half-fill the paper cases with the batter. Place in the centre of the oven and bake for 12–15 minutes until risen and golden. Test by lightly pressing the centre of the cakes; the sponge should spring back. Leave on a wire rack to cool.

4 To make the icing, mix the sugar with hot water to make a soft icing. Tint one-third of it with the food colouring and spoon over four cakes. Ice the remaining cakes with the white icing.

5 Set aside one-third of the fondant and colour the rest red. Roll both out and stamp out 10 red and 4 white snowflakes. Stick one on each cake before the icing sets.

Christmas Star Cakes

Mascarpone and Marsala add a delicious nuance to these cakes, which are topped with a smooth velvety cream and decorated with festive stars and holly leaves.

Makes 8–10
150g/5oz/10 tbsp butter, softened
200g/7oz/scant 1 cup golden caster (superfine) sugar
3 eggs
175g/6oz/³/₄ cup mascarpone
5ml/1 tsp grated lemon rind
30ml/2 tbsp buttermilk
15ml/1 tbsp unsweetened cocoa powder, plus extra for dusting
25ml/1¹/₂ tbsp espresso coffee

15ml/1 tbsp Marsala
250g/9oz/2¹/₄ cups self-raising (self-rising) flour

For the topping
250ml/8fl oz/1 cup double (heavy) cream
225g/8oz/1 cup mascarpone
15ml/1 tbsp golden caster (superfine) sugar
15ml/1 tbsp Marsala
seeds from ¹/₂ vanilla pod (bean)
25g/1oz milk chocolate, melted

For the stars and leaves
100g/3³/₄oz plain (semisweet) chocolate
100g/3³/₄oz milk chocolate

1 Preheat the oven to 180°C/350°F/Gas 4. Line the cups of a bun tin (pan) with paper cases.

2 Beat the butter and sugar together until light and creamy. Gradually beat in the eggs, one at a time, beating well after each addition. Stir in the mascarpone, lemon rind, buttermilk, cocoa, coffee and Marsala, then fold in the flour.

3 Fill the prepared cases. Bake for 25 minutes, or until firm to the touch. Turn out on to a wire rack to cool.

4 Meanwhile, make the topping. Beat the cream with the mascarpone, sugar, Marsala and vanilla seeds. Lightly fold in the melted milk chocolate.

5 For the decorations, melt the chocolates separately. Spread on baking parchment and chill until set. Cut out the shapes.

6 Spoon the topping on to the cakes, and press on the festive stars and leaves. Dust with cocoa powder.

Christmas Star Cakes Energy 718kcal/2990kJ; Protein 8g; Carbohydrate 56.8g, of which sugars 36.7g; Fat 53.7g, of which saturates 32.1g; Cholesterol 167mg; Calcium 146mg; Fibre 1g; Sodium 297mg.
Christmas Spice Cakes Energy 272kcal/1153kJ; Protein 2g; Carbohydrate 56g, of which sugars 49.7g; Fat 6.1g, of which saturates 3.4g; Cholesterol 40mg; Calcium 43mg; Fibre 0.4g; Sodium 52mg.

Christmas Tree Cakes

These chocolate cakes have a crème fraîche icing, which can be made using either dark or white chocolate. Cut the tree decorations out of contrasting chocolate, and bake the cakes in gold cases to sparkle on the festive table.

Makes 20

150g/5oz dark (bittersweet) chocolate
175ml/6fl oz/³⁄₄ cup single (light) cream
5ml/1 tsp vanilla extract
225g/8oz/1 cup golden caster (superfine) sugar
200g/7oz/scant 1 cup butter
3 eggs
225g/8oz/2 cups plain (all-purpose) flour
20g/³⁄₄oz/2 tbsp unsweetened cocoa powder
10ml/2 tsp baking powder

For the icing and decoration

200g/7oz dark (bittersweet) or white chocolate
50g/2oz/4 tbsp butter
250ml/8fl oz/1 cup crème fraîche
75g/3oz/³⁄₄ cup icing (confectioners') sugar, sifted
225/8oz white or dark (bittersweet) chocolate, to decorate

1 Preheat the oven to 190°C/375°F/Gas 5. Line the cups of two bun tins (pans) with paper cases. Melt the chocolate with the cream over low heat, stirring. Stir in the vanilla and set aside.

2 Beat the sugar and butter together until light and fluffy, then beat in the eggs one at a time. Sift the flour, cocoa powder and baking powder over the butter mixture and fold in, alternating with the chocolate cream, until the batter is combined. Half-fill the prepared cups and lightly smooth the tops level. Bake for 20–25 minutes, until the centres are firm. Cool on a wire rack.

3 To make the icing, melt the chocolate and butter over a pan of simmering water, stirring, until smooth. Leave to cool a little, then stir in the crème fraîche followed by the sugar. Spread the icing over the cupcakes with a metal spatula.

4 Melt the chocolate for the trees over a pan of simmering water and pour on to a tray lined with baking parchment. Chill until just set, then cut out the shapes and chill again until firm. Stick the decorations on to the cakes.

Ginger Cupcakes with Lemon Icing

Lemon icing offsets the ginger flavour of these delicious cakes, which are decorated with figures cut out of spiced marzipan.

Makes 12–14

175g/6oz/³⁄₄ cup butter, softened
175g/6oz/generous ³⁄₄ cup golden caster (superfine) sugar
3 eggs, lightly beaten
25ml/1¹⁄₂ tbsp black treacle (molasses)
35ml/2¹⁄₂ tbsp syrup from a jar of preserved ginger
225g/8oz/2 cups self-raising (self-rising) flour, sifted
10ml/2 tsp ground ginger
25ml/1¹⁄₂ tbsp ground almonds
30ml/2 tbsp single (light) cream

For the icing

350g/12oz/3 cups icing (confectioners') sugar
60ml/4 tbsp lemon juice
10ml/2 tsp water

For the decoration

115g/4oz golden marzipan
2.5ml/¹⁄₂ tsp mixed (apple pie) spice
a few drops ginger-brown food colouring

1 Preheat the oven to 180°C/350°F/Gas 4. Line the cups of a large bun tin (pan) with paper cases.

2 Beat the butter and sugar together until light and creamy. Gradually beat in the eggs in batches, beating well between each addition. Fold in the black treacle and the ginger syrup. Sift in the flour with the ground ginger and fold in lightly. Add the ground almonds, then the cream, and stir until well combined.

3 Half-fill the cases and bake for 20 minutes, or until springy to the touch. Leave for a few minutes. Turn out on to a wire rack.

4 To make the icing, sift the icing sugar into a bowl and gradually mix in the lemon juice until the mixture is smooth, adding the water if necessary to get the correct consistency. When the cakes are completely cold, spoon the icing on to each one and smooth it level with a metal spatula.

5 To make the figures, knead the mixed spice and food colouring into the marzipan and roll it out thinly. Using a small figure cutter, cut out the shapes and stick on each iced cake.

Christmas Tree Cakes Energy 419kcal/1751kJ; Protein 4.2g; Carbohydrate 43.8g, of which sugars 33.6g; Fat 26.5g, of which saturates 16.4g; Cholesterol 79mg; Calcium 57mg; Fibre 0.5g; Sodium 125mg.
Ginger Cupcakes Energy 314kcal/1320kJ; Protein 3.9g; Carbohydrate 45.6g, of which sugars 33.3g; Fat 14.1g, of which saturates 7.6g; Cholesterol 71mg; Calcium 64mg; Fibre 0.8g; Sodium 115mg.

Passion Cake

Although traditionally eaten at Easter, this cake is suitable for any occasion and looks great on the Christmas table.

Makes one 20cm/8in round cake

200g/7oz/1¾ cups self-raising (self-rising) flour
10ml/2 tsp baking powder
5ml/1 tsp cinnamon
2.5ml/½ tsp freshly grated nutmeg
150g/5oz/10 tbsp butter, softened, or sunflower margarine
150g/5oz/generous 1 cup soft light brown sugar
grated rind of 1 lemon
2 eggs, beaten
2 carrots, coarsely grated
1 ripe banana, mashed
115g/4oz/¾ cup raisins
50g/2oz/½ cup chopped walnuts or pecan nuts
30ml/2 tbsp milk
6–8 walnuts, halved, to decorate
coffee crystal sugar, to decorate

For the icing

200g/7oz/scant 1 cup cream cheese, softened
30g/1½oz/scant ⅓ cup icing (confectioners') sugar
juice of 1 lemon
grated rind of 1 orange

1 Line and grease a deep 20cm/8in round cake tin (pan). Preheat the oven to 180°C/350°F/Gas 4. Sift the flour, baking powder and spices into a bowl.

2 In another bowl, cream the butter or margarine and sugar with the lemon rind until it is light and fluffy, then beat in the eggs. Fold in the flour mixture, then the carrots, banana, raisins, chopped nuts and the milk.

3 Spoon the mixture into the prepared cake tin, level the top and bake in the oven for about 1 hour, or until risen and the top is springy to the touch. Turn the tin upside down and allow the cake to cool in the tin for 30 minutes. Then turn out on to a wire rack and leave to cool completely. When cold, split the cake in half.

4 To make the icing, cream the cheese with the icing sugar, lemon juice and orange rind, then sandwich the two halves of the cake together with half of the icing. Spread the rest of the icing on top and decorate with walnut halves and the coffee crystal sugar before serving.

Festive Victoria Sandwich

A light sponge cake is given a Christmas theme with a pattern of festive stars. This recipe can be used as the base for other cakes.

Makes one 18cm/7in round cake

175g/6oz/1½ cups self-raising (self-rising) flour
a pinch of salt
175g/6oz/¾ cup butter, softened
175g/6oz/scant 1 cup caster (superfine) sugar
3 eggs

To finish

60–90ml/4–6 tbsp raspberry jam
caster (superfine) sugar or icing (confectioners') sugar

1 Preheat the oven to 180°C/350°F/Gas 4. Grease two 18cm/7in shallow round cake tins (pans), line the bases with baking parchment and grease the paper.

2 Put the flour, salt, butter, caster sugar and eggs into a large bowl. Whisk the ingredients together until smooth and creamy.

3 Divide the mixture between the prepared cake tins and smooth the surfaces. Bake for 25–30 minutes, or until a skewer inserted into the centre of the cakes comes out clean.

4 Turn out on to a wire rack, peel off the lining paper and leave to cool. Place one of the cakes on a serving plate and spread with the raspberry jam. Place the other cake on top.

5 Cut out paper star shapes, place on the cake and dredge with sugar. Remove the paper to reveal the pattern.

Variation

Outside of the festive season, this sponge cake is delicious with strawberries and cream. Whip 300ml/½ pint/1¼ cups double (heavy) cream with 5ml/1 tsp icing (confectioners') sugar until stiff. Wash and hull 450g/1lb/4 cups strawberries, then cut in half. Spread one of the cakes with half of the cream and sprinkle over half of the strawberries. Top with the other cake, spread with the remaining cream and arrange the remaining strawberries.

Passion Cake Energy 4318kcal/18033kJ; Protein 50.9g; Carbohydrate 456.2g, of which sugars 300.8g; Fat 267.4g, of which saturates 144.1g; Cholesterol 890mg; Calcium 798mg; Fibre 14.7g; Sodium 1777mg.
Victoria Sandwich Energy 2965kcal/12419kJ; Protein 37.5g; Carbohydrate 361.3g, of which sugars 227.9g; Fat 162.8g, of which saturates 96.2g; Cholesterol 944mg; Calcium 462mg; Fibre 5.4g; Sodium 304mg.

Apricot Brandy-snap Roulade

A magnificent combination of soft and crisp textures, this cake looks impressive after a Christmas meal and is easy to prepare.

Makes one 33cm/13in roll
4 eggs, separated
7.5ml/1½ tsp fresh orange juice
115g/4oz/generous ½ cup caster (superfine) sugar
175g/6oz/1½ cups ground almonds
4 brandy snaps, crushed, to decorate

For the filling
150g/5oz canned apricots, drained
300ml/½ pint/1¼ cups double (heavy) cream
25g/1oz/¼ cup icing (confectioners') sugar

1 Preheat the oven to 190°C/375°F/Gas 5. Base-line and grease a 33 × 23cm/13 × 9in Swiss roll tin (jelly roll pan).

2 Beat together the egg yolks, orange juice and sugar until thick and pale, about 10 minutes. Fold in the ground almonds.

3 Whisk the egg whites until they hold stiff peaks. Fold them into the almond mixture, then transfer to the Swiss roll tin and smooth the surface with a knife.

4 Bake in the preheated oven for 20 minutes, or until a skewer inserted into the centre comes out clean. Leave to cool in the tin, covered with a just-damp dish towel.

5 To make the filling, process the apricots in a blender or food processor until smooth. Whip the cream and icing sugar until it holds soft peaks. Fold in the apricot purée.

6 Spread the crushed brandy snaps over a sheet of baking parchment. Spread about one-third of the cream mixture over the cake, then carefully invert it on to the brandy snaps. Peel off the lining paper.

7 Use the remaining cream mixture to cover the whole cake, then gently roll up the roulade from a short end, being careful not to disturb the brandy snap coating. Transfer the roulade to a serving platter.

Chocolate Chestnut Roulade

A traditional version of Bûche de Noël, the delicious French Christmas gateau.

Makes one 33cm/13in long roll
225g/8oz plain (semisweet) chocolate
50g/2oz white chocolate
4 eggs, separated
115g/4oz/generous ½ cup caster (superfine) sugar, plus extra for dusting

For the chestnut filling
150ml/¼ pint/⅔ cup double (heavy) cream
225g/8oz can chestnut purée
50–65g/2–2½oz/4–5 tbsp icing (confectioners') sugar, plus extra for dusting

1 Preheat the oven to 180°C/350°F/Gas 4. Line and grease a 33 × 23cm/13 × 9in Swiss roll tin (jelly roll pan).

2 For the chocolate curls, melt 50g/2oz of the plain and all of the white chocolate in separate bowls set over pans of simmering water. Spread on a non-porous surface and leave to set.

3 Hold a long sharp knife at a 45-degree angle to the chocolate and push it along the chocolate, using a sawing motion. Put the curls on baking parchment.

4 Melt the remaining plain chocolate. Beat the egg yolks and caster sugar until thick and pale. Stir in the chocolate.

5 Whisk the egg whites until they form stiff peaks, then fold into the chocolate mixture. Turn into the prepared tin and bake for 15–20 minutes. Leave to cool, covered with a just-damp dish towel, on a wire rack.

6 Sprinkle a sheet of baking parchment with caster sugar. Turn the roulade out on to it. Peel off the lining paper and trim the edges of the roulade. Cover with the dish towel.

7 To make the filling, whip the cream until softly peaking. Beat together the chestnut purée, icing sugar and brandy until smooth, then fold in the cream. Spread over the roulade and roll it up. Top with chocolate curls and dust with icing sugar.

Apricot Roulade Energy 3674Kcal/15272kJ; Protein 69.4g; Carbohydrate 208.1g, of which sugars 193.9g; Fat 291.3g, of which saturates 114.1g; Cholesterol 1172mg; Calcium 809mg; Fibre 14.7g; Sodium 511mg.
Chocolate Roulade Energy 3752kcal/15688kJ; Protein 49g; Carbohydrate 428g, of which sugars 359g; Fat 217g, of which saturates 121g; Cholesterol 1304mg; Calcium 544mg; Fibre 13.6g; Sodium 456mg.

Stollen

Stollen is a fruity yeast bread traditionally served at Christmas time.

Makes one loaf

150ml/¼ pint/⅔ cup lukewarm milk
40g/1½oz/3 tbsp caster (superfine) sugar
10ml/2 tsp easy-blend (rapid-rise) dried yeast
350g/12oz/3 cups plain (all-purpose) flour, plus extra for dusting

1.5ml/¼ tsp salt
115g/4oz/½ cup butter, softened
1 egg, beaten
50g/2oz seedless raisins
25g/1oz cup sultanas (golden raisins)
40g/1½oz/⅓ cup candied orange peel, chopped
25g/1oz/¼ cup blanched almonds, chopped
5ml/1 tbsp rum
40g/1½oz/3 tbsp butter, melted
50g/2oz/½ cup icing (confectioners') sugar

1 Mix together the warm milk, sugar and yeast and leave it in a warm place until it is frothy.

2 Sift together the flour and salt, make a well in the centre and pour on the yeast mixture. Add the softened butter and egg and mix to form a soft dough. Mix in the raisins, sultanas, peel and almonds and sprinkle on the rum. Knead the dough on a lightly floured board until it is pliable.

3 Place the dough in a large, greased mixing bowl, cover it with baking parchment and set it aside in a warm place for about 2 hours, until it has doubled in size.

4 Turn the dough out on to a floured board and knead it lightly until it is smooth and elastic again. Shape the dough to a rectangle about 25 × 20cm/10 × 8in. Fold the dough over along one of the long sides and press the two layers together. Cover the loaf and leave it to stand for 20 minutes.

5 Heat the oven to 200°C/400°F/Gas 6. Bake the loaf in the oven for 25–30 minutes, until it is well risen. Allow it to cool slightly on the baking sheet, then brush it with melted butter. Sift the sugar over the top and transfer the loaf to a wire rack to cool. Serve the stollen in thin slices.

Vegan Christmas Cake

As it contains neither eggs nor dairy products, this cake is suitable for vegans and will prove to be a real treat at Christmas.

Makes one 20cm/8in square cake

350g/12oz/3 cups plain (all-purpose) wholemeal (whole-wheat) flour
5ml/1 tsp mixed (apple pie) spice
175g/6oz/¾ cup soya margarine
175g/6oz/¾ cup muscovado (molasses) sugar, plus 30ml/2 tbsp
175g/6oz/generous 1 cup sultanas (golden raisins)
175g/6oz/¾ cup currants
175g/6oz/generous 1 cup raisins

75g/3oz/½ cup mixed chopped (candied) peel
150g/5oz/generous ½ cup glacé (candied) cherries, halved
finely grated rind of 1 orange
30ml/2 tbsp ground almonds
25g/1oz/¼ cup chopped blanched almonds
5ml/1 tsp bicarbonate of soda (baking soda)
120ml/4fl oz/½ cup soya milk
75ml/2½fl oz/⅓ cup sunflower oil
30ml/2 tbsp malt vinegar

To decorate
mixed nuts
glacé (candied) cherries
angelica
60ml/4 tbsp clear honey, warmed

1 Preheat the oven to 150°C/300°F/Gas 2. Grease a deep 20cm/8in square loose-based cake tin (pan) and double-line with baking parchment.

2 Sift together the flour and mixed spice in a large mixing bowl. Rub in the soya margarine. Stir in the sugar, sultanas, currants and raisins, mixed peel, cherries, orange rind, ground almonds and blanched almonds.

3 Dissolve the bicarbonate of soda in a little of the milk. Warm the remaining milk with the oil and vinegar, and add the bicarbonate of soda mixture. Stir into the flour mixture.

4 Spoon into the tin and smooth the surface. Bake for about 2½ hours, until a skewer inserted in the centre comes out clean. Leave in the tin for 5 minutes, then turn out and cool on a wire rack. Decorate with the nuts, cherries and angelica, and brush with the warmed honey to glaze the cake.

Vegan Cake Energy 6098kcal/25669kJ; Protein 74.3g; Carbohydrate 977.4g, of which sugars 759.6g; Fat 236.7g, of which saturates 38.2g; Cholesterol 12mg; Calcium 1047mg; Fibre 55.6g; Sodium 2160mg.
Stollen Energy 3828kcal/16064kJ; Protein 55.8g; Carbohydrate 511.7g, of which sugars 256.5g; Fat 178.8g, of which saturates 95.2g; Cholesterol 393mg; Calcium 1064mg; Fibre 21.5g; Sodium 1590mg.

Spiced Christmas Cake

This light cake mixture is flavoured with spices and fruit. It can be served with a dusting of icing sugar and decorated with holly leaves for a festive look.

Makes one 20cm/8in ring cake

225g/8oz/1 cup butter, plus extra for greasing
15g/½oz/1 tbsp fresh white breadcrumbs
225g/8oz/generous 1 cup caster (superfine) sugar
50ml/2fl oz/¼ cup water
3 eggs, separated
225g/8oz/2 cups self-raising (self-rising) flour
7.5g/1½ tsp mixed (apple pie) spice
25g/1oz/2 tbsp chopped angelica
25g/1oz/2 tbsp mixed chopped (candied) peel
50g/2oz/¼ cup chopped glacé (candied) cherries
50g/2oz/½ cup chopped walnuts
icing (confectioners') sugar, for dusting

1 Preheat the oven to 180°C/350°F/Gas 4. Brush a 20cm/8in, 1.5 litre/2½ pint fluted ring mould with melted butter and coat with breadcrumbs, shaking out any excess.

2 Place the butter, sugar and water into a pan. Heat gently, stirring occasionally, until the sugar has dissolved. Boil for 3 minutes until syrupy, then allow to cool.

3 In a clean bowl, whisk until the egg whites until stiff. Sift the flour and spice into another bowl, add the angelica, mixed peel, cherries and walnuts and stir well to mix. Add the egg yolks.

4 Pour the cooled syrup mixture into the bowl and beat to form a soft batter. Gradually fold in the egg whites, until the mixture is evenly blended.

5 Pour the mixture into the prepared mould and bake in the preheated oven for about 50–60 minutes or until the cake springs back when pressed in the centre.

6 Leave the cake in the mould for a few minutes, then turn out and allow to cool on a wire rack. Dust with the icing sugar and decorate with holly leaves to serve.

Moist and Rich Christmas Cake

This festive cake can be made 4–6 weeks ahead.

Makes one 20cm/8in cake

225g/8oz/1⅓ cups sultanas (golden raisins)
225g/8oz/1 cup currants
225g/8oz/1⅓ cups raisins
115g/4oz/1 cup pitted and chopped prunes
50g/2oz/¼ cup halved glacé (candied) cherries
50g/2oz/⅓ cup mixed chopped (candied) peel
45ml/3 tbsp brandy or sherry
225g/8oz/2 cups plain (all-purpose) flour
pinch of salt
2.5ml/½ tsp ground cinnamon
2.5ml/½ tsp grated nutmeg
15ml/1 tbsp unsweetened cocoa powder
225g/8oz/1 cup butter
225g/8oz/1 cup brown sugar
4 large (US extra large) eggs
finely grated rind of 1 orange
50g/2oz/⅔ cup ground almonds
50g/2oz/½ cup chopped almonds

To decorate

60ml/4 tbsp apricot jam, warmed
450g/1lb ready-made almond paste
450g/1lb ready-to-roll fondant icing
225g/8oz ready-made royal icing

1 Put the dried fruits, cherries and peel in a bowl with the brandy or sherry, covered, overnight. The next day, grease a 20cm/8in round cake tin (pan) and line it with baking parchment.

2 Preheat the oven to 160°C/325°F/Gas 3. Sift together the flour, salt, spices and cocoa powder. Whisk the butter and sugar until fluffy and beat in the eggs, then mix in the orange rind, all the almonds, soaked fruits and liquid, and the flour mixture. Spoon into the cake tin and level the top. Bake for 3 hours. Cool in the tin on a wire rack for an hour, then turn out, leaving the paper on. When cold, wrap in foil and store.

3 Strain the apricot jam. Remove the paper from the cake, place on a cake board and brush it with apricot glaze. Cover with almond paste, then fondant icing. Pipe a border around the base of the cake with royal icing. Tie a ribbon around the sides.

4 From the trimmings, make a bell motif, leaves and holly berries. Dry for 24 hours. Attach all to the cake with a dab of royal icing.

Spiced Cake Energy 4813kcal/20022kJ; Protein 88.5g; Carbohydrate 322.9g, of which sugars 277.4g; Fat 355.2g, of which saturates 51.2g; Cholesterol 13mg; Calcium 800mg; Fibre 28.2g; Sodium 497mg.
Moist Rich Cake Energy 8145kcal/34415kJ; Protein 74.4g; Carbohydrate 1528.9g, of which sugars 1385.8g; Fat 204.6g, of which saturates 105.4g; Cholesterol 1154mg; Calcium 1859mg; Fibre 38.1g; Sodium 2326mg.

Gingerbread Family

You can have great fun with these cookies at Christmas by creating characters with different features. To add variation, use plain or milk chocolate for decorating.

Makes about 12
350g/12oz/3 cups plain
 (all-purpose) flour
5ml/1 tsp bicarbonate of soda
 (baking soda)
5ml/1 tsp ground ginger
115g/4oz/½ cup unsalted butter,
 chilled and diced
175g/6oz/scant 1 cup light
 muscovado (brown) sugar
1 egg
30ml/2 tbsp black treacle
 (molasses) or golden
 (light corn) syrup
150g/5oz white chocolate,
 to decorate

1 Preheat the oven to 180°C/350°F/Gas 4. Grease two large baking sheets. Put the flour, bicarbonate of soda, ginger and diced butter into a food processor. Process until the mixture begins to resemble fine breadcrumbs. If necessary, scrape down the sides of the food processor bowl with a wooden spoon or spatula to remove any crumbs that have become stuck to the sides and process a little more.

2 Add the sugar, egg and black treacle or golden syrup to the food processor and process the mixture until it begins to form into a ball. Turn the dough out on to a lightly floured surface, and knead until smooth and pliable.

3 Roll out the dough on a lightly floured surface (you might find it easier to roll half of the dough out at a time). Cut out figures using people-shaped cutters, then transfer to the baking sheets. Re-roll any trimmings and cut out more figures.

4 Bake in the oven for 15 minutes until slightly risen and starting to colour around the edges. Leave for 5 minutes, then transfer to a wire rack to cool.

5 To decorate, put the chocolate into a bowl over a pan of simmering water and heat, stirring, until melted. Spoon the melted chocolate into a paper piping (icing) bag, snip off the tip, then pipe faces and clothes on to the cookies. Leave to set.

Christmas Tree Cookies

These simple cookies are not too rich, and are always popular with children, to make as well as to eat.

Makes 30
175g/6oz/¾ cup unsalted butter,
 at room temperature
275g/10oz/1½ cups caster
 (superfine) sugar
1 egg
1 egg yolk
5ml/1 tsp vanilla extract
grated rind of 1 lemon
1.5ml/¼ tsp salt
275g/10oz/2½ cups plain
 (all-purpose) flour

For decorating (optional)
175g/6oz/1½ cups icing
 (confectioners') sugar
small decorations

1 Preheat the oven to 180°C/350°F/Gas 4. With an electric mixer, cream the butter until soft. Add the sugar gradually and continue beating until the mixture is light and fluffy.

2 Using a wooden spoon, gradually beat in the whole egg and the egg yolk. Add the vanilla extract, lemon rind and salt. Stir to mix well. Gradually add the flour, stirring between each addition, until blended.

3 Gather the mixture into a ball, wrap in baking parchment and chill for 30 minutes.

4 On a floured surface, carefully roll out the mixture until it is about 3mm/⅛in thick. Stamp out shapes with a Christmas tree cutter.

5 Bake the cookies for about 8 minutes, or until they are lightly coloured. Using a spatula, transfer them to a wire rack and leave to cool completely. The cookies can be left plain, or iced and decorated.

6 To ice the cookies, mix the icing sugar with enough water to make a thick icing consistency.

7 Fill a piping (icing) bag fitted with a fine nozzle with the icing and pipe dots, lines and patterns on to the cookies. Finish with small decorations such as edible silver balls.

Gingerbread Family Energy 305kcal/1281kJ; Protein 4.1g; Carbohydrate 47.6g, of which sugars 25.2g; Fat 12.2g, of which saturates 7.3g; Cholesterol 37mg; Calcium 71mg; Fibre 1.2g; Sodium 71mg.
Christmas Cookies Energy 118kcal/495kJ; Protein 1.3g; Carbohydrate 17.3g, of which sugars 10.1g; Fat 5.3g, of which saturates 3.2g; Cholesterol 26mg; Calcium 21mg; Fibre 0.3g; Sodium 39mg.

Apple and Elderflower Stars

These delicious, crumbly apple cookies are topped with a sweet yet very sharp icing. Packaged in a pretty box, they would make a delightful festive gift for someone special.

Makes 18
115g/4oz/½ cup unsalted butter, at room temperature, diced
75g/3oz/scant ½ cup caster (superfine) sugar
2.5ml/½ tsp mixed (apple pie) spice

1 large (US extra large) egg yolk
25g/1oz dried apple rings, finely chopped
200g/7oz/1¾ cups self-raising (self-rising) flour
5–10ml/1–2 tsp milk, if necessary

For the topping
200g/7oz/1¾ cups icing (confectioners') sugar, sifted
60–90ml/4–6 tbsp elderflower cordial
sugar, for sprinkling

1 Preheat the oven to 190°C/375°F/Gas 5. Cream together the butter and sugar until light and fluffy.

2 Beat the mixed spice and egg yolk into the butter and sugar. Add the chopped apple and flour and stir together. The mixture should form a stiff dough but if it is too dry, add some milk.

3 Roll the dough out on a lightly floured surface to a 5mm/¼in thickness. Draw a five-pointed star on cardboard. Cut out and use as a template for the cookies. Alternatively, use a star biscuit (cookie) cutter.

4 Place the cookies on non-stick baking sheets and bake for about 10–15 minutes, or until just beginning to brown around the edges. Carefully transfer the cookies to a wire rack to cool.

5 Meanwhile, make the topping. Sift the icing sugar into a bowl and add just enough elderflower cordial to mix the icing to a thick but pourable consistency.

6 When the cookies are cold, trickle the icing over them in a random crisscross pattern. Sprinkle them with a little sugar and leave to set.

Festive Holly Cookies

Dainty, hand-painted cookies look delightful served at Christmas. These are great fun for children to make as presents, and any shape of cookie cutter can be used.

Makes about 12
75g/3oz/6 tbsp butter
50g/2oz/½ cup icing (confectioners') sugar

finely grated rind of 1 small lemon
1 egg yolk
175g/6oz/1½ cups plain (all-purpose) flour
a pinch of salt

To decorate
2 egg yolks
red and green food colouring

1 Beat the butter, icing sugar and lemon rind together until pale and fluffy. Beat in the egg yolk, and then sift in the flour and salt. Knead together to form a smooth dough. Wrap and chill in the refrigerator for 30 minutes.

2 Preheat the oven to 190°C/375°F/Gas 5 and lightly grease two large baking sheets.

3 On a lightly floured surface, roll out the dough to 3mm/⅛in thick. Using a 6cm/2½in fluted cutter, stamp out as many cookies as you can, with the cutter dipped in flour to prevent it from sticking to the dough.

4 Transfer the cookies to the prepared baking sheets. Mark the tops lightly with a 2.5cm/1in holly leaf cutter and use a 5mm/¼in plain piping (icing) nozzle for the berries. Chill for 10 minutes, until firm.

5 Meanwhile, to make the decoration, put each egg yolk into a small cup. Mix red food colouring into one and green food colouring into the other. Using a small, clean paintbrush, carefully paint the colours on to the cookies.

6 Bake the cookies in the preheated oven for 10–12 minutes, or until they begin to colour around the edges. Let them cool slightly on the baking sheets, then carefully transfer them to a wire rack to cool completely.

Apple Stars Energy 157kcal/659kJ; Protein 1.4g; Carbohydrate 26.6g, of which sugars 18.1g; Fat 5.7g, of which saturates 3.4g; Cholesterol 25mg; Calcium 27mg; Fibre 0.4g; Sodium 42mg.
Festive Holly Cookies Energy 118kcal/494kJ; Protein 1.7g; Carbohydrate 15.7g, of which sugars 4.6g; Fat 5.8g, of which saturates 3.4g; Cholesterol 30mg; Calcium 26mg; Fibre 0.5g; Sodium 39mg.

Macaroons

These little macaroons can be served as petits fours with coffee after a special festive feast or other meal. Dust with icing sugar or unsweetened cocoa powder before serving.

Makes 30

50g/2oz/²/₃ cup ground almonds
50g/2oz/¹/₄ cup caster
 (superfine) sugar
15ml/1 tbsp cornflour
 (cornstarch)
1.5–2.5ml/¹/₄–¹/₂ tsp
 almond extract
1 egg white, whisked
15 flaked (sliced) almonds
4 glacé (candied) cherries, cut
 into quarters
icing (confectioners') sugar or
 unsweetened cocoa powder,
 to dust

1 Preheat the oven to 160°C/325°F/ Gas 3. Line two baking sheets with baking parchment.

2 Place the ground almonds, sugar, cornflour and almond extract into a large mixing bowl and mix together well to combine, using a wooden spoon.

3 Stir just enough egg white into the bowl with the other ingredients to form a soft piping consistency.

4 Place the mixture into a nylon piping (icing) bag fitted with a 1cm/¹/₂in plain piping nozzle.

5 Pipe about 15 rounds of the mixture on to each prepared baking sheet, spaced well apart to allow for any spreading while they are cooking in the oven.

6 Press a flaked almond on to half the macaroons and glacé cherries on to the remainder. Bake for 10–15 minutes.

Variation
You can make chocolate-flavoured macaroons, if you prefer. Simply replace the cornflour (cornstarch) with the same amount of unsweetened cocoa powder.

Truffle Christmas Puddings

Truffles disguised as Christmas puddings are great fun both to make and receive. Make any flavour truffles, and decorate them as you like.

Makes 20

15ml/1 tbsp unsweetened
 cocoa powder
15ml/1 tbsp icing
 (confectioners') sugar
20 plain (semisweet)
 chocolate truffles
225g/8oz/1 cup white
 chocolate chips, melted
50g/2oz/¹/₄ cup white marzipan
green and red food colourings
yellow food colouring dust

1 Sift the cocoa powder and icing sugar together in a bowl and use it to coat the chocolate truffles.

2 Spread two-thirds of the white chocolate over a piece of non-stick baking paper. Using a small daisy cutter, stamp out 20 rounds. Place a truffle on the centre of each daisy shape, secured with a little of the reserved melted chocolate.

3 Colour two-thirds of the marzipan green and one-third red using the food colourings. Roll out the green marzipan thinly and stamp out 40 leaves, using a tiny holly leaf cutter. Mark the veins with a sharp knife.

4 Mould lots of tiny red beads. Colour the remaining white chocolate with yellow food colouring dust and place in a paper piping (icing) bag. Fold down the top, cut off the tip and pipe the marzipan over the top of each truffle to resemble custard.

5 Arrange the holly leaves and berries on the top of the puddings. When the truffle puddings have set, arrange them in gift boxes, label and tie with ribbon.

Cook's Tip
These little truffles are fun to make at home and children will love to help. They may be able to coat the truffles, do some stamping, or pack the finished puddings in a box as a present.

Macaroons Energy 102kcal/426kJ; Protein 2.8g; Carbohydrate 7.8g, of which sugars 7.5g; Fat 6.9g, of which saturates 0.6g; Cholesterol 13mg; Calcium 33mg; Fibre 0.9g; Sodium 5mg.
Truffle Christmas Puddings Energy 148kcal/616kJ; Protein 1.3g; Carbohydrate 11.9g, of which sugars 10.3g; Fat 10.5g, of which saturates 6.2g; Cholesterol 22mg; Calcium 19mg; Fibre 0.5g; Sodium 31mg.

Christmas Tree Angels

Why not make these charming edible decorations to brighten your Yuletide?

Makes 20–30

90g/3¹/₂oz/scant ¹/₂ cup demerara (raw) sugar
200g/7oz/scant 1 cup golden (light corn) syrup
5ml/1 tsp ground ginger
5ml/1 tsp ground cinnamon
1.5ml/¹/₄ tsp ground cloves
115g/4oz/¹/₂ cup unsalted butter, cut into pieces
10ml/2 tsp bicarbonate of soda (baking soda)
1 egg, beaten
500g/1¹/₄lb/4¹/₂ cups plain (all-purpose) flour, sifted

For the decoration

1 egg white
175–225g/6–8oz/1¹/₂–2 cups icing (confectioners') sugar, sifted
silver and gold balls
fine ribbon

1 Preheat the oven to 160°C/325°F/Gas 3. Line two baking sheets with baking parchment. Bring the demerara sugar, syrup, ginger, cinnamon and cloves to the boil over low heat, stirring constantly. Remove from the heat.

2 Put the butter in a bowl and add the sugar mixture. Add the bicarbonate of soda and stir until the butter has melted. Beat in the egg, then stir in the flour. Mix, then knead to form a dough.

3 Divide the dough into four and roll out between sheets of baking parchment, to a thickness of 3mm/¹/₈in. To make angels, stamp out rounds using a plain cutter. Cut off two segments from either side of the round to give a body and wings. Place the wings, rounded side down, behind the body and press.

4 Roll a small piece of dough for the head, place at the top of the body and flatten. Make a wide hole in the cookies for threading ribbon. Place on the sheets. Bake for 10–15 minutes until golden brown. Transfer to a wire rack to cool.

5 For the decoration, beat the egg white with a fork. Whisk in the sugar until it forms soft peaks. Put the icing in a piping (icing) bag fitted with a small nozzle and decorate the cookies. Add silver and gold balls. Finally, thread the ribbon.

Christmas Star Cookies

These spiced biscuits may be used as edible festive decorations: thread them with coloured ribbon and hang on the branches of the Christmas tree.

Makes 30

50g/2oz/¹/₄ cup butter
15ml/1 tbsp golden (light corn) syrup or clear honey
50g/2oz/¹/₄ cup soft light brown sugar
225g/8oz/2 cups plain (all-purpose) flour
10ml/2 tsp ground cinnamon
5ml/1 tsp ground ginger
1.5ml/¹/₄ tsp grated nutmeg
2.5ml/¹/₂ tsp bicarbonate of soda (baking soda)
45ml/3 tbsp milk
1 egg yolk
30ml/2 tbsp sugar crystals

1 Preheat the oven to 180°C/350°F/Gas 4. Line two baking sheets with baking parchment. Melt the butter, syrup or honey and brown sugar in a pan. Leave to cool for 5 minutes.

2 Sift the flour, cinnamon, ginger, nutmeg and bicarbonate of soda into a bowl. Make a well in the centre. Pour in the melted butter mixture, milk and egg yolk. Mix to a soft dough.

3 Knead the dough until smooth, then roll out between two sheets of baking parchment until 5mm/¹/₄in thick. Stamp out stars using biscuit (cookie) cutters.

4 Place the cookies on the baking sheets. Make a hole in each with a skewer if you wish to hang them up later. Sprinkle with coloured sugar crystals.

5 Bake in the preheated oven for 10 minutes, until a slightly darker shade. Cool slightly on the baking sheets, then transfer to a wire rack and leave to cool completely.

Cook's Tip
Roll out the dough while it is still warm, since it becomes hard and quite brittle as it cools.

Christmas Tree Angels Energy 147kcal/622kJ; Protein 1.9g; Carbohydrate 28.7g, of which sugars 16g; Fat 3.6g, of which saturates 2.1g; Cholesterol 15mg; Calcium 31mg; Fibre 0.5g; Sodium 45mg.
Star Cookies Energy 118kcal/495kJ; Protein 1.3g; Carbohydrate 17.3g, of which sugars 10.1g; Fat 5.3g, of which saturates 3.2g; Cholesterol 26mg; Calcium 21mg; Fibre 0.3g; Sodium 39mg.

Orange, Mint and Coffee Meringues

These tiny, crisp meringues are flavoured with orange, coffee and mint chocolate sticks and liqueurs. Pile them into dry, airtight glass jars or decorative tins for a festive gift.

Makes 90
25g/1oz/8 chocolate mint sticks
25g/1oz/8 chocolate orange sticks
25g/1oz/8 chocolate coffee sticks
2.5ml/½ tsp crème de menthe
2.5ml/½ tsp orange curaçao
  or Cointreau
2.5ml/½ tsp Tia Maria
3 egg whites
175g/6oz/¾ cup caster
  (superfine) sugar
5ml/1 tsp unsweetened
  cocoa powder

1 Preheat the oven to 110°C/225°F/Gas ¼. Line two or three baking sheets with baking parchment.

2 Chop each flavour of chocolate stick separately and place each into separate bowls, retaining a teaspoonful of each flavour of stick. Stir in the liquid flavourings to match the flavour of the chocolate sticks in the bowls.

3 Place the egg whites in a clean bowl and whisk until stiff. Gradually add the sugar, whisking well until thick.

4 Add one-third of the meringue to each bowl and fold in gently, using a clean spatula, until evenly blended.

5 Place about 30 teaspoons of each mixture on to the baking sheets, spaced apart. Sprinkle the top of each meringue with the reserved chopped chocolate sticks.

6 Bake in the preheated oven for 1 hour or until crisp. Leave to cool, then dust with the cocoa powder.

Cook's Tip
These little meringues are ideal served with coffee after a festive dinner party. Alternatively, they make an original topping

Vanilla Christmas Biscuits

These heart-shaped treats are a traditional Christmas favourite in Norway. They are not only ideal with a cup of tea or coffee but are delicious when served to accompany a dessert such as fruit salad. A little box of them wrapped with a big red bow also makes a delightful present.

Makes about 24
225g/8oz/2 cups plain
  (all-purpose) flour
5ml/1 tsp baking powder
150g/5oz/10 tbsp butter,
  at room temperature
90g/3½oz/½ cup caster
  (superfine) sugar
1 egg, lightly beaten
7.5ml/1½ tsp vanilla extract
120ml/4fl oz/½ cup milk

1 Sift the flour and baking powder together in a large mixing bowl. Put the butter and sugar in a separate large bowl and beat together until light and fluffy.

2 Add the egg and vanilla extract, then add the milk, alternating it with the sifted flour mixture. Mix together, then knead the dough lightly. Chill in the refrigerator for 30 minutes.

3 Preheat the oven to 180°C/350°F/Gas 4. Butter a large baking tray. Transfer the dough to a lightly floured surface and roll it out to 1cm/½in thickness.

4 Using a heart-shaped cutter, cut out hearts from the dough and place on the prepared baking tray. Bring the trimmings together, knead the dough lightly, roll out again and cut out more hearts.

5 Bake the biscuits (cookies) for about 10 minutes until lightly golden brown. Leave on the tray for 2–3 minutes, then transfer to a wire rack and leave to cool.

Cook's Tip
A pretty finish to the biscuits (cookies) could be provided by brushing the hearts with lightly beaten egg white and sprinkling

Orange Meringues Energy 13kcal/54kJ; Protein 0.2g; Carbohydrate 2.6g, of which sugars 2.6g; Fat 0.3g, of which saturates 0.1g; Cholesterol 0mg; Calcium 1mg; Fibre 0g; Sodium 3mg.
Vanilla Biscuits Energy 100kcal/420kJ; Protein 1.4g; Carbohydrate 11.9g, of which sugars 4.8g; Fat 5.6g, of which saturates 3.4g; Cholesterol 22mg; Calcium 24mg; Fibre 0.3g; Sodium 43mg.

Lebkuchen

These sweet and spicy cakes are traditionally baked at Christmas, and are packed with festive flavours.

Makes about 20

115g/4oz/1 cup blanched almonds, finely chopped
50g/2oz/⅓ cup candied orange peel, finely chopped
finely grated rind of ½ lemon
3 cardamom pods
5ml/1 tsp ground cinnamon
1.5ml/¼ tsp grated nutmeg
1.5ml/¼ tsp ground cloves
2 eggs
115g/4oz/generous ½ cup caster (superfine) sugar
150g/5oz/1¼ cups plain (all-purpose) flour
2.5ml/½ tsp baking powder
rice paper (optional)

For the icing
½ egg white
75g/3oz/⅔ cup icing (confectioners') sugar, sifted
5ml/1 tsp white rum

1 Preheat the oven to 180°C/350°F/Gas 4. Set aside some of the almonds for sprinkling and put the remainder in a bowl with the candied orange peel and lemon rind.

2 Remove the black seeds from the cardamom pods and crush using a mortar and pestle. Add to the bowl with the cinnamon, nutmeg and cloves and mix well.

3 Whisk the eggs and sugar in a mixing bowl until thick and foamy. Sift in the flour and baking powder, then gently fold into the eggs before adding to the nut and spice mixture.

4 Spoon dessertspoons of the mixture on to sheets of rice paper, if using, or baking parchment placed on baking sheets, allowing room for spreading. Sprinkle over the reserved almonds.

5 Bake for 20 minutes, until golden. Allow to cool for a few minutes, then break off the surplus rice paper or remove the biscuits from the baking parchment and cool on a wire rack.

6 Put the egg white for the icing in a bowl and lightly whisk with a fork. Stir in a little of the icing sugar at a time, then add the rum. Drizzle over the lebkuchen and leave to set. Keep in an airtight container for up to 2 weeks before serving.

Orange Shortbread Fingers

These are a real tea-time treat at Christmas. The fingers will keep in an airtight container for up to two weeks, meaning you will have some to offer your guests throughout the festive period – as long as you make plenty of them in the first place.

Makes 18

115g/4oz/½ cup unsalted butter, softened
50g/2oz/4 tbsp caster (superfine) sugar, plus a little extra for sprinkling
finely grated rind of 2 oranges
175g/6oz/1½ cups plain (all-purpose) flour

1 Preheat the oven to 190°C/375°F/Gas 5. In a bowl, beat the butter and sugar together until they are soft and creamy.

2 Beat the orange rind into the butter and sugar mixture. Gradually sift in the flour and gently pull the dough together with your hands to form a soft ball.

3 Transfer the dough on to a lightly floured surface and roll it out to about 1cm/½in thick.

4 Cut the dough into 18 fingers with a sharp knife. Sprinkle over a little extra sugar, prick with a fork and bake for 20 minutes, or until the fingers are a light golden colour.

> **Cook's Tip**
> *This recipe is the ideal life-saver for busy cooks at Christmas time. It is a good idea to make extra dough and store it, well wrapped in clear film (plastic wrap), in the refrigerator. When guests arrive unexpectedly over the festive period, you will be able to make up freshly baked fingers in minutes.*

> **Variation**
> *You can cut the dough into whatever shapes you choose. There are also moulds available in attractive designs.*

Lebkuchen Energy 105kcal/444kJ; Protein 2.4g; Carbohydrate 16.3g, of which sugars 11.7g; Fat 3.9g, of which saturates 0.4g; Cholesterol 19mg; Calcium 33mg; Fibre 0.7g; Sodium 16mg.
Orange Shortbread Fingers Energy 92kcal/383kJ; Protein 1g; Carbohydrate 10.5g, of which sugars 3.1g; Fat 5.4g, of which saturates 3.4g; Cholesterol 14mg; Calcium 16mg; Fibre 0.3g; Sodium 39mg.

Glacé Fruits

These sweetmeats are very popular at Christmas. Choose one type or select a variety of fruits.

Makes 24 pieces
450g/1lb fruit
1kg/2¼lb/4½ cups sugar
115g/4oz/1 cup powdered glucose

1 Remove any stones (pits) from stone fruit. Peel and core pineapple and cut into cubes or rings. Peel, core and quarter apples and thinly slice citrus fruits.

2 Place enough fruit in a pan to cover the base. Add water to cover and simmer until almost tender. Repeat, then transfer the fruit to a dish, reserving the liquid and removing any skins.

3 Measure 300ml/½ pint/1¼ cups of the liquid, or make up this quantity with water if necessary. Pour into the pan and add 50g/2oz/4 tbsp sugar and the glucose. Heat gently, stirring occasionally, until dissolved. Bring to the boil and pour over the fruit in the dish, completely immersing it, and leave overnight.

4 DAY 2. Drain the syrup into the pan and add 50g/2oz/4 tbsp sugar. Dissolve the sugar and bring to the boil. Pour over the fruit and leave overnight. Repeat this process each day, draining off the syrup, dissolving 50g/2oz/4 tbsp sugar, boiling the syrup and immersing the fruit. Leave overnight on Days 3, 4, 5, 6 and 7.

5 DAY 8. Drain the fruit, dissolve 75g/3oz/½ cup sugar in the syrup and bring to the boil. Add the fruit and cook gently for 3 minutes. Return to the dish and leave for 2 days. DAY 10. Repeat as for Day 8. The syrup should now look like honey. Leave in the dish for at least 10 days, or up to 3 weeks.

6 Arrange the fruits on a wire rack. Dry the fruit in a warm, dry place until they no longer feel sticky. To coat in sugar, spear each piece of fruit and plunge into boiling water, then roll in sugar. To dip into syrup, place the remaining sugar and 175ml/6fl oz/¾ cup of water in a pan. Heat until the sugar has dissolved, then boil for 1 minute. Dip each piece of fruit into boiling water, then quickly into the syrup. Place on the rack and leave in a warm place until dry. Place in small paper cases and pack into boxes.

Chocolate Citrus Candies

Home-candied peel makes a superb sweetmeat, especially when dipped in chocolate. You can also use bought candied peel for this recipe, but make sure it is the very best quality.

Makes about 100g/4oz petits fours
1 orange or 2 lemons
25g/1oz/2 tbsp sugar
about 50g/2oz good quality plain (semisweet) chocolate

1 Using a vegetable knife, peel the rind from the fruit, without taking too much of the pith. Slice into matchsticks.

2 Blanch in boiling water for 4–5 minutes, until beginning to soften, then refresh under cold water and drain thoroughly.

3 In a small pan, heat the sugar and 30ml/2 tbsp water gently together until the sugar has dissolved.

4 Add the strips of rind and simmer for about 8–10 minutes, or until the water has evaporated and the peel is transparent.

5 Lift out the peel with a slotted spoon and spread out on baking parchment to cool. When cold the peel can be stored in an airtight container for up to 2 days before using, if required.

6 To coat, melt the chocolate carefully in a double boiler or in a bowl over a pan of hot water. Spear each piece of peel on to a cocktail stick (toothpick) and dip one end into the chocolate.

7 To dry the candies, stick the cocktail sticks into a large potato. When the chocolate is completely dry, remove the sticks and then arrange the citrus candies attractively on a dish to serve after dinner or with drinks.

> **Variation**
> *A mixture of the three types – chocolate- and sugar-coated peel, and ginger – makes an attractive selection of sweet nibbles for a special occasion such as Christmas.*

Chocolate Candies Energy 438kcal/1845kJ; Protein 4.4g; Carbohydrate 74g, of which sugars 72.6g; Fat 15.8g, of which saturates 8.9g; Cholesterol 15mg; Calcium 208mg; Fibre 3.6g; Sodium 270mg.
Glacé Fruits Energy 18kcal/78kJ; Protein 0g; Carbohydrate 4.8g, of which sugars 4.8g; Fat 0g, of which saturates 0g; Cholesterol 0mg; Calcium 2mg; Fibre 0g; Sodium 0mg.

Champagne Truffles

Real gold dust has been used for an opulent and festive look to these truffles.

Makes 50

250g/9oz dark (bittersweet) chocolate (70% cocoa solids), chopped or broken
200g/7oz milk chocolate (40% cocoa solids), chopped
150ml/¼ pint/⅔ cup double (heavy) cream
50g/2oz unsalted butter
100ml/3½fl oz/scant ½ cup champagne or other sparkling wine
15ml/1 tbsp brandy
700g/1lb 10oz dark chocolate (70% cocoa solids)
icing (confectioners') sugar for rolling
edible gold dust (optional)

1 Butter a 20cm/8in square baking tin (pan) and line with clear film (plastic wrap). Line a baking sheet with baking parchment. Put the dark and milk chocolate in a heatproof bowl. Set aside.

2 Put the cream and butter in a heavy pan and heat to just under a boil over medium heat. Pour over the chocolate and leave for a minute before adding the champagne and brandy. Whisk by hand until all the chocolate is melted and you have a smooth ganache. Pour into the tin. Leave to firm up.

3 To form the truffles, scrape the ganache up into a piping (icing) bag fitted with a 1cm/½in plain nozzle. Pipe out even little blobs on to the lined baking sheet. Place in the refrigerator for about 20 minutes or until firm. Dust your hands with icing sugar and roll the blobs into balls. Chill for 10 minutes, until firm.

4 Line another baking sheet with parchment paper. Using a dipping fork, dunk each ball of ganache into the dark chocolate and place it on a cooling rack to set.

5 Dip a clean, dry pastry brush into the pot of gold dust. Hold it over the truffles and tap the handle to release the dust and allow it to fall evenly over the truffles. Serve immediately or store the truffles in the refrigerator in an airtight container. Remove from the refrigerator at least 30 minutes before serving, as chocolate should be eaten at room temperature.

Chocolate Christmas Cups

These festive treats are a perfect way of using up any Christmas pudding left-overs.

Makes 30–35

275g/10oz/2½ cups plain (semisweet) chocolate, broken into pieces
70–80 foil or paper sweet (candy) cases
175g/6oz cooked, cold Christmas pudding
75ml/2½fl oz/⅓ cup brandy or whisky
chocolate holly leaves and crystallized cranberries, to decorate

1 Place the chocolate in a bowl over a pan of barely simmering water until it melts, stirring until smooth. Using a pastry brush, coat melted chocolate on to the inside of about 35 sweet (candy) cases. Allow to set, then apply a second coat, reheating the chocolate if necessary. Leave for 4–5 hours to set. Reserve the remaining chocolate.

2 Crumble the cooked Christmas pudding into a small bowl. Sprinkle with brandy or whisky and leave to stand for about 30–40 minutes, until the brandy or whisky has been absorbed by the pudding crumbs.

3 Spoon a little of the pudding mixture into each chocolate cup, smoothing the top. Reheat the remaining chocolate and spoon over the top of each cup to cover the surface right to the edge. Leave to set.

4 When the chocolate cups are completely set, carefully peel off the sweet cases and replace them with clean ones. Decorate the tops of the cups with chocolate holly leaves and crystallized cranberries.

> **Cook's Tip**
> To crystallize cranberries, beat an egg white until frothy; dip each cranberry in the egg white, then in caster (superfine) sugar. Place the coated cranberries on sheets of baking parchment and leave until dry.

Champagne Truffles Energy 144kcal/601kJ; Protein 1.3g; Carbohydrate 14.8g, of which sugars 13.7g; Fat 9.2g, of which saturates 5.4g; Cholesterol 9mg; Calcium 18mg; Fibre 0g; Sodium 16mg.
Chocolate Christmas Cups Energy 59kcal/249kJ; Protein 0.6g; Carbohydrate 7.5g, of which sugars 6.6g; Fat 2.7g, of which saturates 1.3g; Cholesterol 0mg; Calcium 7mg; Fibre 0.3g; Sodium 10mg.

Piccalilli

The piquancy of this relish partners well with sausages, as well as with most bacon or ham dishes.

Makes 3 × 450g/1lb jars
675g/1½lb cauliflower
450g/1lb baby (pearl) onions
350g/12oz/2 cups French
    (green) beans
5ml/1 tsp ground turmeric
5ml/1 tsp dry mustard powder
10ml/2 tsp cornflour (cornstarch)
600ml/1 pint/2½ cups
    cider vinegar

1 Cut the cauliflower into tiny florets. Peel the onions and top and tail the French beans.

2 In a small pan, measure in the turmeric, mustard powder and cornflour. Pour the vinegar into the pan. Stir well and simmer for 10 minutes over low heat.

3 Pour the vinegar mixture over the vegetables in a large pan, mix well and simmer for 45 minutes.

4 Carefully pour the piccalilli into sterilized jars. Seal each jar with a wax disc and a tightly fitting cellophane top. Store the jars in a cool, dark place. The piccalilli will keep well, in unopened jars, for up to a year.

> **Cook's Tips**
> • *Piccalilli is perfect for serving with slices of Christmas ham or left-over turkey for a quick festive lunch.*
> • *Once opened, store the piccalilli in the refrigerator and consume within one week.*

> **Variation**
> *Other vegetables can be used in this relish. Try adding some chopped courgettes (zucchini). Fruit such as chopped pears also goes well in this condiment. Simply cook any extra ingredients with the other vegetables in the vinegar as above.*

Christmas Chutney

This savoury mixture of spices and dried fruit takes its inspiration from mincemeat, and makes a delicious addition to a buffet during the holidays.

Makes 900g–1.5 kg/2–3½lb
450g/1lb cooking apples, peeled, cored and chopped
500g/1¼lb/3 cups luxury mixed
    dried fruit
grated rind of 1 orange
30ml/2 tbsp mixed
    (apple pie) spice
150ml/¼ pint/⅔ cup
    cider vinegar
350g/12oz/1½ cups soft light
    brown sugar

1 Place the chopped apples, dried fruit and grated orange rind in a large, heavy pan.

2 Stir in the mixed spice, vinegar and sugar. Heat gently, stirring until all the sugar has dissolved.

3 Bring the mixture to the boil, then lower the heat and simmer for about 40–45 minutes, stirring occasionally, until the mixture has thickened.

4 Ladle the chutney into warm sterilized jars, cover and seal. Keep for 1 month before using.

> **Cook's Tip**
> *Watch the chutney carefully towards the end of the cooking time, as it has a tendency to catch on the bottom of the pan. Stir frequently at this stage.*

> **Variation**
> *If you like, you can use a combination of apples and pears in this recipe. There is a glut of both these fruits over the festive season when they are at their best, so it is an ideal time to make this recipe. Simply replace half the quantity of the apples in the recipe with pears.*

Piccalilli Energy 453kcal/1919kJ; Protein 11.4g; Carbohydrate 100.3g, of which sugars 88.7g; Fat 4g, of which saturates 0.4g; Cholesterol 0mg; Calcium 185mg; Fibre 6.9g; Sodium 1337mg.
Chutney Energy 1299kcal/5525kJ; Protein 10.9g; Carbohydrate 299.5g, of which sugars 297.7g; Fat 14.9g, of which saturates 1.1g; Cholesterol 0mg; Calcium 254mg; Fibre 10.4g; Sodium 3974mg.

Cranberry and Red Onion Relish

This wine-enriched relish is perfect for serving with hot roast game at a celebratory meal. It is also good served with cold meats or stirred into a beef or game casserole for a touch of sweetness. It can be made several months in advance.

Makes about 900g/2lb

450g/1lb small red onions
30ml/2 tbsp olive oil

225g/8oz/generous 1 cup soft
   light brown sugar
450g/1lb/4 cups cranberries
120ml/4fl oz/½ cup red
   wine vinegar
120ml/4fl oz/½ cup red wine
15ml/1 tbsp yellow
   mustard seeds
2.5ml/½ tsp ground ginger
30ml/2 tbsp orange liqueur
   or port
salt and ground black pepper

1 Halve the red onions and slice them very thinly. Heat the oil in a large pan, add the onions and cook over a very low heat for about 15 minutes, stirring occasionally, until softened.

2 Add 30ml/2 tbsp of the sugar and cook for a further 5 minutes, or until the onions are brown and caramelized.

3 Meanwhile, put the cranberries in another pan with the remaining sugar, and add the vinegar, red wine, mustard seeds and ginger. Stir in well and heat gently, stirring constantly, until the sugar has dissolved, then cover and bring to the boil.

4 Simmer the relish for about 12–15 minutes, then add in the caramelized onions. Stir them into the mixture. Increase the heat slightly and cook the relish uncovered for a further 10 minutes, stirring the mixture frequently, until it is well reduced and nicely thickened.

5 Remove the pan from the heat, then season to taste with salt and pepper. Allow to cool completely before pouring.

6 Transfer the relish to warmed sterilized jars. Spoon a little of the orange liqueur or port over the top of each, then cover and seal. This relish can be stored for up to 6 months. Store in the refrigerator once opened and use within 1 month.

Caramelized Onion Relish

The slow, gentle cooking reduces the onions to a soft, caramelized relish to serve with everything from baked cheese to left-over turkey or ham.

Serves 4

3 large onions
50g/2oz/4 tbsp butter

30ml/2 tbsp olive oil
30ml/2 tbsp light muscovado
   (brown) sugar
30ml/2 tbsp pickled capers
30ml/2 tbsp chopped
   fresh parsley
salt and ground black pepper

1 Peel the onions and halve them vertically, through the core, then slice them thinly.

2 Heat the butter and oil together in a large pan. Add the onions and the sugar and cover the pan with a tight-fitting lid. Cook gently for about 30–40 minutes over very low heat, stirring occasionally, until the onions and sugar have reduced to a soft rich brown caramelized mixture.

3 Roughly chop the capers and stir them into the onions. Allow the mixture to cool completely.

4 Stir in the chopped fresh parsley and season with salt and ground black pepper to taste. Cover and chill in the refrigerator until ready to serve.

> **Cook's Tip**
> When cooking the onions, the heat should be very low to prevent the onions from catching and burning on the bottom of the pan. Using a good-quality heavy pan will also deter this.

> **Variation**
> Try making this recipe with red onions or shallots for a subtle variation in the flavours.

Cranberry Relish Energy 1532kcal/6486kJ; Protein 8g; Carbohydrate 314.6g, of which sugars 304.2g; Fat 23.3g, of which saturates 3.1g; Cholesterol 0mg; Calcium 259mg; Fibre 13.5g; Sodium 46mg.
Caramelized Onion Relish Energy 225kcal/933kJ; Protein 1.9g; Carbohydrate 19.7g, of which sugars 16.3g; Fat 16g, of which saturates 7.5g; Cholesterol 29mg; Calcium 43mg; Fibre 2.1g; Sodium 99mg.

Apple and Sultana Chutney

Use wine or cider vinegar for this chutney to give it a subtle and mellow flavour. For a mild chutney, add only a little cayenne, for a spicier one increase the quantity to taste. The chutney is perfect served with farmhouse cheese and freshly made rustic bread.

Makes about 900g/2lb
350g/12oz cooking apples
115g/4oz/²⁄₃ cup sultanas
  (golden raisins)

50g/2oz onion
25g/1oz/¹⁄₄ cup almonds,
  blanched
5ml/1 tsp white peppercorns
2.5ml/¹⁄₂ tsp coriander seeds
175g/6oz/scant 1 cup sugar
10ml/2 tsp salt
5ml/1 tsp ground ginger
450ml/³⁄₄ pint/scant 2 cups
  cider vinegar
1.5ml/¹⁄₄ tsp cayenne pepper
red chillies (optional)

1 Peel, core and chop the apples. Chop the sultanas, onion and the blanched almonds.

2 Tie the peppercorns and coriander seeds in muslin (cheesecloth), using a long piece of string, and then tie to the handle of a preserving pan or stainless-steel pan.

3 Put the sugar, salt, ground ginger and vinegar into the pan, with the cayenne pepper to taste. Heat gently, stirring, until the sugar has completely dissolved.

4 Add the chopped fruit. Bring to the boil and simmer for 1¹⁄₂–2 hours, or until most of the liquid has evaporated.

5 Spoon into warmed, sterilized jars and place one chilli in each jar, if using. Leave until cold, then cover, seal and label.

Cook's Tip
Store in a cool dark place. The chutney is best left for a month to mature before use and will keep for at least 6 months, if it is correctly stored.

Tomato Chutney

This spicy, dark, sweet-sour chutney is delicious served with a selection of well-flavoured cheeses after a festive feast. It is also popular in sandwiches and chunky rolls packed with cold roast meats such as ham or turkey.

Makes about 1.8kg/4lb
900g/2lb tomatoes, skinned
225g/8oz/1¹⁄₂ cups raisins
225g/8oz onions, chopped
225g/8oz/generous 1 cup caster
  (superfine) sugar
600ml/1 pint/2¹⁄₂ cups malt
  vinegar or red wine vinegar
  or sherry vinegar

1 Chop the tomatoes roughly and place in a preserving pan. Add the raisins, onions and caster sugar.

2 Pour the vinegar into the pan and bring the mixture to the boil over a medium heat. Reduce the heat and simmer for 2 hours, uncovered, until soft and thickened.

3 Transfer the chutney to warmed sterilized jars. Top each jar with waxed discs to prevent moulds from growing. Use good airtight lids, especially if you mean to store them for a long period. Store the jars in a cool, dark place and leave to mature for at least 1 month before use.

Cook's Tip
The chutney will keep unopened for up to 1 year if properly airtight and stored in a cool place. Once the jars have been opened, store in the refrigerator and use within 1 month.

Variations
• Dried dates may be used in place of the raisins. Stone (pit) and chop them into small pieces. You can also buy stoned cooking dates that have been compressed in a block and these will need chopping finely.
• Red wine vinegar or sherry vinegar may be used in place of the malt vinegar, making a more delicate flavour.

Tomato Chutney Energy 1733kcal/7385kJ; Protein 14.9g; Carbohydrate 436.7g, of which sugars 431.6g; Fat 4.1g, of which saturates 0.9g; Cholesterol 0mg; Calcium 342mg; Fibre 16.6g; Sodium 236mg.
Apple Chutney Energy 1299kcal/5525kJ; Protein 10.9g; Carbohydrate 299.5g, of which sugars 297.7g; Fat 14.9g, of which saturates 1.1g; Cholesterol 0mg; Calcium 254mg; Fibre 10.4g; Sodium 3970mg.

Chunky Pear and Walnut Chutney

This chutney recipe is ideal for using up hard windfall pears. Its mellow flavour is well suited to being brought out after a festive dinner with a lovely selection of strong cheeses served with freshly made oatcakes or warm crusty bread.

Makes about 1.8kg/4lb

1.2kg/2½lb firm pears
225g/8oz cooking apples
225g/8oz onions
450ml/¾ pint/scant 2 cups cider vinegar
175g/6oz/ generous 1 cup sultanas (golden raisins)
finely grated rind and juice of 1 orange
400g/14oz/2 cups granulated (white) sugar
115g/4oz/1 cup walnuts, roughly chopped
2.5ml/½ tsp ground cinnamon

1 Peel and core the fruit, then chop into 2.5cm/1in chunks. Peel and quarter the onions, then chop into pieces the same size as the fruit chunks. Place in a large preserving pan with the vinegar.

2 Slowly bring to the boil, then reduce the heat and simmer for 40 minutes, until the apples, pears and onions are tender, stirring the mixture occasionally.

3 Meanwhile, put the sultanas in a small bowl, pour over the orange juice and leave to soak.

4 Add the orange rind, sultanas and orange juice, and the sugar to the pan. Heat gently, stirring constantly, until the sugar has completely dissolved, then leave to simmer for 30–40 minutes, or until the chutney is thick and no excess liquid remains. Stir frequently towards the end of cooking to prevent the chutney from sticking to the base of the pan.

5 Gently toast the walnuts in a non-stick pan over low heat for 5 minutes, stirring frequently, until lightly coloured. Stir the nuts into the chutney with the ground cinnamon.

6 Spoon the chutney into warmed sterilized jars, cover and seal. Store in a cool, dark place and leave to mature for at least 1 month. Use within 1 year.

Cranberry and Claret Jelly

The slight sharpness of cranberries makes this a superb jelly for serving with rich meats such as lamb or game. Together with claret, the cranberries give the jelly a beautifully festive deep red colour.

Makes about 1.2kg/2½lb

900g/2lb/8 cups fresh or frozen cranberries, thawed
350ml/12fl oz/1½ cups water
about 900g/2lb/4½ cups preserving or granulated (white) sugar
250ml/8fl oz/1 cup claret

1 Wash the cranberries, if fresh, and put them in a large heavy pan with the water. Cover the pan and bring to the boil.

2 Reduce the heat under the pan and simmer for about 20 minutes, or until the cranberries are soft.

3 Pour the fruit and juices into a sterilized jelly bag suspended over a large bowl. Leave to drain for at least 3 hours or overnight, until the juices stop dripping.

4 Measure the juice and wine into the cleaned preserving pan, adding 400g/14oz/2 cups preserving or granulated sugar for every 600ml/1 pint/2½ cups liquid.

5 Heat the mixture gently, stirring occasionally, until the sugar has dissolved, then bring to the boil and boil rapidly for about 10 minutes until the jelly reaches setting point (105°C/220°F). Remove the pan from the heat.

6 Skim any scum from the surface using a slotted spoon and pour the jelly into warmed sterilized jars. Cover and seal. Store in a cool, dark place and use within 2 years. Once opened, keep in the refrigerator and eat within 3 months.

> **Cook's Tip**
> When simmering the cranberries, keep the pan covered until they stop 'popping', as they can occasionally explode and jump out of the pan.

Chunky Chutney Energy 3506kcal/14818kJ; Protein 30.9g; Carbohydrate 705.4g, of which sugars 699.5g; Fat 81.4g, of which saturates 6.4g; Cholesterol 0mg; Calcium 634mg; Fibre 40.7g; Sodium 118mg.
Cranberry Jelly Energy 3821kcal/16,290kJ; Protein 5.7g; Carbohydrate 967.7g, of which sugars 967.7g; Fat 0.3g, of which saturates 0g; Cholesterol 0mg; Calcium 506mg; Fibre 4.8g; Sodium 78mg.

Whisky Marmalade

Real home-made marmalade tastes delicious, and flavouring it with whisky makes it a special treat at Christmas time – great for spreading on fresh muffins for breakfast.

Makes 3.6–4.5kg/8–10lb

1.3kg/3lb Seville (Temple) oranges
juice of 2 large lemons
2.75kg/6lb/13½ cups
* sugar, warmed*
about 300ml/½ pint/1¼ cups
* Scotch whisky*

1 Scrub the oranges thoroughly using a nylon brush and pick off the disc at the stalk end. Cut the oranges in half widthways and squeeze the juice, retaining the pips (seeds). Quarter the peel, cut away and reserve any thick white pith, and shred the peel – thickly or thinly depending on your prefererence.

2 Cut up the reserved pith roughly and tie it up with the pips in a square of muslin (cheesecloth) using a long piece of string. Tie the bag loosely, so that water can circulate during cooking and will extract the pectin from the pith and pips. Hang the bag from the handle of the preserving pan.

3 Add the cut peel, strained juices and 3.5 litres/6 pints/15 cups water to the pan. Bring to the boil and simmer for 1½–2 hours, or until the peel is very tender.

4 Lift up the bag of pith and pips and squeeze it out well between two plates over the pan to extract as much of the juices as possible. Add the sugar to the pan and stir over a low heat until it has completely dissolved.

5 Bring to the boil and boil hard for 15–20 minutes or until setting point is reached. To test, allow a spoonful to cool slightly, and then see if a skin has formed. If not, boil a little longer.

6 Skim, if necessary, and leave to cool for 15 minutes, then stir. Divide the whisky among 8–10 warmed, sterilized jars and swill it around. Using a heatproof jug (pitcher), pour in the marmalade.

7 Cover and seal while still hot. Label when cold, and store in a cool, dark place for up to 6 months.

Mulled Claret

This mull is a blend of claret, cider and orange juice. It can be varied to suit the occasion by increasing or decreasing the proportion of fruit juice or, to give the mull more pep, by adding up to 150ml/ ¼ pint/⅔ cup brandy.

Makes 16 × 150ml/
¼ pints/⅔ cup glasses
1 orange
75ml/5 tbsp clear honey

30ml/2 tbsp seedless raisins
2 clementines
a few cloves
whole nutmeg
60ml/4 tbsp demerara
* (raw) sugar*
2 cinnamon sticks
1½ litres/2½ pints/6¼ cups
* inexpensive claret*
600ml/1 pint/2½ cups medium
* (hard) cider*
300ml/½ pint/1¼ cups
* orange juice*

1 With a sharp knife or a vegetable peeler, pare off a long strip of the orange rind.

2 Place the orange rind, honey and raisins in a large heavy pan. Stud the clementines all over with the cloves and add them to the pan with the fruit and honey.

3 Grate a little nutmeg into the sugar and then add it to the pan along with the cinnamon sticks. Pour on the wine and heat over low heat, stirring until the sugar has completely dissolved and the honey has melted.

4 Pour the cider and the orange juice into the pan and continue to heat the mull over low heat. Do not allow it to boil or all the alcohol will evaporate.

5 Warm a punch bowl or other large serving bowl. Remove the clementines and cinnamon sticks from the pan and strain the mull into the bowl to remove the raisins.

6 Add the clementines studded with cloves, and serve the mull hot, in warmed glasses or in glasses containing a silver spoon (to prevent the glass breaking). Using a nutmeg grater, add a little nutmeg over each serving, if you wish.

Whisky Marmalade Energy 10,736kcal/45,734kJ; Protein 22.8g; Carbohydrate 2657.8g, of which sugars 2657.8g; Fat 1.3g, of which saturates 0g; Cholesterol 0mg; Calcium 1.74g; Fibre 15.6g; Sodium 187mg.
Mulled Claret Energy 174kcal/728kJ; Protein 0.2g; Carbohydrate 16.3g, of which sugars 16.3g; Fat 0g, of which saturates 0g; Cholesterol 0mg; Calcium 16mg; Fibre 0g; Sodium 11mg.

Brandied Eggnog

This frothy blend of eggs, milk and spirits definitely comes into the nightcap category of drinks during the festivities.

Serves 4
4 eggs, separated
30ml/2 tbsp caster (superfine) sugar
60ml/4 tbsp dark rum
60ml/4 tbsp brandy
300ml/½ pint/1¼ cups milk (or according to the volume of the glasses), hot
whole nutmeg

1 Beat the egg yolks with the sugar in a bowl. Beat the whites to soft peaks. Mix and pour into four heatproof glasses.

2 Add the rum and brandy to the glasses. You will need about 15ml/1 tbsp of each in each glass.

3 Top up the glass with hot milk. Grate the nutmeg over the top and serve immediately.

Mulled Cider

This hot cider cup is easy to make and traditional at Halloween, but it makes a good and inexpensive warming brew for any winter gathering, particularly for a festive drinks party with lots of finger food.

Makes about 20 glasses
2 lemons
1 litre/1¾ pints/4 cups apple juice
2 litres/3½ pints/9 cups medium sweet cider
3 small cinnamon sticks
4–6 whole cloves
slices of lemon, to serve (optional)

1 Wash the lemons and pare the rinds with a vegetable peeler. Blend all the ingredients together in a large stainless-steel pan.

2 Set the pan over low heat and heat the mixture through to infuse (steep) for 15 minutes; do not allow it to boil.

3 Strain the liquid through a sieve (strainer) and serve with extra slices of lemon, if you like.

Whiskey Punch

Also known as a 'hot toddy', this traditional 'cure' for colds is more often drunk for pleasure as a nightcap, particularly to round off a day's winter sporting activities or a hectic Christmas Day, and it is a great drink to hold and sip on cold winter evenings.

Serves 1
4–6 whole cloves
60ml/4 tbsp Irish whiskey
1 thick slice of lemon, halved
5–10ml/1–2 tsp demerara (raw) sugar, to taste

1 Stick the cloves into the lemon slice, and put it into a large stemmed glass (or one with a handle).

2 Pour the whiskey into the glass and add the sugar. Give the sugar a quick swirl with the whiskey.

3 Put a metal teaspoon inside the glass – this is to prevent the hot water from cracking it – then top it up with boiling water. Stir well to dissolve the sugar and serve immediately.

Cook's Tips
• All three types of Irish whiskey (single malt, pure pot-stilled and a column-and-pot still blend of grain and malt) work well in this recipe.
• The word 'toddy' comes from tari, the Hindu word used for the sap or juice of a palm tree. In Asia, this sap was often fermented to create an alcoholic beverage. British sailors picked up on the idea, which eventually evolved into the toddy.

Variation
You can, of course, use other types of whisky (or whiskey, with an 'e', if Irish or American) in this drink. Scotch, Bourbon and Canadian rye whiskies will all make just as good a drink – it all depends on what you have in the drinks cabinet.

Brandied Eggnog Energy 375kcal/1566kJ; Protein 9.1g; Carbohydrate 29.6g, of which sugars 29.6g; Fat 19.9g, of which saturates 10.7g; Cholesterol 232mg; Calcium 112mg; Fibre 0.1g; Sodium 98mg.
Mulled Cider Energy 61kcal/258kJ; Protein 0.1g; Carbohydrate 9.3g, of which sugars 9.3g; Fat 0.1g, of which saturates 0g; Cholesterol 0mg; Calcium 12mg; Fibre 0g; Sodium 8mg.
Whiskey Punch Energy 149kcal/619kJ; Protein 0g; Carbohydrate 4.2g, of which sugars 4.2g; Fat 0g, of which saturates 0g; Cholesterol 0mg; Calcium 2mg; Fibre 0g; Sodium 0mg.

Grand Marnier, Papaya and Fruit Punch

The term 'punch' comes from the Hindi word *panch* (five), relating to the five ingredients traditionally contained in the drink – alcohol, lemon or lime, tea, sugar and water. The ingredients may have altered somewhat over the years, but the best punches still combine a mixture of spirits, flavourings and an innocent top-up of fizz or juice. Make a bowl of this drink for a festive gathering of friends and family.

Serves 15
2 large papayas
4 passion fruit
300g/11oz lychees, peeled and stoned (pitted)
300ml/½ pint/1¼ cups freshly squeezed orange juice
200ml/7fl oz/scant 1 cup Grand Marnier or other orange-flavoured liqueur
8 whole star anise
2 small oranges
ice cubes
1.5 litres/2½ pints/6¼ cups soda water (club soda)

1 Halve the papayas and discard the seeds. Halve the passion fruit and press the pulp through a sieve (strainer) into a small punch bowl or a pretty serving bowl.

2 Push the papayas through a juicer, adding 100ml/3½fl oz/ scant ½ cup water to help the pulp through. Juice the lychees.

3 Add the juices to the bowl with the orange juice, liqueur and star anise. Thinly slice the oranges and add to the bowl. Chill for at least 1 hour or until ready to serve.

4 Add plenty of ice cubes to the bowl and top up with soda water. Ladle into punch cups or small glasses to serve.

Cook's Tip
Cointreau is one of the most famous orange liqueurs but there are others to choose from. Look out for bottles labelled 'curaçao' or 'triple sec'.

Pineapple and Rum Crush with Coconut

This thick and slushy tropical cooler is unbelievably rich thanks to the combination of coconut milk and thick cream. The addition of sweet, juicy, slightly tart pineapple, and finely crushed ice, offers a refreshing foil, making it all too easy to sip your way through several glasses at a Christmas party.

Serves 4–5
1 pineapple
30ml/2 tbsp lemon juice
200ml/7fl oz/scant 1 cup coconut milk
150ml/¼ pint/⅔ cup double (heavy) cream
200ml/7fl oz/scant 1 cup white rum
30–60ml/2–4 tbsp caster (superfine) sugar
500g/1¼lb finely crushed ice

1 Trim off the ends from the pineapple, then cut off the skin. Cut away the core and chop the flesh. Put the chopped flesh in a blender or food processor with the lemon juice and whizz until very smooth.

2 Add the coconut milk, cream, rum and 30ml/2 tbsp of the sugar. Blend until thoroughly combined, then taste and add more sugar if necessary.

3 Pack the crushed ice into serving glasses and pour the drink over. Serve immediately.

Cook's Tip
This is a great cocktail for making ahead of time. Blend the drink in advance and chill in a jug (pitcher). Store the crushed ice in the freezer ready for serving as soon as it's required.

Variation
If you prefer, you can use a dark rum or even a spiced rum, such as that made by Morgans, instead of the white rum.

Grand Marnier Punch Energy 65kcal/274kJ; Protein 0.5g; Carbohydrate 11.6g, of which sugars 11.6g; Fat 0.1g, of which saturates 0g; Cholesterol 0mg; Calcium 10mg; Fibre 0.9g; Sodium 6mg.
Pineapple Rum Crush Energy 336kcal/1400kJ; Protein 1.3g; Carbohydrate 24.9g, of which sugars 24.9g; Fat 16.5g, of which saturates 10.1g; Cholesterol 41mg; Calcium 58mg; Fibre 1.9g; Sodium 54mg.

Irish Chocolate Velvet

This smooth, sophisticated drink will always be appreciated on cold Christmas evenings.

Serves 4
120ml/4fl oz/½ cup double (heavy) cream
400ml/14fl oz/1⅔ cups milk

30ml/2 tbsp unsweetened cocoa powder
115g/4oz milk chocolate, broken into squares
60ml/4 tbsp Irish whiskey
whipped double (heavy) cream, for topping
plain (semisweet) chocolate curls, to decorate

1 Whip the double cream in a mixing bowl until it is thick enough to hold its shape.

2 Put the milk into a pan and whisk in the cocoa powder. Add the chocolate squares and heat gently, stirring, until the chocolate has melted. Bring the chocolate milk to the boil.

3 Remove the pan from the heat and add the whipped double cream and Irish whiskey. Stir the mixture gently for about 1 minute to blend well.

4 Pour the drink quickly into four heatproof mugs or serving glasses and add to each one a generous spoonful of the whipped cream for topping. Decorate the tops with chocolate curls and serve the drinks immediately.

Cook's Tip
Make chocolate curls for decorating the drinks by running a vegetable peeler down the side of a chilled bar of chocolate. You can also use a grater to create them.

Variation
If Irish whiskey is not available, you can use brandy instead for this drink. Any liqueur that uses Irish whiskey, Scotch whisky or brandy as its base will also work.

Cranberry Frost

A non-alcoholic cocktail with the colour of holly berries will delight younger and older guests alike at Christmas time. It is the perfect 'one-for-the-road' drink to serve at the end of a festive gathering.

Serves 10
115g/4oz/generous ½ cup caster (superfine) sugar

juice of 2 oranges
still water, enough to dissolve the sugar
120ml/4fl oz/½ cup fresh cranberry juice
1 litre/1¾ pints/4 cups sparkling mineral water
45ml/3 tbsp fresh cranberries, to decorate
handful fresh mint sprigs, to decorate

1 Put the caster sugar, orange juice and still water into a small pan and stir the mixture over a low heat until the sugar has completely dissolved.

2 Bring the mixture to the boil and boil vigorously for about 3 minutes. Set aside to cool.

3 Pour the syrup into a chilled serving bowl, pour on the cranberry juice and mix well to combine.

4 To serve, pour on the mineral water and decorate with cranberries and mint leaves.

Cook's Tip
This is a great drink to make during the festivities because the syrup can be made in advance and stored in a covered container in the refrigerator.

Variation
To make this fabulous non-alcoholic drink the very essence of festive colour, chill with ice cubes made by freezing fresh red cranberries and tiny mint leaves in the water.

Irish Velvet Energy 390kcal/1623kJ; Protein 7.5g; Carbohydrate 22.4g, of which sugars 21.6g; Fat 28.3g, of which saturates 17.3g; Cholesterol 54mg; Calcium 208mg; Fibre 1.1g; Sodium 145mg.
Cranberry Frost Energy 56kcal/237kJ; Protein 0.1g; Carbohydrate 14.6g, of which sugars 14.6g; Fat 0g, of which saturates 0g; Cholesterol 0mg; Calcium 8mg; Fibre 0.1g; Sodium 2mg.

Index